AF443271

CITIES IN TRANSITION

ANGLO-GERMAN FOUNDATION FOR THE STUDY OF INDUSTRIAL SOCIETY

The Anglo-German Foundation for the Study of Industrial Society was established by an agreement between the British and German governments after a state visit to Britain by the late President Heinemann, and incorporated by Royal Charter in 1973. Funds were initially provided by the German government; since 1979 both governments have been contributing.

The Foundation aims to contribute to the knowledge and understanding of industrial society in the two countries and to promote contacts between them. It funds selected research projects and conferences in the industrial, economic and social policy areas designed to be of practical use to policymakers.

Titles include:

Bernhard Blanke and Randall Smith (*editors*)
CITIES IN TRANSITION
New Challenges, New Responsibilities

John Bynner and Rainer K. Silbereisen (*editors*)
ADVERSITY AND CHALLENGE IN LIFE IN THE NEW
GERMANY AND IN ENGLAND

Maurie J. Cohen (*editor*)
RISK IN THE MODERN AGE
Social Theory, Science and Environmental Decision-Making

Stephen Frowen and Jens Hölscher (*editors*)
THE GERMAN CURRENCY UNION OF 1990
A Critical Assessment

Eva Kolinsky (*editor*)
SOCIAL TRANSFORMATION AND THE FAMILY IN
POST-COMMUNIST GERMANY

Howard Williams, Colin Wight and Norbert Kapferer (*editors*)
POLITICAL THOUGHT AND GERMAN REUNIFICATION
The New German Ideology?

Anglo-German Foundation
Series Standing Order ISBN 0–333–71459–8
(*outside North America only*)

You can receive future titles in this series as they are published by placing a standing order. Please contact your bookseller or, in case of difficulty, write to us at the address below with your name and address, the title of the series and the ISBN quoted above.

Customer Services Department, Macmillan Distribution Ltd
Houndmills, Basingstoke, Hampshire RG21 6XS, England

Cities in Transition

New Challenges, New Responsibilities

Edited by

Bernhard Blanke
Professor of Public Policy
University of Hanover

and

Randall Smith
Reader in Policy Studies
University of Bristol

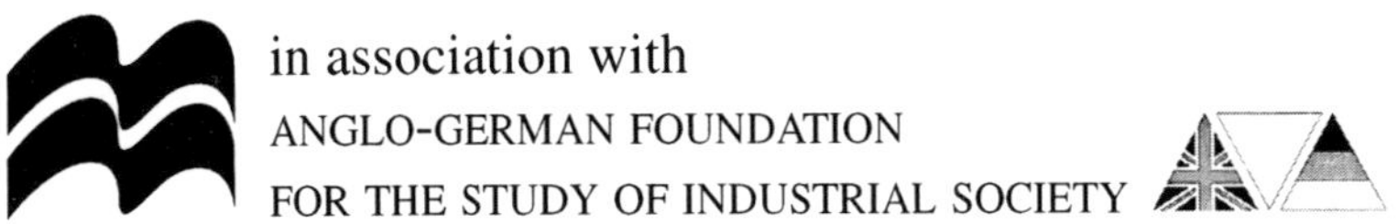

in association with
ANGLO-GERMAN FOUNDATION
FOR THE STUDY OF INDUSTRIAL SOCIETY

First published in Great Britain 1999 by
MACMILLAN PRESS LTD
Houndmills, Basingstoke, Hampshire RG21 6XS and London
Companies and representatives throughout the world

A catalogue record for this book is available from the British Library.

ISBN 0–333–74660–0 hardcover

First published in the United States of America 1999 by
ST. MARTIN'S PRESS, INC.,
Scholarly and Reference Division,
175 Fifth Avenue, New York, N.Y. 10010

ISBN 0–312–22215–7

Library of Congress Cataloging-in-Publication Data
Cities in transition : new challenges, new responsibilities / edited
by Bernhard Blanke and Randall Smith.
p.   cm.
Includes bibliographical references and index.
ISBN 0–312–22215–7 (cloth)
1. Cities and towns—Great Britain—Congresses.   2. Cities and
towns—Germany—Congresses.   3. Urban policy—Great Britain–
–Congresses.   4. Urban policy–Germany–Congresses.   I. Blanke,
Bernhard, 1941–   .   II. Smith, Randall.
HT133.C492   1999
307.76'0941—dc21   99–18873
                                                                              CIP

Selection, editorial matter, Introduction and Chapter 17 © Bernhard Blanke and
Randall Smith 1999
Chapter 11 © Randall Smith 1999
Chapters 2–10, 12–16 © Macmillan Press Ltd 1999

All rights reserved. No reproduction, copy or transmission of this publication may be made
without written permission.

No paragraph of this publication may be reproduced, copied or transmitted save with
written permission or in accordance with the provisions of the Copyright, Designs and
Patents Act 1988, or under the terms of any licence permitting limited copying issued by
the Copyright Licensing Agency, 90 Tottenham Court Road, London W1P 0LP.

Any person who does any unauthorised act in relation to this publication may be liable to
criminal prosecution and civil claims for damages.

The authors have asserted their rights to be identified as the authors of this work in
accordance with the Copyright, Designs and Patents Act 1988.

This book is printed on paper suitable for recycling and made from fully managed and
sustained forest sources.

10   9   8   7   6   5   4   3   2   1
08   07   06   05   04   03   02   01   00   99

Printed and bound in Great Britain by
Antony Rowe Ltd, Chippenham, Wiltshire

vi   *Contents*

Contents

Notes on the Contributors

Bernhard Blanke is Professor of Public Policy, University of Hanover.

Arno Brandt is an economist at the North German State Bank (Nord LB).

Paul Burton is a Research Fellow at the School for Policy Studies, University of Bristol.

Colin Fudge is Dean of the Faculty of the Built Environment, University of the West of England, Bristol, and Chair of the European Union Urban Environment Expert Group.

Dietrich Fürst is a Professor at the Institute for Regional Planning, University of Hanover.

Hubert Heinelt is a Professor at the Institute for Political Science, Technical University of Darmstadt.

Sabine Kunst is a Professor in the Institute of Waste Water Treatment and Waste Management, University of Hanover.

Christine Lambert is a Reader in the Housing and Urban Studies School, Faculty of the Built Environment, University of the West of England, Bristol.

Nick Oatley is a Senior Lecturer in the Housing and Urban Studies School, Faculty of the Built Environment, University of the West of England, Bristol.

Henning Schridde is a Lecturer at the Centre for Social and Public Policy, University of Hanover.

Herbert Schubert is a Research Fellow at the Developmental Planning Research Institute, University of Hanover.

Walter Siebel is a Professor in the Centre for Urban Research at the University of Oldenburg.

Randall Smith is Reader in Policy Studies at the School for Policy Studies, University of Bristol. He is also editor of the journal, *Policy and Politics*.

Nicola Staeck is a Lecturer in the Faculty of Sociology, University of Bielefeld.

Murray Stewart is Professor of Urban and Regional Governance in the Faculty of the Built Environment, University of the West of England, Bristol.

Nigel Thrift is a Professor in the School of Geographical Sciences, University of Bristol.

Adelheid von Saldern is Professor of Modern History in the Department of History, University of Hanover.

Sophie Watson is a Professor in the Department of Cultural Studies, University of East London.

List of Figures

List of Plates

By IBA Emscher Park

Acknowledgements

We are deeply grateful to a wide range of organizations for making possible the symposium upon which this publication is based. Our thanks go to the cities of Bristol and Hanover for their essential contributions, to the Anglo-German Foundation for the Study of Industrial Society for their unstinting support, to the Universities of Bristol, West of England and Hanover which provided both practical support and great encouragement, and to other bodies, including the North German State Bank and the Deutsche Messe AG Hanover.

We are also indebted to our interpreters, Udo Jorg and Claudia Malitzki; our translators, Peter Bennett and Penny Price; our other language and administrative support, Isabella Aboderin; our secretarial help, Jenny Capstick and Angela Torrington in Bristol and Judith Jungfels in Hanover; and the staff at Rodney Lodge, who provided comfortable surroundings for our deliberations.

Finally, our warmest thanks go to our colleagues who were put under great pressure to produce their papers on time, and an extra thank you to those who delivered their contributions by the due date.

Bernhard Blanke
Randall Smith

Foreword

The Anglo-German Foundation for the Study of Industrial Society is delighted that the proceedings of the symposium held in Bristol in May 1997 are being published by Macmillan, with whom the Foundation has a publishing arrangement. This research symposium, held during the fiftieth anniversary of the twinning between Hanover and Bristol (one of the first to be created after 1945) was a worthy successor to an earlier symposium, held in Hanover in 1991, on this occasion as part of the celebrations of the 750th anniversary of the foundation of the City of Hanover. It is heartening to see the close and productive links between the administrations of the two cities and the universities in their midst. The Foundation's congratulations go to Bernhard Blanke and his colleagues in Hanover and to Randall Smith and his colleagues in Bristol.

Connie Martin
Secretary-General, Anglo-German Foundation

1 Introduction

Bernhard Blanke and Randall Smith

In 1991 the Universities of Bristol and Hanover organized a successful symposium on The Future of the Medium-Sized City. Much of the financial support came from the Anglo-German Foundation, though the two universities and the British Council also contributed. It was held in Hanover in May 1991 as part of the celebrations of the 750th anniversary of the founding of the city of Hanover. This symposium became the occasion for the formal signing of a cooperation agreement between the Universities of Bristol and Hanover. A number of papers presented were brought together in a book published by the Anglo-German Foundation in 1993. It has been well received in the academic journals.

Since 1991 there has been increased cooperation in the social sciences between the two universities. Student exchanges have developed, joint research has been undertaken and the German co-editor (Bernhard Blanke) of the 1993 publication has both published in the Bristol-based journal, *Policy and Politics* and become a valued member of its International Advisory Board. The current editor of the journal (Randall Smith) was the English co-editor of the 1993 book. Both Blanke and Smith were encouraged by their respective universities to organize a second symposium to be held in Bristol in 1997 as part of the fiftieth anniversary celebrations of the twinning between the cities of Bristol and Hanover, reputedly the first Anglo-German twinning following the end of the Second World War.

The theme of the 1997 symposium was 'cities in transition'. The event took further analysis of the key role of urban centres in the economy and polity of twenty-first-century Europe. Cities are both engines of growth and, at the same time, the focus for social polarization and exclusion. Thus, the central tenets of present patterns of city development in the light of global economic change should be the subject of analysis, from both an analytical perspective and in terms of praxis.

The process of globalization goes hand in hand with a re-evaluation of the role of the region. Thus, the conurbation is tied into a developed global network of cities, hierarchically structured according to their economic functions, while at the same time a cumulative process is taking place whereby functions are pushed down to the local level. The important themes arising from these dual processes are: the relationship between urban core and region, the nature of institutional structures in the regions and, in particular, their influence upon economic activity and their democratic legitimation. In particular, it remains to be seen if regional cities such as Bristol and Hanover will play a central part within a polynucleated network of urban settlements or if they will be driven by the economic power of world cities such as London and Berlin.

As far as the inter- and intra-regional division of labour is concerned, conurbations are faced with many conflicting demands. There is no longer a unified urban civic culture through which conflicts arising from such functional divisions can be resolved. The revival of regional identities becomes the medium through which the regions are better able to address the economic and social challenges confronting them.

Economic growth and a buoyant labour market are the key requirements for social integration within urban society. They enable the individual to assume an independent and secure economic existence and a socially useful role. This central mechanism of integration breaks down if there are structural problems within the labour market. In addition to such economic and material exclusion, a general value shift has brought about a more profound social and cultural exclusion.

The international profile of the city is essential to the maintenance of its stability. Medium-sized cities in particular need to make the most of their strengths. Marketing and management strategies, internationally recognized and competitive economic and service structures, as well as the optimisation of transport and telecommunications links provide an important starting point for the promotion of a conurbation's international profile. In addition, it is absolutely essential to harness the entire 'endogenous potential' of the region, in other words the extent to which coordination, cooperation and the capacity for innovation exists within the domains of politics, administration, economics and society.

The issues of competitiveness and the quality of life must be assessed with regard to the lasting effect upon the environment. Modern industrial society produces massive ecological damage, some of which – such as climate change – is evident at the global level while other effects – such as noise and air pollution – are evident at the level of the city. Ecological questions can have an important impact upon social and economic questions. The innovative, socially-oriented, democratic and ecological city is the role model for a sustainable form of city development which will be able to reconcile its conflicting aims and functions in the twenty-first century.

These issues were woven into a three-day programme for the symposium and this volume comprises revised versions of the papers presented. The core ideas for the symposium were addressed through two themes: (a) local issues and global implications, and (b) global concerns and local strategies. This structure has also been used to compile this edited book. Some of the topics are addressed at a broad level; others illustrate themes by examples from the cities of Bristol and Hanover. We hope that the various chapters will interest both academics and policy practitioners.

Part I
The Urban Future

2 20/40 Vision –
Urban Futures to Avoid
and Urban Futures to Admire

Nigel Thrift

INTRODUCTION

The future is always unknown to us. Yet the urge to know the future – from economic forecasting and time series analysis through to science fiction and astrology – has probably never been stronger. In this chapter I shall look at the future of British cities. I will want to start by looking at the form that British cities were thought likely to take in the year 2000 by writers in the 1960s. Of course, these writers got some things right and some things wrong but I am more concerned to draw a lesson from these attempts to see the future than to praise them or scoff at them.

Then, in the second part of the chapter, I will suggest that since these attempts were made, there has been a sea change in attitudes to the business of prediction. Instead of attempting to sketch one possible world, writers have become more concerned, spurred on by developments in computer simulation, to etch out many 'would-be worlds', to use Casti's (1997) efficacious phrase, with the intent of acknowledging the social and cultural complexity of cities. In turn, I will argue that the production of these would-be worlds can be seen as a sign of important political and institutional changes.

In the final part of the chapter, I want to turn to Europe and to suggest that across Europe now there is a vast reservoir of material which can act to suggest many would-be worlds which those who run British cities can use to enrich their models of urban futures. And then, just for fun, I will present three models of how Bristol might look in the year 2040, thereby entirely negating the message of the chapter!

1960–2000

The 1960s often seem like a foreign country now, even for those of us who lived through them. They are like an old diary whose contents we can only vaguely remember. That feel of distance and displacement becomes all the greater when one looks at two of the best known attempts to predict what life in a large British city would look like in the year 2000 – Peter Hall's *London 2000* and Colin Leicester's *Life in the Year 2000*.

One might argue that Peter Hall's account of London in 2000 is remarkably prescient. He foresees a future in which the economy of London will become dependent upon industries like higher education, entertainment (including restaurants) and the like. He foresees the importance of gentrification, though he exaggerates its extent. And in presenting his ideal 2000 family as people for whom long-distance commuting has become a normal activity he foresees something that has occurred, although not on the scale that Hall looked to (with daily commuters into London from Boulogne and Paris). Where Hall goes awry, it is hardly his fault. He foresees a London ruled by planners, split up into combined shopping and office centres connected by expressways but surrounded by mixed use development. He foresees expanded networks of new towns around London, run by New Town Corporations. And he foresees Londoners for whom

> distance is no longer an object. They learned to do without cars for much for their working day, but for living their own lives the car has become part of themselves. Just as they no longer can work in isolated communities, so they no longer form their friendships and social lives within bounds of space. For them Hammersmith to Dover has no more significance than would Hammersmith to Hampstead in 1960. (Hall, 1963, p. 206)

Colin Leicester's 'Manbirlon' is more influenced by science and science fiction. This is a city of robots and rocket jets, sometimes nearer to Dan Dare than the future. The account is uncannily accurate in its forecasts of the adoption of information technology. It foresees a world of 'visual telephones', 'phonetic typewriters' and data transmission via 'light pipes' (fibre optic cables) which is not so far from our own. It is less prescient in other ways. Like Hall he foresees the conquest of space – but by hovercar and rocket jet. Unlike Hall, he foresees that by the year 2000 technology will have produced more free time for everyone: his leading character, a manager, is looking forward to his two-month holiday and then to a sabbatical year!

As we can see with the benefit of hindsight, these two accounts fall down in three ways. First, there is the faith in planning. But, in reality, much of what has happened in British cities might be interpreted as nearer to Hall's 'nightmare scenario' of

> a different London 2000. It also would be recognisable, but chiefly through the ugliness and frustration which have been maintained, and intensified from the London we have now. We could have a formless, inadequately planned sprawl of offices out from London, as suburbs sprawled between the wars; traffic gradually congealing to a stop in the centre and along the main arteries; ugly, dispiriting, demoralising suburbs sprouting like fungi from every old town within sixty miles of St. Pauls. (Hall, 1963, p. 209)

Second, there is the faith in mobility. For both Hall and Leicester (even in the days of Plowden) traffic growth was something that could be solved. Third – and this is the point I want to concentrate on – they miss out the social: it is suppressed by a pervasive technological determinism which depends on technology both to imagine the future and to provide a sense of progress towards that future. Therefore, they fail to foresee a whole set of issues. Their accounts are a middle-class vision – there is no sense that the future might hold information technology *and* beggars. Their accounts are heavily gendered – their future families are firmly nuclear; there is no sense of the enormous changes in British cities that have been driven by the rise of different forms of household structure. And their accounts are ethnocentric. There is no sense of ethnicity as an important urban determinant. There is, in other words, little sense of the social and cultural richness and complexity of cities which so many commentators from Jane Jacobs (1961) in the 1960s to Richard Sennett (1994) today have been concerned to celebrate and, indeed, protect.

SENSING THE FUTURES

Yet what is clear about the current urban literature has been its attempts to incorporate that social richness into how we think about the future of cities. These attempts have been of three kinds which together, I think, add up to a quite new stance towards the urban future.

The first of these attempts has been the growth of interest in what might be called 'would-be' or 'possible' worlds (Casti, 1997; Dyson, 1997). Using a combination of computer technology and insights from complexity theory, urban theorists are trying to sense the future possibilities in our current urban worlds, rather than simply extra-polating in a linear fashion, on the principle that these possible worlds can be productive guides. In other words, these theorists start from the premise that the future is inherently unpredictable. Dyson (1997), for example, argues that ten years is the outer limit of social forecasting. But it is possible, even so, these theorists go on to argue, to sense what is new and how it will impact on cities by generating a range of possible computational worlds. These worlds are based on three principles. First, they are not attempts to produce exact replicas of the future. Rather, they are attempts to sense complex *processes* in which interaction between a number of different variables produces higher order organization. Often then, the quality and exactness of the data are less important than being able to sense a process or processes at work. Second, it follows that these worlds are often purposely vague, acknow-ledging not only that it is impossible to know everything (see Stewart, 1997), but also that it is often impossible to know even a few things well. Third, these worlds are perceived as embedded in the processes they are attempting to sense. What we see then is the growth of creative computing with a strong interpretative bias, bent on producing worlds with which to think about the future but not making claims that these worlds are the future.

In turn, this expansion in thinking about possibilities can be linked to developments in the practice of urban planning and, in particular, the rise of so-called collaborative or associationist planning (Healey, 1997; Amin and Thrift, 1995). This kind of planning, the second attempt to incorporate social richness into how we think about the future of cities, is intent on giving voice to the populations who are the subjects of the planning system by pushing the process of decision to the front of the stage rather than the goals, and in that *process* con-structing solidary institutions of discourse, dialogue and dissent which demand a more active citizenship. The goal, in other words, is

> to give a community (local or otherwise) sufficient potential for strategic action ... through a process of negotiation, in which the process of negotiation is itself a vital part of the institution-building process. Thus, the social consciousness of a community is changed, and not just its institutional framework, and, in the process, the community is endowed with agency.
>
> (Amin and Thrift, 1995, p. 55)

A potential part of this collaborative strategy is an orientation towards 'intermediate forms of governance' as a means of building institutional thickness. These intermediate institutions are the third and final attempt to incorporate social richness into thinking about the future of cities. Such institutions are based on the notion of an active citizenship forged in the fires of process. But since the 1960s there has, in fact, been a flowering of these kinds of 'alternative' institutions in Britain, based in part on the growth of religious institutions, in part on new growth in the old-style voluntary and charitable sector (as in the rise of institutions for palliative care like hospices and Macmillan nurses (Bosanquet, 1997)), in part on the growth of 1960s counter-cultural institutions (but now with a dose of 1980s financial hardheadedness) and in part on the institutions of a burgeoning environmental movement. When put together, these institutions have begun to produce new ideas of organization around which to locate ideas which are both old and new (see Leadbeater, 1997).

My particular concern has been with alternative financial institutions which, in the 1980s in particular, began to take root (Leyshon and Thrift, 1997). Ranging from institutions which are rapidly becoming a part of the formal economy, like ethical investment funds and community development banks, through to institutions which are clearly a part of the informal economy, like local exchange trading schemes (LETS), what is remarkable about these different bodies is their democratic ethos and their attempt to redefine money according to that ethos, both by attaching new cultural values to money and by 'relocalizing' money.

These financial institutions present all kinds of problems. But they also provide all kinds of alternative practices and inspirations (Leyshon and Thrift, 1996). Four of these come to mind. First, they are a means, however modest, of fighting back against a 'Gradgrind' mindset which assumes that money is only ever about harvesting profits. Second, nearly all alternative financial institutions have begun as 'bottom-up' and largely practical initiatives, and, unusually, they are often examples of institutional 'templates' which have moved from the Third World to the First World. Third, they are a means of providing the kind of democratic associationism already mentioned, by stressing that money and finance is as much a part of civil society as of the economy. Fourth, and finally, their emergence is symbolic of a wider movement which is re-evaluating the role of money and finance (Leyshon and Thrift, 1997), and which is intent on bringing it back to the social and cultural realm from which it should never have been allowed to escape.

The point is that each of these three approaches to the city is about a much greater sense of contingency and possibility, about openness to the future and a future of openness (Taussig, 1997).

2000–2040: BRISTOL IN THE FUTURES

What, then, of the future of cities like Bristol in this perspective on the future? Three rules seem to pertain. The first is that we cannot know the future, though we can know some things which are slow moving, like certain kinds of physical infrastructure. The second is that we must force the social into any account, rather than leaving it to technology to drive us forward. Then, third, we must realize that open systems are always open, and therefore we need to emphasize the likelihood of imports of peoples, ideas and capital which make it even more difficult to sense the future. For example, in the last few years, numerous ideas have circulated in city and regional planning which have been copied in cities around the world – the urban cultural strategy, the 24-hour city and so on, and which have had determinate effects on urban landscapes.

I want to continue with this last point for a little longer. For what is striking about many of these 'planning fads' in Britain, like the management fads which circulate in the business community (to which planning has become increasingly aligned in many countries), is that so many of them have come from North America. Very few of them have come from the rest of Europe. But that situation is now changing. European networks are producing new connections and, in turn, an archive of new practices for British urban planners to draw on. For example, work on alternative financial institutions has become a trans-European exercise which, with the help of Directorate-General XIII of the European Commission, is leading to tangible results such as the proposal for a new EU social banking directive. Much of this work has been driven from Germany with its tradition of intermediate financial institutions (such as the regional savings banks) by writers like Udo Reifner (Rossiter, 1997). Then, as another example, there is the emphasis on working with time in order to plan space better. The Italian experiments with time plans for cities which involve attempting to change the temporal capacity of a city by, for example, staggering work hours, school hours and the like in order to attack traffic growth, have now spread to other European cities. Similarly, in Germany temporal planning is at least beginning to occur. There is, in other words, a vast archive of European experiments which can enliven our sense of the future and enable us to sense it better (see, for example, Lassave and Querrien, 1997).

Let me now negate almost everything I have said and offer, as an entertaining end piece, some futures for Bristol that are in line with the key message of this chapter – that urban futures are not determined. Therefore, there can never be just one future to be described but only a series of more or less ghostly possibilities. As Ferguson (1997, p. 86) puts it:

> As has often been said, what we call the past was once the future; and the people of the past no more knew what their future was than we can know our own. All they could do was consider the likely future, the plausible outcome. It is possible that some people in the past had no interest in the future whatsoever. It is also true that many people in the past have felt quite sure that they did not know what the future would be, and that sometimes they have even got it right. But most people in the past have tended to consider more than one possible future. And although no more than one of these actually has come about, at the moment *before* it came about it was no more real (though it may now seem more probable) than the others.

In this spirit, I will present three of these possible visions of how Bristol might appear in the year 2040. The first of these is taken from the growing body of work by young and highly influential science fiction writers like Simon Ings, Paul McAuley and Jeff Noon, who have piggybacked on the work of North American writers like Bruce Sterling, William Gibson and Neal Stephenson but given it a distinctively British twist. For these writers, the large British city of 2040 is an urban hell. Global warming has produced a city that is parched and sweaty. Disparities of income have markedly increased producing a vast underclass which spends most of its time either high on exotic new drugs, like Noon's 'feathers', or attempting to get hold of them, often through criminal acts. Information technology, biotechnology and nanotechnology have run riot, producing exotic new forms of human, animal and artificial intelligencies which, in Ings' work, extend to cities that think. Strange religious cults abound. In other words, 2040 is a world of dysfunctional cities and in this future Bristol is a heated-up, tripped-out and high-tech version of today in which Peter Hall's ideal family has become a gang of drug dealers, hustling their way through the day and high as a kite at night (see, in particular, Beckett, 1997).

The second future is an ecological city. Bristol has become a truly eco-friendly city, recycling everything. The city's parks and gardens have been turned into allotments to support urban dwellers. Many work from home, but those who cycle to work (and everyone now cycles) travel to low-energy workplaces based on solar power, fibre optics and the like. The city is run by a patchwork of local communes who decide everything by electronic vote. Vast office spaces like Abbey Wood to the north of the city have been turned into communes surrounded by their own agricultural space. Compared with today, what would strike a visitor from the past is the lack of traffic noise and the massive plantings of trees – the city is now ringed by the Bristol community forest. The ideal Bristol family is one of the elite, descended from the Earth Firsters of the 1990s. Its members spend their days in tasks like software development and their evenings in community cultural events, often based on the official state religions of Buddhism and Gaia.

Finally, there is Bristol as a neo-liberal 'learning city'. European Union policy has been successful and Britain has become one of the capitals of the 'Atlantic arc'. This success is built on the city having been able to produce a vast array of civic institutions bent on pushing its economy towards constant innovation, based on networks of small firms in industries like aerospace, medicine, management consultancy and multimedia. It has become a kind of Silicon Valley of Europe. But it has also become a cultural capital, based on the Lottery money buildings of the 1990s, a large and well-educated middle class, and a Bohemian fringe of artists and virtual reality jocks. The outskirts of Bristol now feature a vast network of small 'factories' but since much of the work of organizations is done from home the size of these factories is no guidance to the size of the organization. The ideal family consists of two same-sex partners, one working in world wide web advertising, the other in menotic materials. Their days are taken up in a whirl of constant electronic and face-to-face interaction. Their religion is making money.

These are only three possible urban futures out of many plausible alternatives. What we can be sure of is that none of these futures will happen but that all of them could happen in some measure and to some degree. In a sense, they are all deeply unattractive but, given the emphasis on contingency as a fundamental element of causation, which has been the main message of this chapter, they provide a set of 'might-bes' which we can now work hard to make sure 'might-not'.

References

A. Amin and N.J. Thrift, 'Institutional issues for the European regions: from markets and plans to socioeconomics and powers of association', *Economy and Society*, 24 (1995) 41–66.

C. Beckett, 'The welfare man', in Pringle, P. (ed.), *The Best of Interzone* (London: HarperCollins, 1997) pp. 341–60.

N. Bosanquet, 'Palliative care', *British Medical Journal*, 314 (1997) 1.

J. Casti, *Searching for Certainty: What Science Can Know About the Future* (New York: William Morrow, 1991).

J. Casti, *Would-Be Worlds: How Simulation is Changing the Frontier of Science* (New York: John Wiley, 1997).

F. Dyson, *Imagined Worlds* (Cambridge, Mass.: Harvard University Press, 1997).

N. Ferguson (ed.) *Virtual History, Alternatives and Counterfactuals* (London: Picador, 1997).

P. Hall, *London 2000* (London: Faber & Faber, 1963).

P. Healey, *Collaborative Planning* (London: Jessica Kingsley, 1997).

J. Jacobs, *The Death and Life of Great American Cities* (New York: Random House, 1961).

P. Lassave and A. Querrien (eds) Special issue on 'Emplois du temps/time schedules', *Les Annales de la Recherche Urbaine*, 77 (1997) 1–152.

C. Leadbeater, *The Rise of the Social Entrepreneur*, Paper No. 25 (London: Demos, 1997).

C. Leicester, 'Life in the year AD 2000', in Blowers, A., Hamnett, C. and Sarre, P. (eds) *The Future of Cities* (London: Hutchinson/Open University, 1974; original 1970) pp. 304–9.

A. Leyshon and N.J. Thrift (eds) 'Theme issues on financial exclusion', *Environment and Planning A*, 28:7, 8 (1996).

A. Leyshon and N.J. Thrift, *Money/Space: Geographies of Monetary Transformation* (London: Routledge, 1997).

J. Rossiter (ed.), *Financial Exclusion* (London: New Policy Institute, 1997).

R. Sennett, *Flesh and Stone: The Body and the City in Western Civilization* (New York: Norton, 1994).

L. Stewart, 'Crashing the barriers', *New Scientist*, 29 March 1997, pp. 40–3.

M. Taussig, *The Magic of the State* (New York: Routledge, 1997).

Part II
Local Issues and Global Implications

3 The Politics of Interdependence – Risk and Uncertainty in the City-Region

Murray Stewart

INTRODUCTION

This chapter addresses the theme of Local Issues and Global Implications. Its thesis is that towards the end of the twentieth century successful cities must reflect, and at the same time reinforce, a regional identity since, with the possible exception of the largest world cities – of which there is only one in Britain – cities are too small to create a sense of economic or political identity appropriate to the twenty-first century. In terms of politics and governance the issue is whether the locality – the city-region in general but the Bristol city-region in particular – has sufficient political and administrative capacity to secure the necessary coordination and control for 'global' competition, yet is also sufficiently flexible to sustain the 'local' identity necessary for success in that competition.

The City and County of Bristol (population 356 000) sits within a wider functional economic ('travel to work') area of around 600 000 population. It is the largest of four unitary authorities formed in April 1996 from the former County of Avon (population one million), which in turn was one of the seven counties of the South West Region of England (total population of almost five million). Bristol is thus nested in a regional setting. It cannot stand alone but must draw from its regional base and contribute to that base. It is dependent on its neighbours as they are on it. The contemporary political challenge is the management of territorial and institutional interdependence.

From April 1996 the new Council of the City and County of Bristol, reinstated following local government reorganization as the largest most-purpose non-metropolitan authority in England, has responded to this political challenge. A set of core values was agreed emphasizing the role of the Council in giving community leadership with due regard given to the contributions of public, private and voluntary partners. Joint arrangements with other local authorities and a code of good practice for relations with the voluntary sector have been developed. Appropriate 'rules of engagement' for the negotiation and conduct of collaborative and partnership arrangements have been considered. The city is seeking to reassert its identity and autonomy as a unitary authority while recognizing its interdependence with others in the region.

This assertion of 'sense of identity – sense of place' is hampered, however, by the historic weakness of regionalism in England. It is currently fashionable to argue a regional renaissance in England as political and economic pressures force regionalism up the agenda, but the second part of this chapter suggests a deeper and long-standing basis for more negative views of regionalism. The third part of this chapter explores the nature and extent of regional identity and regional collaboration in the South West of England as a whole and in the Bristol/West of England subregion in particular, while the fourth part argues that the interdependence now evident in the Bristol city-region, as elsewhere, is less a consequence of a rediscovery of regional identity and more a defence against the risks inherent in the competitive culture of urban and regional policy in England.

In presenting this interpretation of the history and nature of English territorial politics and administration, this chapter offers an analysis which is open to comparative analysis – comparison with other cities and regions in England, but more particularly cross-national comparison in general and comparison with the position of Hanover in particular.

ENGLISH REGIONALISM

Analysis of the English region is analysis in a vacuum. There is no democratic governmental form at the regional level, little struggle for power or resources, and – until recently – negligible political debate. There is little agreement about the existence or nature of regional identities. There are overlapping and confusing definitions of regions, with a multiplicity of mutually inconsistent boundary overlays. The region has seldom been seen as a focus for the exercise of administrative discretion or professional expertise; in terms of civil service careers it has been at best a stepping stone, at worst a graveyard.

The Thatcher years exaggerated the decline of the regional idea. A philosophical attachment to the unitary state and parliamentary sovereignty, a fierce dislike of Europe (with its obvious attempts to build a Europe of the Regions), and the dismantling of all machinery concerned with strategic or long-term planning (including most obviously the Greater London Council and the Metropolitan County Councils), all militated against any revival of regionalism. Small wonder then that there is often observed to be a regional vacuum in England. The city-region in turn has been even more neglected in research and discussion. With minor exceptions (Senior, 1969; City Region Campaign, 1996) the concept and practical potential of city-regions has been squeezed out of debate by the competing interests of town and country.

There has been, however, a revival of regionalism fuelled as ever by debate about Scottish, and to a lesser extent Welsh, devolution but also by recognition of the need to maintain a presence within, and draw down resources from, European programmes (Roberts, 1996). There is an active regional debate stimulated not simply by political interest and the experience of referenda, but by a range of concerns relating to democracy and accountability, economic competitiveness, and administrative efficiency (Harding et al., 1996; John and Whitehead, 1997; Bradbury and Mawson, 1997). Under the new Labour administration attention has focused primarily upon Regional Development Agencies rather than regional government. Should the latter emerge, however, they may well follow a model of Regional Chambers, probably confederations of local authorities, and thereafter optional or staged Regional Assemblies. Even without elected regional government, however, a continued impetus towards the regionalization of administration will be driven from Brussels, Westminster and Whitehall (Stewart, 1997b). In Scotland and Wales the debates about regionalism, nationalism and devolution are linked to a clear political agenda, but England is ill prepared for a new regionalism, uncertain about whether it promises a devolution of influence, power and resources from the centre or whether it might involve rather the aggregation of role and function upwards from local government and hence represent the dilution of established political power bases. The tensions evident in debate about the role, function, resources and membership of Regional Development Agencies well illustrate this uncertainty.

In some English regions the debate has been well rehearsed and structures established to exploit the potential of any new regional arrangements. In other regions – and notably the South West of England – there has been an ambivalent, half-hearted and often fragmented response to the potential arrival of a regional dimension to governance. There have been moves towards concertation and coordination (the politics of interdependence) but there has also been complacency, conflict and inaction (what might be termed the politics of unease).

The weakness of English regionalism derives in part from the absence of regional democratic government, in part from the lack of regional identity, and in part from the absence of even administrative coherence. Hogwood (1996) reminds us of the massive variation in the scale and scope of the regional structures of English government, as well as of the incompatibility between regional boundaries. There are differing regional structures for over a hundred executive functions. Several policy areas (e.g. transport, education, health) have more than one regional structure. Within the agriculture policy area there are 18 different regional structures, within law and order 13. There are variations in the subregional arrangements within regions and in the extent to which within-regional staff are dispersed or centralized in a regional centre. Although two (non-identical) structural sets of regions dominate (the 'standard' regions used for planning guidance and for statistical purposes, and the regions designated for economic development, industry, employment and regeneration under an integrated government office) no other government function uses all of the regions from either of these two sets. Even in the medium term 'New Labour: New Regions' seems unlikely to shake this established base.

A key feature of English political culture affecting the long-term viability of the regional idea is that territorial politics is inherently weak. This can be argued to stem from the absence of a constitution which guarantees the position of subnational tiers of democracy combined with the presence of the Westminster model which gives primacy to Cabinet, Ministers and Parliament. In addition, for eighty years since Haldane (1918), England has been dominated by machinery of government which is functionally rather than territorially based (Scotland and Wales are, of course, different). Thus the lack of congruency in regional boundaries discussed above (Hogwood, 1996) stems neither from accident nor oversight, but from the fact that for Whitehall the organization of government on a territorial basis is a secondary consideration. Functional efficiency is more important than territorial integrity; the region has little significance for the organization of public administration in England.

New Government Offices for the Regions have begun to give some coherence to regionalism but as yet remain ambiguously balanced between centre and periphery. Indeed they can be argued to have made as great a contribution to creeping centralization in England as to the enhancement of localization (Stewart, 1994; Hogwood, 1995). It is, however, in their potential challenge to the long-term culture of functionalism that the integrated government office could represent a radical shift rather than the simple rationalization (and resource cutback) of the government's urban programmes.

The existence of this functional as opposed to territorial tradition in English government is echoed in political and administrative cultures. There is far less of the interaction between local and national politics and politicians in England than elsewhere in Europe. There is no interpenetration of subnational and national roles of the kind reflected in the (albeit reduced) French 'cumul des mandats' (the simultaneous holding of multiple positions of power at local, regional and national level). Nor historically has there been any clear advantage to high-flying civil servants in holding posts in the regions, since the Whitehall village (Heclo and Wildavsky, 1981), though now reduced in size, maintains its core executive role and its high policy functions. There is potential for change. Members of Parliament could be ex-officio members of a Regional Chamber and indeed find more scope for constructive work and political reward at regional level than in a disempowered Palace of Westminster. Regional Director roles could become essential stepping stones to the most senior civil service posts. Genuine central/local, vertical partnerships could become the accepted mode of allocating resources as opposed to the horizontal local or regional partnerships which now enjoy a subservient and contractual relationship with the centre rather than any shared identity of interest. Proposed legislation on Regional Development Agencies will enhance the administrative status of regions, but there is growing recognition that in establishing a weakly accountable quango as the first step to regionalism rather than creating directly elected Regional Chambers which would demand a political response, the government has reinforced rather than weakened traditional power structures. Despite the excitement of the arrival of a more active regionalism under the 1997 Labour government, the centralist tendencies inherent in the traditional practice of English politics and administration must be remembered.

Nor did the recent review of the structure of local government in shire England reinforce any sense of regionalism. In an early overview the Local Government Commission for England argued that

> The Commission believes that ... the size of the [new unitary] author-
> ities will best be determined by reference to the need to ... facilitate
> strategic approaches to regional economic development and infra-
> structure, transportation co-ordination and environmental issues.
> (Local Government Commission, 1993)

This implied that the Commission was well aware of the need to build a system of local government which incorporated a capacity to operate at a strategic subregional or regional level and which countered the forces of centralism. In terms of specific proposals as to how such capacity might in practice emerge, however, the Commission said very little, and in consequence, although the review of local government offered the opportunity to develop a debate about the way in which local authority activities could be aggregated into a regional or sub-regional dimension, the outcome of the review was to demote the regional issue (Leach, 1994). The conclusion from research on the work of the Commission is that it contributed nothing to long-term debate about the territorial distribution of power and function in England (Stewart, 1997a).

In much of England (though not Avon) the impact of the review has been to strengthen the existing county-based structure, the disappearance of which many see as the prerequisite for regional government. Indeed the outcome of reorganization has been to resurrect old tensions between town and country, around which many of the conflicts inherent in city-regional politics revolve. There is a long history of anti-urbanism in England, the belief that the city is the source of social evil while rural, suburban or exurban development offers the benefits of well ordered social and economic life. Much English town planning was rooted in this belief with the Garden City and New Towns movement offering concrete examples in practice. The distinction between town and country has been exacerbated by debates about boundaries. Such debates are fuelled by concerns about local taxation, local services, housing development and transportation, but are also rooted in the long-standing wish of many households to get out of cities. The local politics of cities with tightly drawn boundaries (of which Bristol is one) are often coloured by the fiscal and electoral politics of potential boundary review. In England the recent local government review did nothing to address, far less resolve, such tensions, and indeed by reinventing the county borough but largely preserving the English counties (in its recommendations for 'hybrid' structures involving unitary urban authorities within otherwise two-tier counties), the Local Government Commission has done much to rekindle the old town versus country debate and consequently to relegate the regional issue.

There have been attempts to redefine the whole region/city-region issue and to identify new areas for territorial administration. If the existing standard regions offer little consistency, is there scope for developing an entirely new interpretation of the 'city-region' based on functional analysis of commuting, retail, and economic and leisure activities? A recent analysis (Coombes, 1996) identifies 53 such city-regions in England, many matching existing areas of county government but others offering new definitions of the relationship between cities and their hinterlands. But the post-reorganization fatigue currently being experienced by central and local government alike is such as to deter attempts to interpose a new level of government between existing district authorities and new regions (as the city-regions would).

BRISTOL, THE WEST OF ENGLAND AND THE SOUTH WEST

These ambiguities and uncertainties about regional futures are compounded in the South West of England. The region itself has a strong rural dimension. Seventy per cent of the region's land area is used for agriculture; 47 per cent of the population lived in rural areas in 1994; more than half the region's population live in towns of less than 20 000 people; 37 per cent is designated as National Park or Area of Outstanding Natural Beauty. On the other hand, a third of the region's population live in towns and cities over 100 000 in which are concentrated 58 per cent of the region's jobs and 61 per cent of its unemployment. The region has 14 per cent of the country's derelict land, and the cities (Bristol and Plymouth) as well as much of the County of Cornwall and many smaller seaside tourist-oriented towns, experience significant multiple disadvantages. These differences in the socio-economic position of differing parts of the region are accentuated by its size and length. At 386 kilometres from end to end, it is a shorter distance from the northern edge of the region to Scotland than to its southern tip – and considerably quicker in travel time.

The region has attracted high levels of inward migration. From 1991 to 1994, the population increased by 80 000 (the fastest rate of increase in England) and is projected to continue to increase to 5.25 million by 2011. The number of households will rise even faster as household size falls, with 545 000 new households predicted for the period 1991–2016

(South West Regional Planning Conference, 1996). The region illustrates, perhaps above all others in England, the tension between environmental sustainability and economic growth, with demand for housing, employment and movement increasing and inevitably posing threats to the quality of life.

The geographical spread of the South West Region accentuates a duality of function. On the one hand there is the 'Far South West' – Cornwall and Devon – much of it with European Union Objective 5b status. The disappearance of traditional mining, agriculture and the seasonal nature of much of the tourist and services sector economic activity, reinforced by geographical peripherality, poses severe problems. In the northern part of the region, good communications have brought massive population and housing expansion, along the northern edge of Bristol in particular.

The West of England hovers between peripherality and centrality. In European terms South West England lies within the newly defined Atlantic Arc Region, defined by the European Commission as being largely peripheral, 'having a weak and unbalanced urban system, and with its productive sectors in decline' (European Commission, 1995). By contrast Bristol – one of the major cities along the Atlantic Rim – is close to the edge of the Central Cities Region triangulated by London, Paris and Brussels, a region of high potential and spatial concentration. Within the UK, the South West is equally ill at ease as improved communication with the rest of Europe increases the relative advantage of the south and east of England, while structural funds allocated under Objectives 1, 2, and 5b assist many other subregional locations.

This ambiguity about the nature of the region is reflected in its structures of governance. There are two Government Offices (one based in Bristol, one in Plymouth), reflecting the size and length of the region, as well as two Regional Development Agencies. For health purposes, the South and West Region extends eastwards to include Hampshire; conversely, Gloucestershire falls within the Midlands Region for the purposes of the Environment Agency. Thus both formally and informally there are distinct subregional groupings of interests, reflecting both the difference between the 'Far South West', 'West of England' and 'South East' subregions, and the differing roles of their main urban centres. Plymouth rivals Bristol as a regional capital in the 'far South West'; Bournemouth and Poole in the 'South East' subregion have strong links with Southampton and Portsmouth in the South East Standard Region and with Le Havre and Rouen in northern France. Bristol itself straddles the M4 growth corridor as a crucial north/south, east/west transportation node.

At the same time Coombes' (1996) analysis of the city-regional structure of England identifies seven city-regions falling within the current standard South West Region (just as there are seven counties currently within the region). None of these city-regions, however,[1] is coterminous with an existing county area. These variations within regional conditions and circumstances are reflected in very different interpretations of what could or should be 'regional' objectives, and in a very incoherent and shifting agenda of regional politics.

A number of factors have led, therefore, to some recognition of a wider political and economic interdependence in a subregion larger than an immediate Greater Bristol but smaller than the South West Region. The vulnerability of the defence and financial service sectors, increased pressure of demand for housing, office, commercial and industrial land and buildings, the revitalization of the Port of Bristol and the opening of a second road bridge crossing over the River Severn have all accentuated the significance of a range of strategic planning issues. The experience of the last five years, therefore, has been one of the proliferation of interorganizational initiatives designed to provide identity and coherence to subregional economic and strategic land use planning. The West of England Development Agency (WEDA), integrating five county areas within a government-sponsored arrangement and directed primarily at the capture of inward investment, has joined the longer-standing Western Development Partnership (WDP) which, within the former county of Avon area, also addresses issues of inward investment, but additionally provides a forum for discussion of the needs of particular sectors, of strategic sites for economic development, and of European programmes such as KONVER which span local authority boundaries. The authorities of Bristol, Swindon and Gloucester are linked into the West of England Initiative (WEI) which focuses on the common and interrelated questions faced by the urban authorities of the subregion.

In the area now covered by the four unitary authorities of the former Avon county there is recognition that economic, planning, transportation and waste management issues can best be managed on a collaborative basis, and a Joint Committee of Strategic Planning and Transportation (supported by a Joint Unit) is preparing a revised structure plan for the four-authority area. Despite fears about the disruption to strategic planning likely to be caused by the abolition of Avon County Council in 1996, the Joint Committee has made a strong beginning to its complex task and a formal protocol has equal membership, equally shared costs and rotating chairmanship as the basis for joint working (Joint Strategic Planning and Transportation Unit, 1996). Equally evident has been the liaison between senior officers of the four unitary authorities. As if unburdened by the disappearance of the county council and confident in their new base of responsibility for all the functions of local government, the four new unitary authorities have begun to act responsibly and collaboratively.

Within the city itself a wide range of partnerships have been established linking public, private and non-statutory sectors in a variety of ways and for a variety of purposes. Some – the Cultural Development Partnership, the Western Partnership for Sustainable Development, for example – focus on activities which, either because Bristol acts as a focus for subregional-wide activity (as in the arts) or because the issue is not confined by administrative boundaries (environment), have implications for neighbouring authorities. In other areas, Bristol partnerships are more directly competitive with, as well as complementary to, edge-city and other subregional developments. The Broadmead Board, a public/private partnership company with responsibilities in the retailing and commercial core of the city, is one example, fighting to re-establish central Bristol in the face of fierce out-of-town competition.

Partnership building in and around Bristol has inevitably been undertaken in the shadow of past relationships, a past characterized by suspicion between public and private sectors, tension between local and central government, uncertainty between the local authority and non-statutory groups, and (in the 1980s) competition between the local authority and newly created local quangos. Bristol City Council has a strong tradition of service provision while both the council and the private sector have had reputations for independence (and sometimes for complacency). In the run up to reorganization, relations with neighbouring authorities were inevitably difficult, but partnerships in Bristol and the West have begun to challenge the stereotype of local infighting and territorial jealousies (Snape and Stewart, 1996). There are of course ambiguous messages about the image of Bristol in the surrounding subregion, and with respect to its 'regional capital' role the city is seen by some as being introspective. There remains resistance from those who fear what might be perceived as a new

Bristol imperialism within the West of England. Nevertheless drawing regional stakeholders into partnership may be an important way in which these tensions and fears can be addressed and resolved.

COMPETITION, RISK AVOIDANCE AND INTERDEPENDENCE

The earlier sections of this chapter point to a precarious framework within which the politics of the city-region are exercised. In practice, two additional factors cement the interdependence of the local actors – uncertainty (bordering on unease) and risk.

It is clear from the above arguments that the nature and future of English regions, of the South West region and of the Bristol and West of England subregion in particular is uncertain. Political uncertainty surrounds the future of regionalism regardless of the colour of national political control; there is uncertainty about the future shape of regional policy throughout Europe and of the impact of any 'Europe of the Regions' project; there is uncertainty about the role and function both of the Regional Development Agencies and of the still young Government Offices for the Regions (not least in the South West where there are two such offices for different parts of the region); there are uncertainties about the machinery of strategic planning following local government reorganization; there are uncertainties about the role of the various regional and subregional organizational innovations designed to coordinate and rationalize the disparate efforts of local actors; and there are uncertainties in the Bristol/West of England subregion about the joint arrangements for working across new unitary authorities. There are in addition uncertainties about substantive issues such as the future of economic growth, the increase in housing demand, and the quality of the environment and sustainability.

Uncertainty is mixed with concern. In a number of the above areas some actors feel not simply uncertain, but also uneasy, fearing the adverse consequences on their organizations of some of the factors identified above, but believing that uncertainty shared is uncertainty reduced. In the wake of the fragmentation of institutional form experienced in the 1980s and the proliferation of new organizations and agencies during that decade, there is now a new recognition of the significance of integration and of the interdependence of local organizations. Inter-sectoral interdependence has been addressed as public, private and non-statutory sectors form partnerships. Local authorities recognize the interdependence of strategic planning interests. Even the client/contractor relationship inherent in service provision is recognized to be an interdependence determined not solely by market factors.

In terms of urban and regional governance these interdependencies have been recognized in attempts to build local capacity. Oatley and Lambert in Chapter 13 explore the routes through which Bristol has sought to increase local capacity, drawing on a range of studies (Miller, 1958a and b; Clements, 1969; DiGaetano, 1997; Bassett, 1996; Stewart, 1996) and identifying the implications for UK regional analysis of the application of growth mechanisms, urban coalitions and regime theory. The sprouting of partnership activity in Bristol is without doubt a proactive response to a perceived need to build local capacity, not least because partnerships are now a prerequisite for resource acquisition.

In the last five years the government, inherently distrustful of public sector bureaucracy, has sought to institutionalize inter-urban competition. Two rounds of City Challenge set the tone for what is now a pervasive culture of public sector resource allocation, and while City Challenge has been superseded by the Challenge Fund element of Single Regeneration Budget (SRB) funding, this is now open to all authorities, thus introducing a new intra-regional element of inter-locality competition.

The evidence is that City Challenge, and more particularly its SRB successor, has won grudging acknowledgement that the competitive process has had an impact and indeed brought some advantage. The impact on both winners (de Groot, 1992) and losers (Malpass, 1994; Oatley and Lambert, 1995) has been significant, and even opponents acknowledge the new regime to have had a significant positive impact upon the mobilization of local leadership and collaborative capacity building. The formalized competition which now characterizes urban policy has had a series of consequences, therefore, running far beyond simplistic 'some win, some lose' outcomes. These consequences include the fact that participation in competition must be supported by partnerships representing all those with a key interest, and the building of local coalitions is therefore a condition of entry to the many competitions. Partnerships vary in structure and behaviour but within the competitive regime as a whole consensual, multi-sector coalitions and partnerships are the most likely winners, thus diminishing the potential of SRB as a vehicle for the expression of local political aspirations. Partnership in the mid-1990s effectively depoliticizes regeneration strategy building.

Additionally the capacity to deliver has become more crucial than ever, with the winning of approval in principle being followed by preparation of a delivery plan and subsequent detailed appraisal of all the elements of the plan. Resources are conditional upon the delivery of agreed outputs and although competition offers the route to success, in practice the operation of the Single Regeneration Budget through the Challenge Fund process also represents the contractualization of policy implementation. Indeed capacity to deliver has superseded local needs as the primary criterion for support. Although in practice the correlation between deprivation as measured by the Index of Local Conditions (Department of the Environment, 1994) and resources allocated has been reasonably close, with almost half of Challenge Fund II being allocated to districts with scores in the top two deciles of the Index, there remained significant allocations of resources to districts with below average Index scores (£141 million in the Challenge Round II). All these tendencies have significantly altered the practice of urban policy delivery. They are encapsulated in the underlying shift towards a general culture of markets and competition, and towards the legitimation of place marketing. Although the Labour government now argues that the rationale for regeneration programmes is largely social, and has shifted the guidelines for regeneration funding to give greater emphasis to areas of need (Department of the Environment, Transport and the Regions, 1997), the competitive edge has been retained with recognition that 'competition for resources is unavoidable in some form if resources are not distributed entirely by formula'.

Historically competition between localities has been regarded as a zero sum game and has been frowned on by government. Unfettered competition between cities (or regions) was thought likely to be inefficient insofar as free competition is likely to result in oversupply, underused resources and therefore inefficiencies in the provision and use of resources (King, 1990; Stewart and Underwood, 1984). In the 1990s, however, competition is perceived as a healthy incentive and several of the Bristol partnerships – the Bristol Regeneration Partnership and Bristol 2000, for example – were established primarily to draw down resources from the national Regeneration Challenge Fund and the National Lottery Funds respectively.

Partnership building, however, can also be seen in terms of risk avoidance and/or risk management. The entry of risk into what have traditionally been areas of non-risk public administration represents a further shift in the culture of urban policy management. Under conditions of uncertainty organizations will look to joint activity in order to spread risk or indeed in order to take risks. Thus much of the rationale of partnership building in Bristol has been the recognition that the local authority has neither the resources, the legal right nor perhaps the will to take risks inherent in much contemporary urban boosterism. Equally, the private sector is unwilling to make risky investments without some form of civic underwriting. It is well known from the organizational literature that groups take riskier decisions than individuals and it is clear that the activities of the several Bristol Partnerships have produced more innovation, adventure and risk than Bristol has enjoyed in recent decades.

It is also clear that the competitive route towards winning resources involves risk management. The investment of time and money in civic ventures that may not come to fruition if resources are not won involves risk and uncertainty. The partnerships can be likened to new business ventures, in that they require risk-taking among the partners who come together, each contributing something and hoping for greater individual and collective profit or civic benefit as a return on their investment. Understanding partnership working as a strategy of collective risk avoidance adds a second dimension to that of simple capacity building and helps to explain the nature of interdependence in the city-region.

A number of strategies have been adopted by various partners to 'minimize' the risks of partnership working. These have included use of the company structure with limited liability, with stability inherent in the legal framework and an important element of psychological commitment linked to company directorship. In other situations partners join together in cooperative groupings for the pragmatic purpose of getting a specific job done, but not entering into the legal 'marriage' of the company structure, e.g. Bristol 2000. This structure has been adopted in instances where the partners do not require an ongoing cooperative relationship and have come together only for a specific, time limited, mutually beneficial end. The use of 'trading' whereby one party gives a commodity to another with the understanding that it will be returned to the original party in an improved condition or with interest offers another route to risk minimization, while some potential partners will wait to see what other partners have to offer before individual organizations commit their own resources (i.e. as a means of ensuring that all partners are contributing on an equitable basis). Finally a number of partnerships have shown reliance upon feasibility studies in an attempt to have as much information as possible about the potential success of an initiative before committing substantial time, energy or resources to a project. Mutually generated and owned information about risks and opportunities goes some way to building the trust essential to collaborative working.

CONCLUSION

This chapter has pointed to a precarious framework within which the politics of the city-region are exercised. Unified regional administration is illusory, while there is lack of clarity about the role of the region in debates about subnational structure. The South West Region is large, heterogeneous and divided with little sense of regional purpose or vision. The impending establishment of a Regional Development Agency has as yet provided no coherence to the debate. In the Bristol/West of England subregion (whether defined as several counties or the former County of Avon area), the legacy of local government structural reform and the initial momentum of public/private partnership provide a platform for the reconciliation of long-term strategic vision with short-term management of economic and social change. This is a fragile platform, however, with any new city-regional governance very much on probation. Risk and uncertainty cement the interdependence of the local actors. There is, therefore, very little 'sense of identity, sense of place' upon which city-regional governance can build.

The politics of interdependence in the West of England, therefore, rely much less on the assertion of common regional or urban values of history, heritage, culture, language or even administration than do many regions elsewhere in Europe. Important as these are to the place marketing and economic development of the city, they do not form the basis for a robust interdependence of political interest reflecting a sense of 'identity and place'. Instead this chapter argues that in the face of global competition and the domestic institutional-ization of a 'winners and losers' culture of competitive resource allocation, the dominant values are rather those of pragmatism and risk minimization. The politics of interdependence in the Bristol city-region are the politics of the head not the heart.

Note

1. The seven city-regions are based on Plymouth, Exeter, Taunton, Bristol, Bath/Swindon, Bournemouth/Poole and Gloucester/Cheltenham.

References

K. Bassett, 'Partnerships, business elites and urban politics: new forms of governance in an English city', *Urban Studies*, 33 (1996).

J. Bradbury and J. Mawson (eds), *British Regionalism and Devolution* (London: Jessica Kingsley, 1997).

City Region Campaign, *Building a New Britain: an Alternative Democratic Vision for the United Kingdom and its Constitution* (London: The City Region Campaign, 1996).

R. Clements, *Local Notables and the City Council* (London: Macmillan, 1969).

The Constitution Unit, *Regional Government in England* (London: The Constitution Unit, 1996).

M. Coombes, 'Definition of city regions in the United Kingdom', Appendix to *Building a New Britain: an Alternative Democratic Vision for the United Kingdom and its Constitution* (London: The City Region Campaign, 1996).

L. DeGroot, 'City Challenge: competing in the urban regeneration game', *Local Economy*, 7:3 (1992).

Department of the Environment, *Index of Local Conditions* (London: DoE, 1994).

Department of the Environment, Transport and the Regions, *Regeneration Programmes: The Way Forward* (London, DETR, 1997).

A. DiGaetano, 'Urban governing alignments and realignments in comparative perspective: developmental politics in Boston, Massachusetts, and Bristol, England 1980–86', *Urban Affairs Review*, 32:6 (1997).

European Commission, *Europe 2000+ Co-operation for European Territorial Development* (Luxembourg: Office for the Official Publications of the European Commission, 1995).

Haldane, *Report of the Machinery of Government Committee* (The Haldane Report), Cmnd 9230 (London: HMSO, 1918).

A. Harding, R. Evans, M. Parkinson and P. Garside, *Regional Government in Britain: an Economic Solution* (Bristol: The Policy Press, 1996).

H. Heclo and A. Wildavsky, *The Private Government of Public Money* (London: Macmillan, 1981).

B.W. Hogwood, *The Integrated Regional Offices and the Single Regeneration Budget*, Research Paper 13 (Commission for Local Democracy, 1995).

B.W. Hogwood, *Mapping the Regions: Boundaries, Co-ordination and Government* (Bristol: The Policy Press, 1996).

P. John and A. Whitehead (eds), 'Regionalism in England: current trends and future prospects', *Policy and Politics*, 25:1 (1997).

Joint Strategic Planning and Transportation Unit, *Service Plan and Budget 1996–97 and 1997–98* (Bristol: Joint Committee for Strategic Planning and Transportation, 1996).

D. King, 'Economic activity and the challenge to local government', in D. King and J. Pierre (eds), *Challenges to Local Government* (London: Sage, 1990).

R. Leach, 'The missing regional dimension to the local government review', *Regional Studies*, 28:8 (1994).

Local Government Commission, *Renewing Local Government in the English Shires: A Progress Report* (London: HMSO, 1993).

P. Malpass, 'Policy making and local governance: how Bristol failed to secure City Challenge funding (twice)', *Policy and Politics*, 22:4 (1994).

J. Mawson et al., *The Single Regeneration Budget: Stocktake: A Review of Challenge Round II* (Birmingham: Centre for Urban and Regional Studies, University of Birmingham, 1996).

D.C. Miller, 'Decision making cliques in community power structures: a comparative study of an American and an English City', *American Journal of Sociology*, LXI (1958a).

D.C. Miller, 'Industry and community power structure: a comparative study of an American and an English city', *American Sociological Review*, XXIII (1958b).

N. Oatley and C. Lambert, 'Evaluating competitive urban policy: the City Challenge Initiative', in R. Hambleton and H. Thomas (eds), *Urban Policy Evaluation* (London: Paul Chapman Publishing, 1995).

P. Roberts, *Regional Strategy and Partnership in European Programmes: Experience in Four UK Regions* (York: York Publishing Services, 1996).

D. Senior, *The Royal Commission on Local Government in England 1966–1969 Report*, Cmnd 4040, Vol. II (Memorandum of Dissent) (London: HMSO, 1969).

D. Snape and M. Stewart, *Keeping up the Momentum: Partnership in Bristol and the West of England*, Report to the Bristol Chamber of Commerce and Initiative (Bristol, 1996).

South West Regional Planning Conference, *Revised Regional Strategy: Priority Issues Report* (Taunton: South West Regional Planning Conference, 1996).

M. Stewart, 'Between Whitehall and town hall: the realignment of urban regeneration policy in England', *Policy and Politics*, 22:2 (1994).

M. Stewart, 'The politics of local complacency', *Journal of Urban Affairs*, 18:2 (1996).

M. Stewart, *The Work of the Local Government Commission for England 1991–96*, Joseph Rowntree Foundation (York: York Publishing Services, 1997a).

M. Stewart, 'The shifting institutional framework', in J. Bradbury and J. Mawson (eds), *British Regionalism and Devolution* (London: Jessica Kingsley, 1997b).

M. Stewart and J. Underwood, 'Inner cities policy', in K. Young and C. Mason (eds), *Urban Economic Development* (London: Macmillan, 1984).

4 Commentary on Murray Stewart's Thesis

Dietrich Fürst

STEWART'S THESIS

Murray Stewart puts forward the thesis that despite the advantages of the new forms of inter-municipal cooperation (improved regional division of labour, increased innovation in dealing with problems, etc.), such links are particularly precarious in the UK because they primarily constitute strategic 'risk avoidance partnerships'. Consequently he considers 'a unified regional administration illusory'. As Stewart suggests, the main reasons for problems encountered with cooperation in England are:

- the absence of a democratically elected regional tier of government, of a tradition of regional policy formulation and even of regional identities;
- the political system characterized by sectoralization and centralization while a territorial dimension of policy-making has no tradition;
- territorial elements of national government policies which are too heterogeneous and particularistic to form the core of regional cooperation;
- the abolition by central government of new forms of regional cooperation initiatives under the Thatcher government.

Furthermore, the local authorities encouraged to become involved in partnerships lack experience of cooperation, all the more so since:

- there is a history of tensions between rural and urban areas plus a long-standing antipathy towards cities;
- public and private sectors mistrust each other;
- tensions between local and central governments are common;
- relationships between local authorities and non-statutory bodies are characterized by uncertainty;
- and, in addition, there is competition between local administrations and newly created 'quangos' (quasi-autonomous non-governmental organizations).

If, under such circumstances, regional cooperation does emerge, this is primarily due to the fact that:

- functional regional interrelations increase the need for cooperation;
- under the new national funding mechanisms (City Challenge, Single Regeneration Budget, Challenge Fund) local authorities have to compete for state funds and can improve their competitive position by cooperation.

Stewart's thesis is startling. However, what are its consequences? The motivation to act is undoubtedly an important but underestimated element influencing cooperation. It not only affects the initiative to take action but also affects the process and may strongly influence the outcome. This is because the motivation in part determines the interpretation of the need for action, influences the assessment of opportunities for action and thus the actors' commitment and, what is more, impacts on the internal dynamics of the partnership. If risk avoidance is the dominant motive it might have the effect that:

- the initial situation is regarded by local government as just another chance to receive public funds;
- the organizational devices considered relevant are either very 'weak' and short-lived forms of cooperation, i.e. project-oriented strategic alliances, or the collaboration is 'externalized' by creating organizations which are less 'politicized' yet can be controlled, such as a development agency (with limited competences and managed through a set of clear rules by a 'board of directors' which draws its members from the partners involved);
- the internal dynamics of the partnership do not lead to the kind of closer relationships which could in turn develop into a more sustained network of cooperation. For, if the partnership does not evolve beyond risk avoidance, it lacks the inherent dynamism of development. Cooperation continues to be seen as a means of obtaining funds rather than as a 'resource' for collective action which would allow problems to be resolved in a more innovative, effective and efficient manner.

Consequently, in England a very different system of regional cooperation would be likely to emerge than in Germany where in many ways the opposite prerequisites for regional cooperation exist, as is outlined below. England (Stewart refers explicitly to England) would be likely to produce either:

- strategic alliances aimed at winning in the competition for state funds; or
- regional development agencies responsible for organizing partnerships between the private sector and local governments; or
- specific regional groups set up to seek remedies for particular problems not otherwise being addressed by public bodies.

THE GERMAN EXPERIENCE

Regional cooperation in Germany operates in an environment which contrasts with Stewart's analysis of England. Indeed, the background for local and regional cooperation is particularly favourable because (see Benz 1996; Fürst, 1996)

- there is a strong territorial tradition enhanced by the federal system of government and in many regions the existence of a feeling of 'regional identity';
- although, as in Britain, the policy-making structures are sectoralized and there is a tendency towards centralization at the federal government level, this is counterbalanced by a strong territorial dimension. This territorial dimension exists not only at the *Länder* and local levels but also at the regional level, i.e. the level between local authorities and the *Länder*. At the regional level the territorial dimension is represented by district governments (*Bezirksregierungen*) or by regional bodies which are responsible for spatial planning and – in part – for infrastructure provision (Fürst, 1996). Furthermore, the political parties, the unions and many non-governmental organizations are also regionalized (have regional decision-making structures), and increasingly the mass media are regionalized, heightening regional identities even further.
- In addition, there is a long-standing commitment to local self-government; following the principle of subsidiarity. Local autonomy allows local authorities to handle their own affairs on a relatively broad canvas.

Nevertheless, cooperation between local authorities in Germany seems to be no easier than it is in England. An assessment of experiences of successful outcomes in regional cooperation in Germany suggests that local authorities do not initiate cooperation with the aim of establishing 'joint regional development concepts' (*Regionale Entwicklungskonzepte*); rather they cooperate on particular projects, and only if required to do so by fiscal or technical demands entailing joint action because:

- some tasks such as public transport and waste disposal extend well beyond local boundaries and require at least regional consultation and coordination of interests;
- severe resource constraints force local authorities to finance public services or local amenities jointly with neighbouring communities.

By contrast, should regional cooperation be aimed at producing 'regional development programmes' (*Regionale Entwicklungskonzepte*)? It is, in the main, initiated by the state. In this case there are basically two different motives for cooperative action. First, the state enforces cooperation by law. This has been the usual way in the past. Second, cooperation is induced by state-controlled fiscal incentives. Similar to the City Challenge programme in England, local authorities receive additional public funds if they cooperate on 'regional development programmes'. EU structural funds, by requiring regional operational programmes, have had a similar effect and undoubtedly enforced this programme approach in Germany.

From the analysis a preliminary conclusion can be drawn. Despite differences in the institutional frameworks, inter-municipal cooperation is very restricted in both England and Germany. The authorities work together only in areas where cooperation produces obvious advantages and where local autonomy is largely unaffected. Thus the promotion of economic development is not very often an element of regional cooperation in Germany because it is considered to be an important field of inter-municipal competition where there is considerable discretion for local action.

Why is cooperation between communities so difficult? Numerous studies have been undertaken to examine the situation in Germany. Their findings come, more or less, to the same principal conclusion. There are adverse institutional conditions for cooperation.

- The logic of action of local politicians is not supportive of regional cooperation in that it is committed to 'local egoism'. Politicians elected to a local council are expected to show strong concern for the welfare of their own community. If they present themselves as 'champions of the region' this is rarely appreciated by the electorate.

- The political transaction costs of decisions to engage in regional cooperation are very high because German local government law as well as the voting system favour coalition governments which tend to lead to higher costs of decision-making.
- The costs of not cooperating in the region are not obvious and not in any way attributable to individual local politicians. Consequently, they are not taken into account in policy-making. Since the failure to solve local problems, which in principle could be tackled regionally, can have many causes, it is easy for politicans to blame such failure on third parties. In the German federal system, they could be the *Land*, the federal level or even the European Union.
- The financial capacity of local authorities is more or less dependent on the size of their populations. This applies to revenues from taxes and rates as well as to the state system of fiscal equalization. Thus, regional cooperation tends to lead to conflicts in the redistribution of costs. This is particularly the case if regional cooperation is a common good from which the entire region benefits, while the expenditures have to be financed by different local authorities. Where cooperation was successful it was because local entities confined themselves to projects where redistribution conflicts could be resolved by the application of the principle of equivalence.
- Additional problems arise in large areas. They are usually structured as follows: a county-free city (*kreisfreie Stadt*) forms the core of a region surrounded by county-dependent local authorities (*kreisangehörige Gemeinden*). This arrangement produces two further obstacles to cooperation, as follows.
- Usually the city has a stronger need to cooperate than the surrounding communities because it lacks suitable sites for land use (which are plentiful in the surrounding region) or because its public services and amenities are used by neighbouring local authorities who do not contribute adequately to them. However, the core city is rarely willing to give up part of its autonomy in favour of a joint approach.
- On the other hand the need for regional cooperation is diminished by the fact that joint statutory authorities already exist which could be a substitute for inter-municipal cooperation. Usually, there are associations of local authorities engaged in spatial planning and other special purpose associations. Also, some agglomerations border the territory of other *Länder* (such as Bremen, Berlin,

Hamburg, Halle/Leipzig) so that cooperation across city boundaries is impeded by different state-laws, raising the transaction costs of cooperation to a prohibitive level.

The arguments refer primarily to project-oriented partnerships. If, however, the focus is on cooperation with the objective of establishing common 'regional development programmes', the styles of cooperation used in Germany hardly differ from those in England:

- 'Weak' organizational devices are chosen, ensuring full autonomy for all partners and providing exit options at any time.
- In most cases strategic alliances are developed. Here the central problem is how to define the limits of the area to be covered and who are the actors to be involved. Usually the problem is solved pragmatically. The actors involved are those interested in cooperation or those whose inclusion is required by functional considerations at the regional level.
- The effectiveness of such partnerships is determined primarily by factors such as (a) the presence of committed advocates; (b) the existence of an institutional framework which encourages or, at least, does not hamper cooperation; (c) basic agreement to cooperate on common projects; (d) the establishment of an efficient management of cooperation, for instance through professional facilitators or development agencies; and (e) rapid achievement of success (see also Van den Berg et al., 1997).

RISK AVOIDANCE AS A REASON FOR COOPERATION?

In contrast to Stewart's findings, German studies have paid relatively little attention to the reasons for cooperation. It is generally assumed that cooperation is either the result of a pragmatic reaction to technical and fiscal requirements or that partnerships simply constitute 'cartels of interest' seeking more effective access to state funding.

Stewart has focused attention on risk avoidance in the context of a competitive system of bidding for state funds. At first sight, this interpretation cannot be corroborated by German findings, where risk avoidance (or risk control) seems to play only a minor role. Local politicians rarely bear the risks of non-cooperation and, in addition, local competition for state funds is far less developed. However, this latter motive cannot be entirely ignored in those circumstances where *Länder* governments have introduced new systems of distributing funds based on regions competing for state funds by putting forward common development programmes. Thus Stewart's assumptions might be applicable to the regional conferences in North Rhine-Westphalia (see Fürst and Kilper, 1995). Here, empirical findings showed that in only a few instances has regional cooperation evolved into a constructive system of 'collective problem-solving'. In most cases regional conferences agreed on 'regional development programmes' on the basis of the lowest common denominator. That is a highly likely outcome since nearly all the regions involved include within them powerful local authorities with strong ties to the *Land* administration,[1] such that they can influence the allocation of resources by bypassing the regions. Despite North Rhine-Westphalia's long history of regional planning – the *Siedlungsverband Ruhrkohlenbezirk* made the Ruhr District the cradle of German regional planning – regional cooperation did not seem to become more popular. In circumstances where constructive cooperation got into the 'take-off phase', this was primarily due to 'institutionalized regional advocates', for instance if a joint regional bureau existed which fostered the cooperative process.

Stewart's argument corresponds to the logic of action of local authorities which, compared to that of enterprises, is much more input- than output-oriented and hence focused on limited problem-solving and risk avoidance rather than on the innovative utilization of new possibilities. Politicians are not rewarded for a job well done; rather they can expect to be 'punished' if the electorate is dissatisfied with their achievements. The principle of the 'politics of blame avoidance' applies to them (see Weaver, 1986).

The logic of actors from the business community is completely different. Competition forces them to make use of available options thus risking bad investments. Hence they cooperate regionally if changing concepts of production techniques and organization (outsourcing, just-in-time, etc.) require such steps on the basis of cost-benefit considerations. To put it in another way: while entrepreneurs' actions are option-orientated, politicians tend to emphasize cost avoidance. This localist view is further supported by the institutional framework favouring a narrow perspective. For local politicians only those costs are relevant which are incurred within local boundaries.

However, if risk avoidance were the main reason for cooperation, the need for cooperation would be much greater in England than in Germany as the uncertainty and risks for local authorities have increased in the 1980s and the 1990s. The financial basis of local government in England is weaker than in Germany, making local authorities more dependent on central government funds than their German counterparts. But government grants are more difficult to obtain since they are subject to a competitive bidding process.[2] In addition, local authorities compete more intensely in England since political entrepreneurs seem to play a more important role than in Germany. In Germany political entrepreneurs are still rare, even though most local government legislation now has provision for a 'strong mayor'.

Hence, the English system of competitive bidding for funds could be seen as ambivalent. On the one hand, it is part of the modern system of 'new public management' to allocate public funds with the effect that:

- questions of redistribution are depoliticized through the competitive approach: the system is no longer dominated by 'an equal share principle' as in Germany, but by a system of merits or by the 'capacity to deliver';
- authorities bidding for resources are required to produce convincing action programmes aimed at targets set by the funding body which also controls the implementation process.

On the other hand, the system has reinforced thinking about strategic alliances as devices created for a specified period of time to secure public funds rather than to generate longer-term cooperation.

THE CONTEXT FOR THE 'POLITICS OF INTERDEPENDENCE'

If one takes for granted that in England regional cooperation is both active and positive and that competition at the local level introduced by central government produces 'political entrepreneurship', creating an outlook similar to that of businessmen and women, the question arises: does the different institutional framework have anything to do with it?

There are a number of clues pointing in this direction. Regional cooperation is the mobilization of collective action under particular circumstances such as:

1. the presence of people promoting such an approach;
2. responsiveness by partners willing to engage in cooperation. Such responsiveness requires a clear awareness of issues and a way of thinking which accepts regional cooperation as a useful problem-solving device;

3. low transaction costs to bring about cooperation without undue use of resources. 'Policy windows' and 'windows of opportunity' (Kingdon, 1984, p. 173) may help to reduce transaction costs;
4. an institutional framework which, on the one hand, lowers transaction costs and, on the other hand, creates opportunities for action.

These circumstances may well vary between England and Germany because the context is different. First, the actors' responsiveness towards cooperation may be more favourable in Germany than in the UK. For instance, the cooperative tradition plays a significant role (Van den Berg et al., 1997, p. 255). Even more important could be paradigmatic changes which have influenced local political action in Germany in the last ten years. For example, the readiness of local authorities to cooperate has been greatly enhanced by the competition between the regions in the EU internal market, as well as by numerous publications and warnings on trends and scenarios dramatizing the precarious future position of the regions in the single common market. The reorganization of the Stuttgart metropolitan region (1994) and the changes underway in the Hanover region[3] illustrate this point.

Secondly, the role played by change agents is particularly significant. Van den Berg et al. (1997, p. 259) argue that the leadership and the entrepreneurial spirit of key figures or key institutions contribute substantially to the successful designing, development and implementation of projects. There must be leadership, whether relying on specific competencies (the position in the administrative hierarchy, financial capabilities, specific know-how or other powers) or on the charisma of public or private individuals who successfully fulfil the function of 'project puller'. In this respect the local/regional level in Germany compares unfavourably with the UK. Institutions/ actors who could provide regional leadership are absent, as are incentives rewarding the 'entrepreneurial policy-maker'. The core cities cannot provide leadership without encountering resistance from surrounding towns and districts. Local politicians rarely receive recognition for taking the lead. And for various reasons private enterprises do not show enough interest for the region to take on leadership roles. Therefore, the provision of leadership rests primarily with the *Land* government which performs this function only reluctantly because of the strong standing of the local authorities. In addition, Land governments are no longer willing to initiate territorial reform discussions after the negative experience of the last local government reform (1965–78) (Thieme and Prillwitz,

1981). The stance is now to shy away from compulsory measures and to use incentives, instead. If compulsory intervention is required the *Land* government waits for signals from the regions rather than initiates legislative action. This can be seen in the regions of Stuttgart and Hanover.

As already noted, the institutional framework in England does promote entrepreneurial strategic alliances while in Germany it tends to enforce 'strong organizations' with negative effects on the dynamics of cooperative problem-solving and innovation. 'Soft' forms of cooperation, such as network-based structures, would not last in Germany. Rather, the context tends to strong institutionalization in the longer run. Reasons for this may be:

- in Germany the political culture is more 'legalistic' (the *Rechtsstaat* principle, Benz 1996) demanding stronger forms of institutional arrangements with the effect that inter-municipal strategic alliances (networks) are perceived as transitory;
- informal network-based structures lack legitimacy. They may structure the decision-making process at the local level, but they cannot be held accountable. Political parties and the public would not tolerate a permanent system of 'pre-decision-makers';
- only 'harder' institutional arrangements can ensure continuity, extending beyond personal linkages. This kind of continuity is, however, of vital importance for political commitment at the local/regional level;
- redistribution conflicts between local authorities cannot be settled without strong institutional arrangements. The latter allow for at least the partial resolution of conflicts by formal rules while 'soft' arrangements leave only the option of negotiation. Thus, stronger institutional arrangements bring together two modes of conflict resolution: hierarchical control and horizontal bargaining;
- finally, 'soft' arrangements are more susceptible to changes in the party political structure of the participating partners.

Hitherto, in Germany the local problem of formal institutional arrangements was 'externalized' to the *Land* government which has organized regional cooperation by introducing appropriate legislation. However, in future the *Land* government is likely to proceed more cautiously and to wait for initiatives to come from the regions before taking action. The local authorities will thus be responsible for the choice of formal arrangements for cooperation. The *Land* just offers different legal ways of formalizing inter-municipal cooperation. Traditionally it has been organized through special-purpose bodies, but lately there has been a shift towards development agencies. Such agencies can act more swiftly and more flexibly than institutions under public law which are subject to lengthy and tedious legal procedures.

CONCLUSIONS

Stewart's interpretation of regional cooperation in England is highly plausible, but less so in the situation of Germany. The argument seems to depend on a specific institutional context, particularly the government-initiated competition between local and regional authorities which in Germany is still at a very early stage. However, it cannot be ruled out that risk limitation is a *latent* key motive in promoting cooperation in areas where increased inter-regional competition is a *manifest* motivation for cooperation. The crucial factor is not whether or not this competition really exists, but rather how it is perceived and thus affects inter-municipal decision-making.

The impact of the risk factor on local decisions in Germany differs from that in England. While in the UK, as Stewart argues, it leads to project-based soft forms of cooperation for a very limited period, in Germany it may contribute to getting cooperation under way which may then develop into strong institutional arrangements for cooperation. In summary, the key factors determining the various impacts of the same motives seem to be:

- the institutional framework (see above);
- the mechanisms for cooperation: there is a wide range of (strong) legal institutional arrangements offered by the state which can be used by local/regional authorities;
- the differences in the transaction costs of cooperation: in Germany high transaction costs constitute a barrier to cooperation. If they can be overcome, cooperation can be introduced more effectively. Factors increasing transaction costs are:
  - the high status of local autonomy as a result of the importance attached to local self-government;
  - the predominance of coalitions in local governments as a result of the specific constitutional and electoral systems;
  - the strongly locally orientated 'logic of local government action' as a result of the system of government incentives;

- the lack of regional entrepreneurship in policy-making as a result of relatively underdeveloped competition between communities.

In addition, one major difference between English and German inter-regional cooperation might be the extent to which the business community is integrated in the partnership. In England business involvement seems to be working relatively well; in Germany the different motivations of participants are seen as a substantial obstacle to cooperation. Entrepreneurs are looking for cooperation on the basis of cost-benefit considerations. Their interest in the region is limited, especially as their traditional close ties in a region are gradually loosening. More and more businesses are subsidiaries of larger corporations with the effect that local management remains in the region only for a limited time. By way of contrast, local political decision-making is primarily based on cost calculations and rarely on estimates of regional potential relative to regional costs. Consequently, local politicians are, in the main, interested in meeting the needs of their communities by means of a project-based approach. Inter-municipal cooperation is considered worthwhile if the projects either reduce local expenditure or require regional cooperation for technical reasons.

In cases where regional cooperation is initiated by the state with the aim of distributing public funds according to 'regional development programmes', the participation of the business community usually is a requirement. However, private sector commitment tends to fade quickly because the cooperative endeavour, more often than not, is dominated by the interests of the local authorities. They control the steering group (the board); the results of the cooperation have to be approved by the local councils; and public funds are by law provided for projects put forward by local authorities and not those put forward by private sector bodies.

Notes

1. Unlike in Britain, in Germany civil servants in the highest ranks of the government hierarchy are members of the ruling parties (Derlien, 1991).
2. In Germany the proportion of general grants not targeted to specific areas/purposes has increased in recent years with a corresponding decline in specific grants.

3. The Hanover region is about to reorganize its local structure. In future, there will be a 'regional county' including the central city of Hanover. But the county will be organized on a two-tier system. The upper tier will have responsibility for regional planning, economic development, mass transit, waste disposal and some further functions, while the local authorities keep responsibility for all functions which are close to the people. A similar reorganization is under way in the Toronto region (Barlow, 1997).

References

M. Barlow, 'Administrative systems and metropolitan regions', *Environment and Planning C: Government and Policy*, 15 (1997) 399–411.

A. Benz, 'Beyond the public–private divide: institutional reform and cooperative policy making', in A. Benz and K.H. Goetz (eds), *A New German Public Sector? Reform, Adaptation and Stability* (Aldershot, 1996), pp. 165–88.

H.U. Derlien, 'Historical legacy and recent development of the German higher civil service', *International Review of Administrative Science*, 57 (1991) 385–401.

D. Fürst, 'The regional districts in search of a new role', in A. Benz and K.H. Goetz (eds), *A New German Public Sector? Reform, Adaptation and Stability* (Aldershot, 1996), pp. 119–36.

D. Fürst, '"Weiche" versus "harte" Kommunalverbände: Gibt es Gründe für eine "härtere" Institutionalisierung der regionalen Kooperation? [Strong or weak links: is there an argument for greater formalization of regional cooperation?', in G. Seiler (ed.), *Gelebte Demokratie: [Democracy in Action]: Festschrift für Oberbürgermeister a.D. Dr. M. Rommel* (Stuttgart, 1997) pp. 131–58.

D. Fürst and H. Kilper, 'The innovative power of regional policy networks: a comparison of two approaches to political modernisation in North Rhine-Westphalia', *European Planning Studies*, 3 (1995) 298–304.

J.W. Kingdon, *Agendas, Alternatives, and Public Policies* (Boston/Toronto, 1984).

W. Thieme and G. Prillwitz, *Durchführung und Ergebnisse der kommunalen Gebietsreform* [Implementation and Impact of Local Government Boundary Reforms] (Baden-Baden, 1981).

I. Van den Berg, I. Braun and J. van der Meer, 'The organising capacity of metropolitan regions', *Environment and Planning C: Government and Policy*, 15 (1997) 253–72.

R.K. Weaver, 'The politics of blame avoidance', *Journal of Public Policy*, 6 (1986) 371–98.

5 Identity, Community and Polity – Thinking about the Future in Bristol

Paul Burton

INTRODUCTION

In early 1997 a booklet was distributed in Bristol containing hundreds of suggestions for how the city might be improved as well as a smaller number of broader and more thematic 'visions' of the future. Later in this chapter I will look in more detail at these suggestions, but at the outset it is worth reflecting more generally on the relationship between identity, community and polity as we approach the new millennium and to link this to the changing role of cities like Bristol and Hanover.

At about the same time as this booklet was published, the urbanist Manuel Castells was interviewed about his life and works and in the course of this he discussed the contrasting fortunes of two Spanish cities, Barcelona and Seville. Both received substantial investments of state capital – to support the Olympics in Barcelona and Expo '92 in Seville. According to Castells, the contrast between the two cities was 'staggering' and he attributed Barcelona's successful transition into one of Europe's leading cities to its enthusiasm for widespread citizen participation and Seville's failure to secure lasting regeneration to 'an extremely bureaucratic government'. If we accept Castells' analysis then the role of local states in encouraging their citizens to engage in local planning and decision-making is crucial to the successful management of cities in transition. However, the powers and autonomy, indeed the very legitimacy, of local states have been subject to great pressure in recent years.

It has become a contemporary orthodoxy to assert that modern processes of development have produced a marked compression of time–space relationships which are inextricably bound up with processes of globalization. As a consequence many of the traditional spatial containers of identity such as the nation-state are perceived to be under threat, from above by the new international groupings of capital and global governance and from below by the resurgence of more focused territories of distinctive identity. To the best of our knowledge cities have existed in various forms for over 5000 years (Mumford, 1961; Childe, 1942) but our understanding of their role in the formation of individual and social identity remains elusive. Giddens has written of the growing separation of space and place in contrast to previous eras in which 'the spatial dimensions of social life are, for most of the population … dominated by presence – by localised activity' (Giddens, 1990, p. 18). Now though, relations are increasingly with 'absent others', located throughout the world but connected by information technologies and global processes of development such that 'what structures the locale is not simply that which is present on the scene; the visible form of the locale conceals the distanced relations which determine its nature' (ibid.). Somewhat paradoxically, one important facet of the process of globalization is a new celebration and indeed commercialization of certain locales (Gold and Ward, 1994) and more generally of the spirit of localism (Lovering, 1995). Thus we see the hard selling of particular locations for a variety of activities ranging from tourist consumption through academic engagement to the location of industrial or commercial business. But we also see the celebration of local action and involvement within a global context captured perfectly in the slogan 'Think global, act local'.

We are still left though with the question of the role played by cities in identity formation, or more precisely the role of cities *vis-à-vis* other spatial containers such as the nation-state or the community. At an empirical level there is clearly going to be a range of answers while a coherent and comprehensive answer at a theoretical level would require more than can be included in a short contribution such as this. However, in the rest of this chapter I want to approach the question by considering very briefly some issues of democracy, of communities and communitarianism and of identity politics before grounding the discussion in a description of a local initiative which sought to involve the citizens of Bristol in an exercise in 'community visioning'. I hope this shows what one group of local citizens thinks about 'their' city and its future prospects and in so doing throws some light on broader questions of identity, community and polity in the future.

THEORIES OF DEMOCRACY

James Fishkin describes his work on democracy and deliberation as 'part of a 2500 year-old quest to adapt the democratic idea, originally suited to populations of several thousands in a Greek city-state, to populations of many millions in a modern mega-state' (Fishkin, 1991, p. 1). Plato described his ideal city as having a population of 5000 citizens while Aristotle argued that each citizen should know each other by sight and that a *polis* of 100 000 would be considered absurd because it could not govern itself properly (Kitto, 1996). Citizenship in ancient Greece meant participation in public affairs and politics and the encouragement to 'active citizenship' heard recently in Britain would have been equally absurd. Of course this conception of direct democracy has been challenged on many grounds over the centuries and representative or liberal forms now prevail in the constitutions of most institutions of government, from the international to the parochial.

But there remains a powerful residual attachment to the virtues of more direct forms of democracy, perhaps because they tend to imply a return to a smaller scale of human organization – contemporary assumptions about the capacity of networked information technologies notwithstanding (e.g. Percy-Smith, 1996). Clearly there are parallels here with the ways in which we often think about communities: assuming a correlation between smallness or intimacy and the effectiveness of politics or social organization. However, it is important also to remember one of the fundamental points in the liberal critique of participatory democracy, namely the assertion made most strongly by Madison that 'pure democracies' – consisting of a small number of citizens who assemble and administer government in person – have always been intolerant, unjust and unstable (Held, 1993). Again, we can see the parallel with notions of community in which the closeness and intimacy of social relations within 'traditional' communities are also often associated with lack of tolerance if not with injustice and instability.

Classic conceptions of liberal representative democracy offered by Madison and by Bentham place less emphasis on active citizenship and more on the role of government in both enhancing the common good and regulating the collective affairs of the population as a whole. More specifically the role of representative democracy included '... securing its members against oppression and depredation at the hands of those functionaries which it employs for its defence' (Bentham, quoted in Held, 1993, p. 19), in short to protect us against the despotic use of power by the institutions of government or indeed by any other powerful groups in society. Hence the state itself has a crucial role to play in the maintenance of democratic forms of politics while at the same time being subject to its checks and balances.

There has been a growing concern voiced in recent years about the state of representative democracy in Britain: the low turnout in elections here has been contrasted with the recent elections in South Africa, where newly enfranchised black citizens often queued for hours to vote; opinion polls regularly show politicians to be held in low esteem, to be seen as untrustworthy and poor guardians of the common good; and it is reported to be increasingly difficult to convince people to stand and remain as candidates in local elections. At the same time an issue of some importance, certainly in the build up to the last general election in the UK, was the need for referenda on the future position of Britain *vis-à-vis* the European Union, on the mechanisms for joining in the establishment and use of a single European currency and for moving forward with the creation of new structures of regional government in Scotland and Wales.

Moreover, there are calls from Charter 88 to strengthen the institutions of democracy more generally and from the Commission for Local Democracy for enhancing democracy at the local level. Greater public involvement in policy debates is advocated in many fields – from 'listening to local voices' in the planning of health services to the establishment of popular planning forums as part of the post-Rio environmental agenda.

It is often taken for granted that 'the people' want to be more involved in policy debates and that if achieved this will lead not only to better debate but to better decisions about what to provide, to whom and in what form. However, there is little research evidence to back up these assumptions, especially those about a desire for greater involvement, and indeed work carried out in Canada (and currently being replicated in Bristol) has shown that while many people would like 'more of a say' in decisions that affect their lives, they are reluctant to take responsibility for making difficult decisions away from established and often directly elected politicians (Abelson et al., 1995). There is, therefore, some space between a commonplace reluctance to get involved in politics as a profession and the desire to have some greater say in local decision-making.

COMMUNITIES AND COMMUNITARIANISM

It is worth remembering Plant's observation that 'community' can be and usually is both a statement of fact and of value and his injunction to base our understanding and application of the notion of community on an awareness of its historical roots and development (Plant, 1974).

To this end he describes the seminal contribution of theorists from the German romantic tradition of the late eighteenth and early nineteenth centuries such as Herder, Schiller and Hegel, who not only celebrated the democratic and communitarian ideal embodied in the political organization of Periclean Athens, but saw in the transition to the modern period a loss of community in which 'whole men' interacted in the totality of their social roles. Instead they saw a more fragmented and indeed segmented set of relationships arising out of an increasingly organized and bureaucratized society. Tönnies' distinction between *Gemeinschaft* and *Gesellschaft* is perhaps the most well known and highly developed expression of this dichotomy (Tönnies, translated by C.P. Loomis, 1940).

We might note also Plant's contrast between German and British historiography in which he suggests:

> whereas the German communitarians tended to look a long way back to the Greek polis for their image of community, British communitarians have more often than not looked back to the village community which was beginning to be destroyed in the second half of the eighteenth century (1974, p. 27)

while remaining aware of more recent urban idealistic images of community in the writings of Young and Willmott (1957) and Jacobs (1961) and seen in French (1969).

The tensions between these different conceptions of community remain and can be seen both in more wide-ranging contemporary debates over the relationship between individualism and communitarianism (e.g. Avineri and de-Shalit, 1992) and in more prosaic debates within local government about the need to move beyond limited conceptions of citizens as mere consumers to more rounded views of local residents as citizens, consumers and electors enjoying complex relations with local state institutions. The intensity of debate provoked by Etzioni's recent work on communitarianism offers further illustration of the ambiguities and complexities surrounding notions of community (Etzioni, 1992). There is a clear tendency to treat community as a 'positive prefix' in its association with policy measures in such fields as policing, architecture, the arts and economic development (Butcher et al., 1993). At the same time there has been a sustained and powerful critique of many of the fundamentally patriarchal assumptions of some brands of communitarianism (e.g. Friedman, 1992).

However, I am especially interested here in questions about the relationship between the local state and the development of community or community spirit. Local authorities often claim a variety of roles in supporting community development and the importance of doing this is well summed up by the Association of Metropolitan Authorities:

> Community development can be seen as a key element in any democracy since it stimulates and supports participation and involvement and thereby encourages effective and responsible citizenship.   (AMA, 1989, p. 7)

This essentially communitarian conception assumes a connection between participation and community which is both descriptively accurate and morally desirable, in other words a sense of community stimulates participation which further builds community. In their more extended discussion of this conception of the relationship between participation and community, Butcher et al. make the important point that

> communitarian democracy therefore stresses the centrality of dialogue as an underlying ethic ... [and that] ... the ethics of participation in decision making should not be confined to the electoral process but should be extended to other aspects of our daily lives.   (1993, p. 226)

Recent research evidence sheds some light on the construction of local identity and identification with local communities: Young, Gosschalk and Hatter (1996) present survey evidence of the ways in which people living in the English shires (i.e. outside the major conurbations) identify with the area in which they live and analyse the factors shaping their sense of local identity. Respondents were asked about their 'sense of belonging' to areas such as neighbourhood, town, district and county and their perception of the 'strength of community' at these levels. The largest single group (31 per cent of the sample) showed no strong attachment whatsoever to any level of place, while the second largest group (26 per cent) described a strong attachment at the neighbourhood level. The remainder of the sample showed much more diversity in both the intensity and the popularity of their level of attachment. The analysis also tackled the question of whether the characteristics of people or of places drive whatever sense of attachment exists and concluded, perhaps surprisingly in relation to popular assumptions, that place characteristics such as historic status and local cultural attributes were relatively insignificant. The characteristics of respondents on the other hand, especially the duration of their residence in a particular area, were much more significant. Clearly there are important implications in these findings for the roles that can be played by local authorities in attempting to construct a sense of local identity and community attachment and we return to some of them in the conclusions.

IDENTITY POLITICS AND LOCAL IDENTITY

Hall (1992) talks of a postmodern subjectivity emerging in recent years in which 'identity becomes a moveable feast: formed and transformed continuously in relation to the ways we are represented or addressed in the cultural systems which surround us' and in which we are able to assume different identities at different times and in different places. In this section I want to touch briefly on the importance of place in the construction of identity – looking not only at the identity of individuals in places, but also at the ways in which individuals construct the identity of particular places. There is a long tradition of examining the relationship between place and identity (e.g. Buttimer and Seamon, 1980) and Money offers a good illustration of a commonly held view:

> We are herd animals, we are tribal animals (or ought to be) and we are territorial animals. We may not be territorial in the ways of some species, we may not need to mark out a new territory each season, but we do need to identify with some particular spot on the planet's surface. Just as we need to identify and find ourselves in the context of family and friends, so we need to know the physical place where we belong. We cherish our place and it nurtures us.
>
> (Money, 1993, p. 3)

On a somewhat more abstract plane, Mouffe and Massey have addressed questions of identity from the traditions of philosophy and geography. Mouffe stresses the importance of resisting 'the ever present temptation to construct identity in terms of exclusion' – can there be an 'us' without a 'them' (Mouffe, 1995, p. 265) – while Massey offers a series of propositions concerning both the spatialization of identity and the construction of identities of place in which 'we make our spaces ... in the process of constructing our various identities' (Massey, 1995, p. 285). For both of them the crucial question for (radical) democrats is how to make tangible the commitment in principle to not only tolerate diversity but also to celebrate it, while recognizing the possibility that some differences will be at or indeed beyond the limits of communal acceptability. Again, a critical issue here is the role played by local political institutions in accommodating and being shaped by the pressures of local identity politics.

CHOICES FOR BRISTOL

The following section presents a case study from Bristol in which many of the issues and questions raised above come together. In 1994 an initiative took shape in Bristol which set out to 'involve large numbers of adults and young people in a series of problem-solving discussions on Bristol's future' with the aim of 'generating a clearer picture of what the people of Bristol would like to see for their city and their communities in the next century'. Drawing on Fishkin's principles of deliberative polling (Fishkin, 1991), Owen's 'open space technology' (Owen, 1992) and Weisbord and Janoff's 'future search' techniques (Weisbord and Janoff, 1995), the Choices for Bristol project built on an earlier initiative involving school children in debates about the future role of Britain in relation to the rest of Europe. Since then it has brought together a steering group drawn from the public, commercial and voluntary sectors to manage a rolling programme of work involving the citizens of Bristol in envisioning their city in the future and identifying actions to link these visions to the present.

In brief the project developed and published a discussion guide to stimulate the generation of plausible but ambitious visions of the future of Bristol. Over two thousand responses were received by the project in time to be collated and discussed further at two 'vision meetings' held in December 1996. At these meetings ideas were grouped into themes and issues and the participants – over three hundred local people – developed vision statements to encompass the ideas under each theme. These efforts were published in a booklet, entitled *Your Ideal Bristol* and launched in February 1997. The project is currently facilitating the development of a limited number of these visions into more tangible programmes of action in collaboration with a variety of partners from across the city and a more detailed evaluation of its impact has recently been published (Burton, 1997).

By looking more closely at the range of ideas put forward by this small group of citizens of Bristol we can begin to develop some further insights on contemporary notions of community and identity and the role of the local state in their development. It is possible to discern at least five different aspects of community in the ideas submitted: spaces and circulation; functions and activities; prominence and perception; spirit of place and history; and political organization. There is some degree of overlap between the categories and it should be borne in mind that they are not the same as the categories developed by participants in the vision meetings. Nevertheless they do help to extend our understanding of the ways in which a particular group of citizens express their conceptions of and proposals for the development of both city-wide and more localized communities.

Spaces and circulation

Various suggestions were made for improving the vibrancy of the city centre and indeed for creating a more civic-minded or public space where citizens could meet for a variety of purposes, for example:

- Create a really vibrant city centre.
- Find a suitable location to restart an open-air and covered market.

It is worth noting that Bristol has a number of 'centres', none of which currently offer the opportunities associated with the main squares and piazzas of many other European cities.

Some ideas also pointed to the benefits of reconnecting living and working spaces in ways redolent of settlements of the past and of improving and connecting smaller-scale centres and focal points of community activities:

- Ensure all new housing areas have a space for small businesses to develop.
- Connect safe and pleasant areas to each other by developing good cycle routes.
- Reduce the speed limit in residential areas to 20 miles per hour.

Functions and activities

An enduring question about communities relates to the regulation of access to any benefits of community membership. A number of ideas advocated the granting of special privileges to citizens of Bristol which would not be enjoyed by others, for example:

- Encourage more use of Harbourside by giving local families free access.
- Ensure that every school-age child, regardless of family circumstances or disability, has opportunities to take part in cheap or free sporting, cultural and leisure activities in the city.

While it is recognized that external threat is often a potent force in encouraging the formation and development of communities of adversity, there were also signs of encouragement for more playful expressions of community solidarity, as in:

- Make it easier for people to hold street parties.

In terms of political or governmental function it was suggested that Bristol should become a seat of regional elected government while a number of suggestions were made about the need for greater involvement of commerce and industry in community development:

- Help businesses give something back to the community and strongly encourage all businesses to become more involved in their communities.

Prominence and perception

Many felt it was important for Bristol to develop its reputation within Britain and beyond, including:

- Emphasize Bristol as a European city by promoting the city more positively in Europe.
- Work for national and international recognition and respect as a city with an excellent record on community safety.

Associated with this desire for Bristol to be more well known were ideas about dealing with some of the consequences of this, namely in increased flow of visitors from beyond the city. The following probably relates to temporary visitors rather than prospective longer-term settlers, but is interesting nevertheless:

- Introduce a formal hospitality scheme for overseas visitors.

However, not all suggestions of this type advocated large-scale or monumental projects so often associated with efforts at increasing the prominence of places and some proposed spending less on prestigious projects at the expense of more parochial initiatives geared to local community development.

Spirit of place and history

In terms of the celebration or commemoration of the city's history, ideas tended to polarize around those adopting a relatively safe or sanitized approach:

- Celebrate Bristol's colourful (sic) history with summer pageants.
- Hold a competition to compose a 'song for Bristol'.

and those taking a more critical or indeed apologetic approach:

- Honour the vital part played in our history by black people and all other immigrants by creating a park of remembrance and having frequent celebratory events.

Again, some adopted a more localized approach and focused instead on smaller areas and issues of diversity:

- Make more of each area's identity by encouraging particular styles of street identification, street decoration and tree planting.

Political organization

Despite the absence more generally of evidence pointing toward any inclination to get more involved in politics at the national or even local scale, a number of participants proposed greater public involvement in city governance:

- Enable citizens to have more say in how council tax is spent.
- Enable children and young people to be represented on the City Council and other major institutions in Bristol.

Other ideas related to the development of a more informed and politically conscious citizenry or polity:

- Run citizenship workshops to involve people in how the city works.
- Set up an 'apprentice citizen' scheme for young people to find out what being a citizen is all about.
- Start a scheme for shadowing other people within the city for a short time so that we can gain a good understanding of lifestyles very different from our own.

Finally some ideas suggested developments at the other end of the scale, as it were, focusing on the political elite:

- Have a Lord Mayor with greater power and responsibility, directly elected by the people of Bristol.

CONCLUSIONS

There is a growing awareness of the value of developing more inclusive systems of politics and equally of the consequences of moving in the opposite direction (King and Stoker, 1996; Burton and Duncan, 1996). This does not mean that there is a marked increase in the number of people with enthusiasm for the conventional forms of political activity; indeed voter registration and turnout in British elections has fallen in recent years and there has been a vociferous rejection of many of the established forms of political protest and engagement. However, the volume of people who are prepared or inclined to engage with various forms of community-based and self-help initiative shows no sign of declining and might even be growing – although the precise measurement of this is notoriously difficult.

Similarly, there are few if any signs of more people wanting to become 'professional politicians' and indeed at the local level in Britain there is evidence of a growing difficulty in recruiting new local councillors. Nor do most people want to take on the full burden of making difficult political decisions about the allocation of public resources.

But there are clearly a great many stages between the extremes of full-time politics and complete political disengagement. It seems reasonable to assume that many people would like some more influence over some of the factors which affect their lives. Furthermore, it seems reasonable to assume that political and governmental institutions – from the local to the global levels – can play a worthwhile role in facilitating and encouraging developments in this direction. This is not to say that movement in the direction of greater inclusiveness and involvement is totally dependent on the support and facilitation of existing political and state institutions – the recent overthrow of apparently impregnable political regimes in the former Soviet Union and its satellite countries provides vivid evidence to the contrary. Nevertheless, the state clearly looks to play various roles in the stimulation of political involvement and local authorities are increasingly supporting a range of measures to enhance democracy at the local level.

While these political initiatives are relatively new departures for many local authorities in Britain, attempts to support community development have a much longer tradition. But for many years a feature of much state-sponsored community development work has been an underlying assumption, often implicit, that it is only certain 'deprived' communities that need support in the form of professional community work. Less attention has been paid to the characteristics of all spatially defined communities within a city, including those assumed to be functioning more effectively and hence less in need of support.

One of the most significant challenges in the coming period will be the ways in which processes of identity formation and community development are managed within cities. The tension between notions of community rooted in homogeneity and shared aspects of identity and political principles which recognize and indeed celebrate difference will not be easy to manage. The limits of acceptable difference will always be contested as we can see in current debates over 'zero-tolerance policing' advocated by the Labour Party and in recent legislation concerning the provision of sites for gypsies and travellers (Hawes and Perez, 1996). While city or urban planning has often embraced the importance of striving for social balance in the planned development of communities, the enduring fact of social and ethnic segregation in many different places has been well documented (e.g. Peach, Robinson and Smith, 1981). And while these patterns of segregation and exclusion are sometimes explained as the unintended consequences of broader processes of urban development, there is evidence too of the growing popularity of walled communities within cities (Davis, 1990) and of communities developed solely for particular groups such as the elderly.

A distinctive feature of much urban policy in Britain in recent years has been an assumption that people living in disadvantaged communities need their 'capacity' building. It may be more appropriate to develop this assumption further and include not just those pushed to the margins of society but those who see themselves as operating closer to the centres of power and social influence. Indeed the capacities of all citizens in any location might be significantly enhanced if the opportunities for dialogue across all points on the social, political or economic spectrum were developed more fully. Creating opportunities for hearing the views of others, seeing how others live their lives and understanding better the constraints that limit their opportunities would appear to offer a worthwhile starting point in the development of greater civic capacity to manage the challenges of the future.

Choices for Bristol came into being to promote a new approach to civic dialogue in the city. In one sense it was misnamed for it devoted relatively little attention to helping or encouraging people to make choices, although it certainly set out with a stronger intention to do so. It has been more successful in providing new opportunities for local dialogue about various aspects of the development of the city and its constituent communities. The ideas put forward reflected a wide range of conceptions of 'community', not least in terms of the spatial scale at which it is held to be of greatest relevance and meaning to its members.

One of the important features of theoretical conceptions of community, especially those developed in association with democratic principles, has been the notion of dialogue and the construction of a sense of community through dialogue. In promoting more informed dialogue and in encouraging a wider range of people to get involved in thinking about the future of their city, Choices for Bristol has contributed to a growing sense of community within Bristol. The magnitude and impact of this contribution has not been great, but it represents nevertheless a positive development for a city in transition.

References

J. Abelson, J. Lomas, J. Eyles, S. Birch and G. Veenstra, 'Does the community want devolved authority? Results from deliberative polling in Ontario', *Canadian Medical Association Journal*, 153: 4 (1995) 403–12.

Association of Metropolitan Authorities (AMA), *Community Development: The Local Authority Role* (London: AMA, 1989).

S. Avineri and A. de-Shalit (eds), *Communitarianism and Individualism* (Oxford: Oxford University Press, 1992).

P. Burton, *Community Visioning: an Evaluation of the 'Choices for Bristol' Project* (Bristol: The Policy Press, 1997).

P. Burton and S. Duncan, 'Democracy and accountability in public bodies: new agendas in British governance', *Policy and Politics*, 24: 1, January (1996) 5–16.

H. Butcher et al. (eds), *Community and Public Policy* (London: Pluto Press, 1993).

A. Buttimer and D. Seamon (eds), *The Human Experience of Space and Place* (London: Croom Helm, 1980).

M. Castells, 'Citizen movements, information and analysis: an interview with Manuel Castells by Bob Catterall', *City*, 7 (1997) 140–55.

G.V. Childe, *What Happened in History* (Harmondsworth: Penguin, 1942).

M. Davis, *City of Quartz: Excavating the Future in Los Angeles* (London: Verso, 1990).

A. Etzioni, *The Spirit of Community: the Reinvention of American Society* (New York: Simon & Schuster, 1992).

J. Fishkin, *Democracy and Deliberation: New Directions for Democratic Reform* (New Haven, Conn.: Yale University Press, 1991).

R.M. French (ed.), *The Community: a Comparative Perspective* (Itasca, Ill.: FE Peacock Publishers, 1969).

M. Friedman, 'Feminism and modern friendship: dislocating the community', in S. Avineri and A. de-Shalit (eds), *Communitarianism and Individualism* (Oxford: Oxford University Press, 1992).

A. Giddens, *The Consequences of Modernity* (Cambridge: Polity Press, 1990).

J.R. Gold and S.V. Ward (eds), *Place Promotion: the Use of Publicity and Marketing to Sell Towns and Regions* (Chichester: John Wiley & Sons, 1994).

S. Hall, 'The question of cultural identity', in S. Hall, D. Held and T. Pettigrew (eds), *Modernity and Its Futures* (Cambridge: Polity Press, 1992).

D. Hawes and B. Perez, *The Gypsy and the State: the Ethnic Cleansing of British Society* (Bristol: The Policy Press, 1996).

D. Held, 'Democracy: from city-states to cosmopolitan order?', in D. Held (ed.), *Prospects for Democracy* (Cambridge: Polity Press, 1993).

J. Jacobs, *The Death and Life of Great American Cities* (New York: Vintage Books, 1961).

D. King and J. Stoker (eds), *Rethinking Local Democracy* (London: Macmillan, 1996).

H. Kitto, 'The Greeks', in R. LeGates and F. Stout (eds), *The City Reader* (London: Routledge, 1996).

J. Lovering, 'Creating discourses rather than jobs: the crisis in the cities and the transition fantasies of intellectuals and policy makers', in P. Healey et al. (eds), *Managing Cities: the New Urban Context* (Chichester: John Wiley & Sons, 1995).

D. Massey, 'Thinking radical democracy spatially', *Society and Space: Environment & Planning D*, 13 (1995) 283–8.

M. Money, 'Introduction to re-inhabitation by Gary Snyder', in M. Money (ed.), *Health and Community: Holism in Practice* (Dartington: Green Books, 1993).

C. Mouffe, 'Post-Marxism: democracy and identity', *Society and Space: Environment & Planning D*, 13 (1995) 259–65.

L. Mumford, *The City in History* (Harmondsworth: Penguin, 1961).

H. Owen, *Open Space Technology: a User's Guide* (Potomac, Md.: Abbott Publishing, 1992).

C. Peach, V. Robinson and S. Smith (eds), *Ethnic Segregation in Cities* (London: Croom Helm, 1981).

J. Percy-Smith, 'Downloading democracy? Information and communication technologies in local politics', *Policy and Politics*, 24: 1, January (1996) 43–56.

R. Plant, Community and Ideology: an Essay in Applied Social Philosophy (London: Routledge & Kegan Paul, 1974).

F. Tönnies, *Fundamental Concepts of Sociology* (New York: American Book, 1940).

M. Weisbord and S. Janoff, *Future Search: an Action Guide to Finding Common Ground in Organizations and Communities* (San Francisco: Berrett-Koehler, 1995).

M. Young and P. Willmott, *Family and Kinship in East London* (London: Routledge & Kegan Paul, 1957).

K. Young, B. Gosschalk and W. Hatter, *In Search of Community Identity* (York: York Publishing Services, 1996).

6 Identities, Communities and Policies – Cities on the Threshold of a New Era

Adelheid von Saldern

INTRODUCTION

It is not easy to make predictions, but we need them. They are normally based on present-day scenarios, from which current trends are projected into the future. Looking back into the past therefore makes it easier for us to approach the twenty-first century. While 'globalization' enlarges the *spatial* dimension of our thinking, the look to the past as well as into the future lengthens our *time* horizon.

In nineteenth- and twentieth-century history, each phase of development has been characterized by particular trends, some of which are mutually compatible while others are diametrically opposed. In addition, there are various time discontinuities and irregularities in the development process which are caused by structures and mentalities. Development is not likely to shed any of this complexity. Therefore, any attempt to try and predict clear trends cannot possibly account accurately for the complexity of future trends. The following comments are designed to illuminate the selected topics of identities, communities and policies, subject to the aforementioned general proviso.

IDENTITIES

Pluralist identities

Establishing identity is not a single finite process, but a continuing infinite one. Associations which are important for shaping individual identity include, for example, nationality, ethnic origin and religion. Over time, their significance for the individual has varied, and today identification processes tend to include several points of reference at the same time, more than in the past. One of these points of reference is likely to be communities. Consequently, we are concerned with pluralist identities. Apart from the followers of certain sects and other religious fundamentalists, the majority of people in Europe tend to identify with some elements of a position rather than take on board everything wholesale. Despite potential revivals of national identity, even nationalistic identification trends look set to remain limited, given the increasing popularity of value relativism. One can therefore safely assume that *partial identification* applies in cities and communities.

Identity, individualization and community

Pluralist identity structures are being challenged by the growing trend in favour of individualization. There are two possible responses. People might try and consolidate their own identity via individualization coupled with privatization and the consumer culture.[1] Alternatively, they might try and enhance their own identity via social involvement (Habermas, 1995, p. 84). Since self-confidence and self-assurance can be increased via active participation, by learning about individual strengths and those of a group, success can stimulate, while failure may reduce activity.

In this age of individualism, social involvement is often based on individual personal motivation which is new in its intensity, though not as a phenomenon in itself. There is a vital difference in comparison with traditional societies. There, this type of activity was primarily characterized by social norms and values, unlike in the present and future, where the individual tends to claim more freedom to make decisions and demands greater autonomy. This also applies to the right to withdraw at short notice purely on personal grounds from individual participation in a specific issue or in the community. In contrast to previous centuries, group or community claims on individuals are seen as inappropriate.

Since the onset of the crisis of the welfare state, trends favouring a self-help society have been strengthening. In 1979/80 there were around 30 000 self-help groups in Germany; by the mid-1980s the figure had reached between 40 and 50 thousand (Jarre and Krebs, 1986, p. 16). Currently, there are around 67 500 self-help groups with around 2.6 million active members (Hepp, 1996, p. 5). Others estimate that between 17 and 20 per cent of over 16 year olds in Germany are involved in unpaid voluntary work, i.e. between 12 and 15 million people, three quarters of whom are women (Lölhöffel, 1997). Nevertheless, self-help groups look set to remain a minority phenomenon in western society in the twenty-first century. Only 1 per cent of the population were involved in community action groups between 1986 and 1995 (Opaschowski, 1997).

Over the past thirty years, the new self-help movement has become part of democracy. It follows in the tradition of the student movement and community action groups of the late 1960s and early 1970s. During the same period, willingness to accept the traditional parties has declined and this is no accident (Hepp, 1995). In Germany, this shift has been the subject of much controversy. Some see opportunities for emancipation in the new civil society, while others warn of the 'vagaries of the public spirited' (Brumlik, 1995). However, it is not a question of either/or but of a new balance.

Identification with local urban areas

For many people part of the identification process is linked to local urban areas, specifically the immediate neighbourhood. The significance of the local area for people depends largely on age and position. Although parents with small children and old people may think in a cosmopolitan way, they are in many respects dependent on their neighbourhoods. As the older sector of the population continues to expand, the local area will become more important for them in the twenty-first century, even if they can still afford to go on holiday to Majorca. The same applies to the poorer sectors of the population, which include an above average proportion of women and the unemployed. With the projected end of the traditional *working society*, the neighbourhood will become more important for all those adversely affected.

(Partial) identification of a person with their local living area can be interpreted as part of a process of 'appropriation' (Miller, 1988) which includes all the senses (Chombart de Lauwe, 1956). However, attempts to get people to identify with a specific social area *purely* by making their living environment more aesthetically pleasing are bound to fail in the long term, unless they are supported by people in their *active life* (*vita activa*). Social involvement is necessary for individual quality of life (Wendt et al., 1996, p. 8). Opportunities for individual co-determination and social involvement at local level facilitate the sense of belonging in an area.

In this context, there are differences between the sexes. Drawing on situational analysis, it is noted that women tend to get more involved at the affective, informal, emotional level, although part of this may be due to their (welfare) care work. Men prefer to act in formal structures with contractual relations and explicit procedures. These findings are problematic. Although gender differences should not be seen as irrelevant, at the same time, women's involvement in community work should not reinforce the traditional hierarchical division of labour between the sexes in society. Otherwise, the structural disadvantage of women is increased rather than reduced.[2]

'Appropriation' in an urban area tends to be based on the *vita reflectiva* (*the reflective life*). This includes memories of situations and residents who are linked to a particular neighbourhood so that it becomes familiar to people. History is part of our cultural memory and the present helps shape our image of the past with an eye to the future. Social areas must be conceived as places of memories. Even negative memories or memories of battles against the power of the state should be included. Knowledge of the history of a neighbourhood is important for the sense of belonging in an urban area. Contemplation of the past should not only take the form of stone memorials with inscriptions. The past should not be fossilized, but should remain open and alive. That is why the popular policy in many cities of presenting their history to the public in the most attractive and flattering way possible is the wrong approach (Häußermann and Siebel, 1987, p. 208). People want to discover history themselves. They want to decide for themselves what they want to remember and what to put on one side. An active and self-determined approach to the history of a local area facilitates thinking in a broader context. Moreover, this also strengthens and improves the chances of the future survival of neighbourhoods and thereby of cities in general.

COMMUNITIES

Communities from a historical perspective

In historical terms, the concept of community has a number of roots. From the early to mid-nineteenth century, setting up associations and cooperatives was encouraged under *liberalism*. In so far as liberalism was concerned with the 'social question' at all and was not tantamount to so-called Manchester liberalism, the social question was to be solved by 'helping people to help themselves'. Today, by contrast, liberalism is primarily viewed in Germany as Thatcherism and is mainly associated with fighting under the banner of individualism and deregulation.[3]

In the nineteenth century under *conservatism*, communities were encouraged more as traditional hierarchical organizations. H.W. Riehl's mid-nineteenth-century lament over the decline of old village communities and the apparently immoral jungle of the cities led to pessimistic cultural visions of the future, as featured in Spengler's *The Decline of the West* published in 1920. Wherever conservatives are involved in community projects today, they still try and integrate them into their canon of values.

In *pre-fascist milieus* in the Weimar Republic, there was a preference for smaller communities of (racist and predominantly masculine) groups based on a leader/follower model which superseded the class-based group hierarchy. In the National Socialist era and before, national socialists adopted the system of a 'national community' (*Volksgemeinschaft*) as a uniform mass collective which was meant to be built upon by many smaller communities at local and regional level. As their means of instituting the 'national community' in the Nazi sense, they employed violence and terror against Jews, 'political enemies' and other 'unwanted persons'. Yet, below the political level there were also a number of 'positive' incentives for non-Jewish Germans to identify with, such as the practical social work undertaken by the *Winter Aid Programme* in cities and local communities.[4] Those who cling to the popular idea that the success of National Socialism was the result of the rootlessness of the people (Barber, 1995, p. 363) have only reproduced conservative models of interpretation of the time which do not stand up to cross-examination in the empirical studies of the closing phase of the Weimar Republic. After 1930 National Socialism, for example, was particularly successful in penetrating some relatively enclosed village groupings.

In contrast to early socialist models (Owen and Fourier), the political strategy and system of values *of social democracy* were designed to address society and the state as a whole. It built an appropriately large-scale party and union organization. Yet that was just one side of the coin. There were also social settings which gave people a stable environment between 1890 and 1933, and a broad socio-cultural network was set up linking neighbourhoods and numerous workers' associations. After 1945, this anti-bourgeois social democratic organization with its welfare net and network of associations was not rebuilt. All that has remained is the commitment to state and society as a whole and a faith in strong, large-scale organization.

There are a great many more examples to be found in nineteenth- and twentieth-century history.[5] Those quoted already clearly indicate, first, that the concept of community has a long tradition, and, second, that all political groups were involved in one way or another. From this we may conclude that communities are polyvalent in (party) political terms, i.e. they may be integrated in a wide range of political contexts. Notions of community are not the ideal way to improve democracy in political terms. Community action groups and self-help organizations do not necessarily embrace such notions *per se* and they, therefore, can trigger either positive or negative potential, the latter specifically in terms of egocentric political interests.[6] In any case, decentralized self-help organizations tend to counteract overcommitment to state and authority in a positive way. There are numerous well known examples of very persistent state-oriented behaviour in Germany.

Self-help and need

In the past, self-help groups were set up in the local neighbourhood particularly in times of crisis. For instance, neighbourhood groups in the barracks areas in the Kaiserreich (empire era) did not just develop purely out of a sense of abstract solidarity with the workers, but also from a pragmatic sense based on a culture of necessity.

To quote a second example from history, anti-fascist committees and other self-help organizations were set up immediately after the Second World War to help people survive the early days before any new official organizational structures could be established. A third example reveals that self-help organizations flourished in the early years following completion of small newly established housing estates. Infrastructure was poor, life in the new environment had no established pattern, 'normality' had not yet appeared and the houses and gardens seemed to be literally open on all sides. The need to help each other was a necessity. Historical findings can be generalized and adapted to the future and the present. There are two factors which are particularly important in terms of activating citizens' groups – the need to act and the opportunity to act (von Saldern, 1995).

The harmony trap

In German political culture, the idea of community is still frequently associated with the idea of harmonious and peaceful living together (coexistence) of a group of people (see Dahrendorf, 1968). The more homogeneous the group, according to this model, the easier it is to achieve this aim. The commitment to social and cultural homogeneity in neighbourhoods and urban areas can be justified on these grounds. Yet these arguments are highly problematic in social policy terms. The opposite should in fact be the aim. The 'other', the strange, must be accepted by communities. Tolerance and conflict management need to be practised. Communities must not separate themselves nor moralize and try and be paragons of virtue, but must respect individual freedom. Fenced in estates with security guards, such as those which are increasingly emerging in the United States, create communities without any positive, progressive consequences for the twenty-first century. Quite the reverse. Communities must be open and not transformed into numerous mini-fortresses, as argued by Walzer (1992, p. 75). In other words, communities should not feel obliged to abide by the values of a separate self-isolated community, but rather should follow the universal values which were developed through the enlightenment conception of society (Habermas, 1995). Otherwise, the outcome would be the end of urban culture and the endangering of society from within and below.

POLICIES

Not replacement but rather a new balance

There is no disputing the fact that existing democratic political principles cannot simply be replaced (Kurbjuweit, 1996). In the twenty-first century we will continue to need party democracy, central administration, the welfare state. Instead, a new balance must be found between the principles of centralization and decentralization, party democracy and non-parliamentary representation of interests, welfare state and self-help possibilities, which will recognize the growing role of citizens in society in the twenty-first century.

Institutional learning process and communication methods

States and cities tend to base their interest in self-help organizations on real or estimated cost-saving grounds (Schridde, 1995). Instead, democratic theory and social structural considerations should be central to their interests (see Gessenharter, 1996, pp. 3–13 for a summary). The question is: how can democracy be revived without damaging the party system which is based on the principle of representation? The public debate about citizens' interests, or 'sub-policy' as Ulrich Beck calls it (1993, p. 162), could revitalize the entire political sphere in the sense of *res publica* and thereby indirectly contribute to the stabilization of party democracy.

Another important issue is competition between urban centres in attracting industry. Whether this trend is welcome or not, the competitive spirit will continue in the early years of the twenty-first century. One good outcome may be that such a trend will stimulate a process of learning about city administration, which can develop through debate with citizens. The successful policies of city administrations, created by a sustained learning process, will become the yardstick by which to judge the overall attractiveness of a city in the twenty-first century. Specific solutions to problems lose their edge rapidly over time. Flexibility will be all the more essential.

We can predict that in the twenty-first century, we will permanently be searching for solutions. Therefore, institutions will have to improve their learning capabilities. In order to accelerate this process, it is essential to find out which institutional structures and processes promote or inhibit learning. Or, to put it another way: what role do cultural, structural and individual factors play in the development of learning processes, particularly at local party level and in urban administration (Diereks, 1996)?

Support measures for promoting communities and citizens' organizations

Communities and citizens' organizations cannot be 'made' or planned for. Nevertheless, measures to promote collective identity and citizens' organizations can be taken. Citizens' commitment, based on individual specific activities, is best developed through projects. However, project sponsors need to create mutual networks and learn to look beyond their own narrow areas of interest. Self-help groups must not become trapped by being inward looking.

Cities should aim to increase the creative potential of citizens in their neighbourhoods, enhance neighbourhood related social policy as well as supporting particular initiatives. More communal rooms, counselling services and contact centres could be created. Urban policy must also be designed to promote equality for women. Wherever possible, a broad range of jobs should be created in the neighbourhoods. Enterprise zones can help to attract companies to the local area too, and companies should be involved in the development of a community strategy. There should also be union support for networking beyond local branch level. In short, in the twenty-first century, cooperative administration will be required on all levels and intensive cooperation with local citizens is a prerequisite. By contrast, patriarchal urban bureaucracy, with traditional compartmentalized thinking, is already out of date.

The search for urban identity

Efforts to transform cities into entities searching for identity are a familiar phenomenon. A city should have a unique image which will then be marketed as such and employed in the growing rivalry between local authorities. This is similar to company policies, practised with varying degrees of success, in the fight for market shares, profit maximization and staff motivation by means of a corporate image. Only companies with the 'right product' have any chance of success. In urban policy terms, this means that although sensational events, such as a world exhibition, can draw public attention to an urban centre, they are not durable. Short-lived and superficial success in recent years have characterized these kinds of celebrations and aesthetic attractions (Häußermann and Siebel, 1993, pp. 7–32; Lipp, 1987, pp. 231–51). Making cities into aesthetic objects only serves to 'sweep the misery aside, not to banish it', according to Häußermann and Siebel (1987, p. 209). The 'festivalization' of cities works in a similar way. Although festivals also offer commercial highlights, sensation and show, which certainly do justice to new technology, they have very little to do with the social reality of people and tend to be of an escapist character. Urban identity cannot be built on escapism.

Furthermore, the search for urban identity is not a new phenomenon. Attempts at shaping urban identity – as a result of inter-city rivalry – were already emerging in the Kaiserreich era. In that period of the newly established conventions of municipal authorities, local services, especially in the infrastructure sector, were emphasized and weak points, such as bad housing in working-class districts were kept hidden as far as possible. Over a number of years figures were collected and then the statistical material was published as a basis for comparative analysis. For example, there was the illuminating book of statistics by Heinrich Silbergleits on *Preußens Städte* (Prussia's cities) published in 1906. Any city levying the lowest supplement on income tax could expect to attract pensioners with the right kind of advertising, as Hanover, Göttingen and Wiesbaden have managed to do effectively. When the longing for nature and the life reform movement (*Lebensreformbewegung*) influenced many citizens in the last years of the Kaiserreich and in the 1920s, Hanover advertised itself with the slogan 'the green city'. In fact, Hanover really did have more green space per head than any other city. Quality of life was part of the city's advertising and was directed not just at pensioners, but at the entire population. Therefore Hanover operated a very modern kind of corporate image strategy at that time.[7]

To sum up, the greatest opportunities for creating a sustainable urban identity in the twenty-first century are clearly to be found in our efforts to improve the quality of life. In order to do so, we need to be innovative and open in our search for solutions to problems, to maintain dialogue during conflicts, to take the initiative on cultural needs and to involve the city in a broader sweep of time and space. This requires a public civic forum and a *collective memory* in the city. In the twenty-first century, the search for true *urban identity*, if it is to be more than a superficial marketing strategy, will be marked by public involvement and a sustained dialogue.

Communities can play a major role in the development of urban identity as contributors to the quality of life. They can help revitalize, expand and rediscover social policy, civic public life and democracy, and promote active participation in civil society in an urban context (Meyer and Reese-Schäfer, 1996, p. 9). This involves pragmatic project planning, which should be networked in a new way so that individuals, groups and urban administrations work together in close cooperation. On this basis an urban identity can be established in the twenty-first century.

Whether a civil society will really emerge in the twenty-first century and whether a new type of urbanity and urban identity can develop out of this remains to be seen. It is just one *option* available in our future history, in view of the complex and contradictory trends mentioned above.

Notes

1. The problems presented for society by this approach to strengthening identity are not considered further in this chapter.
2. This refers to the limited opportunities for women in the economy, in academia and politics compared with men, and to female age-related poverty.
3. The plea by Guido Westerwelle (of the Free Democratic Party) in favour of the family, cooperatives, community action groups, etc. is not discussed further in this chapter. See *Die Zeit*, no. 3, 10 January 1997.

4. The *Winterhilfswerk* (Winter Aid Programme) operated on strictly racist lines as well.
5. Communities and self-help organizations in nineteenth-century history have tended to be overlooked by researchers, apart from the formal associations. Only in the 1980s did a trend begin to examine the history of housing corporations and the cooperative culture in communal life, leading to unexpected findings.
6. This aspect is underrated by the American communitarians. Altvater (1995, pp. 540–1) overemphasizes the negative aspects. He fears exclusion of the problems of a 'two-thirds world'.
7. However, the fact that the green space was not evenly distributed throughout the city and the upper class had access to most of it was not mentioned.

References

E. Altvater, 'Stammeswesen im globalen Dorf [Tribalism in the global village]', *Blätter für deutsche und internationale Politik* [*Bulletin on German and International Politics*], 5 (1995).

B.R. Barber, 'Die liberale Demokratie und der Preis des Einverständnisses [Liberal democracy and the price of consent]', in B. van den Brink and W. van Reijen (eds), *Bürgergesellschaft, Recht und Demokratie* [*Civic Society, Law and Democracy*] (Frankfurt am Main, 1995).

U. Beck, *Die Erfindung des Politischen. Zu einer Theorie reflexiver Modernisierung* [*Reflexive Modernization: Politics, Tradition and Aesthetics*] (Frankfurt am Main, 1993).

M. Brumlik, 'Das Irrlicht des Gemeinsinns [The volatility of the public spirit]', *Die Tageszeitung*, 20 February 1995.

P.H. Chombart de Lauwe, *La Vie quotidienne des familles ouvrières: recherches sur les comportments sociaux de consommation* (Paris, 1956).

R. Dahrendorf, *Demokratie und Gesellschaft* [*Democracy and Society*] (Munich, 1968).

M. Diereks, 'Zukunftsforschung gilt bis heute als akademisch wenig reputierlich [Research into the future is still frowned upon in academic circles]', *Frankfurter Rundschau*, 299, 23 December 1996.

W. Gessenharter 'Warum neue Beteiligungsmodelle auf kommunaler Ebene? Kommunalpolitik zwischen Globalisierung und Demokratisierung [Why new models for participation at local government level? Local governance between globalization and democratization]', *Aus Politik und Zeitgeschichte* [*Politics and History*], 50, 6 December 1996.

J. Habermas, 'Aufgeklärte Ratlosigkeit. Warum die Politik ohne Perspektiven ist. These zu einer Diskussion [Enlightened but helpless: why there is no hope for politics – theses for discussion]', *Frankfurter Rundschau*, 30 December 1995.

J. Habermas, 'Die Normalität einer Berliner Republik [Normality in a Berlin republic]', *Kleine Politische Schriften* [*Brief Political Extracts*], VIII (Frankfurt, 1995).

H. Häußermann and W. Siebel, *Neue Urbanität* [*New Urbanity*] (Frankfurt, 1987).

H. Häußermann and W. Siebel, 'Die Politik der Festivalisierung und die Festivalisierung der Politik. Große Ereignisse in der Stadtpolitik [Politics of "festivalization" and the "festivalization" of politics: great events in urban policy]', *Leviathan*, special issue (1993).

G. Hepp, 'Wertewandel und Bürgergesellschaft [Changing values and civil society]', *Aus Politik und Zeitgeschichte* [*Politics and History*], 20 December 1996, B52–3.

J. Jarre and H. Krebs (eds), 'Soziale Selbsthilfe- und Initiativgruppen in kommunalen Aktionsfeldern [Social self-help groups in local action areas]', *Loccumer Protokolle* 53 (1986).

D. Kurbjuweit, 'Der Sozialstaat ist sein Geld Wert [The welfare state is a worthwhile investment]', *Die Zeit*, 33, 9 August 1996.

W. Lipp, 'Gesellschaft und Festkultur, Großstadtfeste der Moderne [Society and celebration culture: city festivals in modern times]', in P. Hugger (ed.), *Stadt und Fest. Zur Geschichte und Gegenwart europäischer Festkultur* [*The City and Celebrations: European Celebration Culture – Past and Present*] (Stuttgart, 1987).

H. Lölhöffel, 'Unsichtbare Arbeit [Invisible work]', *Frankfurter Rundschau*, 16 January 1997.

T. Meyer and W. Reese-Schäfer, 'Die politische Rezeption des kommunitaristischen Denkens in Deutschland [Political response to communitarian thinking in Germany]', *Aus Politik und Zeitgeschichte* [*Politics and History*], 36, 30 August 1996.

D. Miller, 'Appropriating the state on the council estate', *Man*, new series, 23 (1988).

H.W. Opaschowski, 'Die Generation der Medienkids will alles sehen, hören und erleben [The generation of "media kids" wants to see, hear and experience everything]', *Frankfurter Rundschau*, 11 January 1997.

H. Schridde, *Neue sozialpolitische Tendenzen in deutschen Großstädten* [*New Social Policy Trends in Large German Cities*] (Düsseldorf, 1995).

A. von Saldern, *Häuserleben. Zur Geschichte städtischen Arbeiterwohnens vom Kaiserreich bis heute* [*Home Life: The History of Urban Workers' Living Conditions from Empire to the Present*] (Bonn, 1995).

M. Walzer, *Sphären der Gerechtigkeit. Ein Plädoyer für Pluralität und Gleichheit* [*Spheres of Justice: A Plea for Pluralism and Equality*] (Frankfurt am Main/New York, 1992).

W.R. Wendt et al., *Zivilgesellschaft und soziales Handeln. Bürgerschaftliches Engagement in eigenen und gemeinschaftlichen Belangen* [*Civil Society and Social Action: Citizen Involvement in Personal and Common Causes*] (Freiburg im Bresgau, 1996).

7 The Dual City or the City of Many Parts? Rethinking Differences in Cities in Transition

Sophie Watson

INTRODUCTION

For more than a decade urban analysis and debate has drawn attention to growing social spatial polarization in many cities. As the rich have got richer and the poor poorer, so also there has been a tendency to construct the notion of the divided or dual city (Fainstein, Gordon and Harloe, 1992). In this formulation social and economic divisions are mapped onto urban space in what is sometimes a simplistic fashion. There is ample evidence to suggest that there have been strong polarizing tendencies in cities, which in some cities of the US have been particularly extreme. White people have fled to the suburbs leaving the inner city to black and Hispanic minorities. Yet there is also growing evidence to support the argument that the picture is more complex, and that it may be more helpful to talk in terms of quarters or parts of cities (Marcuse, 1989, 1995) or in terms of fragments or patchwork quilts. Fainstein, Gordon and Harloe (1992), comparing London and New York, initiated this approach. The problem is often that the detailed statistical evidence is either not available or difficult to access.

This chapter sets out to look first at the now relatively familiar reasons behind the growing social spatial polarization witnessed in cities. It then looks at new ways of thinking about the dual model arguing that without concentrated attention on detailed differences and complexities, urban policies will be hampered in their attempts to address inequality. It then explores some aspects of social and demographic differentiation in contemporary Britain and considers the possible implications of this. It finally argues for a need to examine both where differences and divisions lock people into deprivation and where they do not, in order to start thinking about how communities draw on differences in a positive way without denying or homogenizing these diffferences.

GLOBAL RESTRUCTURING

Global restructuring refers to a number of different but interconnected changes which have had considerable impacts on cities. First, the ever increasing internationalization and mobility of capital and greater flexibility of production have had their consequences, as companies seek to find cheaper sources of labour further afield. At the same time, the manufacturing base of many cities has declined or been decimated to be replaced (or not) by a growth in financial and producer services. Cities are thus increasingly reliant on a service sector base which implies a growth in those jobs where many of the unemployed do not have the necessary skills. The technological and information revolution forms another part of the picture where physical distance becomes increasingly meaningless for those cities that are rich in information technology and communications (Castells, 1996). Cities at the top of the urban hierarchy are increasingly those where command and control functions and producer services are located.

The impact of global forces on cities has been highly differentiated with the success of cities depending on their ability to find a niche in the new urban hierarchy (Allen and Massey, 1988). However, many cities are facing similar trends. These trends are economic in terms of changing labour markets, and social and demographic in terms of changing household structures and racial and ethnic composition. There have also been dramatic shifts which reflect a combination of these factors in relation to housing markets and the potential for households to house themselves adequately. There are growing numbers of homeless in many major cities. The argument in this chapter is that the interaction of labour market opportunities as a result of restructuring, housing markets, social demographic factors, and racial and ethnic differences cross cut any simple divisions which can easily be mapped spatially. Thus within one so called 'community' – defined in spatial or other terms – there may be households with different access to resources as well as differences within households themselves. These need to be explored more fully if sense is to be made of the transitions through which cities are currently moving.

Marcuse (1989, 1995) is one theorist who has developed a more complex model of divisions within cities. In his view, cities are increasingly fragmented and chaotic yet behind the chaos he suggests there are patterns. Rather than think in terms of divisions it is useful to think in terms of quartered cities or five-parted ones where the parts are intricately linked, walled in and walled out, hierarchical in power and dependent on outside social forces. In the technologically developed cities of today Marcuse defines five types of city which form independent cities in an ordered and interdependent pattern. The residential city can be seen as comprising the dominating city with its luxury housing; the gentrified city which is occupied by professional, managerial and technical groups; the suburban city with both single family dwellings in the outer-city and inner-city apartment blocks; the tenement city; and the abandoned city. The economic city can similarly be divided into five or more parts: the controlling city as the site of big decisions; the city of advanced services; the city of direct production; the city of unskilled work and informal production; and the residual city where the homeless and unemployed are concentrated. Though there may be other ways of characterizing the city and though these are not discrete, they give us a way of thinking beyond more simple divisions.

Marcuse takes the argument further by considering how these quarters or parts are differentiated by walls. Differences of race, gender, sexuality and class are not simply a question of special needs or lifestyle. They represent differences of power. The different parts of the city are separated by walls which are symbolic or real. Since the days of the medieval city these walls tend to define rather than surround the city. Again he designates a five-part typology. Prison walls, walls defining ghettos or places of confinement and walls built for the re-education of those confined, are one type. Second are the barricades – walls of cohesion or solidarity – which may be marked simply by street signs or in immigrant quarters by language symbols. Third, stockades are walls of aggression which may secure areas of invasion, such as in the gentrified city (Smith, 1996). Fourth are stucco walls sheltering gated estates or residential enclaves, which exclude others to protect social status or to exercise social control. The last kind are the ramparts or walls of fortification. These are walls expressing domination and superiority which may be seen in the tall skyscrapers or the penthouses of wealthy neighbourhoods. This typology is useful for the argument of this chapter since it focuses our attention on the actual, perceived and symbolic ways in which cities are partitioned or divided.

Much of the research in this field focuses more precisely on occupational structure, incomes or notions of class. Mollenkopf and Castells' (1991) study of New York argues for a sixfold division of the occupational structure, since in their view 'the complexity of New York's social structure cannot be reduced to a dichotomy between the two extremes of the income distribution' (p. 401). In their formulation there is an upper stratum of executives, managers and professionals, clerical workers, service sector workers, manufacturing workers, public sector employees and those outside of the labour force; and each of these interrelate in a multiplicity of ways. Yet within this framework, which postulates increasingly fragmented and diverse groups and alliances, they still propose a 'comparatively cohesive core of professionals and a disorganized periphery fragmented by race, ethnicity, gender, occupational and industrial location, and the spaces they occupy' (p. 402). There is thus in play another binary model which obscures the differentiation within those very binaries, which means that there is differential access to jobs, services and provisions within communities and households on the basis of those very differences they mention. They do, however, modify this dualism at a later stage, characterizing New York this time as three cities: the 'metropolitan heaven' – the privileged core; the 'inner city hell' – those outside the labour market; and 'elsewhere' – who are the remaining social groups.

On the basis of their work Fainstein, Gordon and Harloe (1992, pp. 257–61) also conclude by modifying the dualistic account to a tripartite division of the social structure. At the top are the upper class which expanded in the 1980s as a result of the expansion in financial and allied services, who are mainly white and male, and the new service class which is frequently tied to international as well as local labour markets and is also usually white and male. The second group comprises the middle and lower levels of the service class – many of whom are women and/or from ethnic minorities, as well as the contracting skilled working class. The third group comprises the unskilled working class, whose positions are often very insecure and low waged, combined with what they call the underclass – those excluded from participation in the formal labour market, who tend to be women, immigrants, elderly and young unqualified men. In this formulation the social divisions are mapped in relation to labour markets rather than in terms of their spatial distribution in the city.

Each of these different approaches represents a start in unpacking simple divisions and dichotomies and analyses of a growing polarization between the rich and the poor. Sassen in her recent work (1996, pp. 183–97) argues for a more complex way of understanding global forces and their impact on the city and its residents. It is less and less possible, she suggests, to accept the notion of a hierarchical ordering which has created the semblance of a unitary economic system in which individuals are clearly located. Though 'the centre concentrates immense power, a power that rests on the capability for global control' at the same time 'marginality, notwithstanding weak economic and political power has become in Hall's words a "powerful space"' (p. 197). The devalued sectors which rest largely on the labour of women, immigrants and African-Americans in the cities of the US represent a terrain where battles are fought on many fronts and on many sites, and these battles lack clear boundaries. Marcuse's picture is less grounded in empirical work but it gives some pointers to new ways of thinking about social-spatial shifts. Further study at the local level in cities will enable these models to be elaborated. As the conclusion suggests, the current shifts in social and economic factors, the socio-spatial divisions and their interconnectedness in cities, need to be rethought if growing divisions in cities are to be addressed by urban policy.

The sector models of cities, described above, are rather schematic in that they either do not closely define the basis on which cities are being disaggregated or provide clear links between the socio-economic divisions and other forms of difference that relate to identity and community experience. Economic divisions need to be related to notions of identity and difference.

SOCIAL DEMOGRAPHIC FACTORS

There have been dramatic shifts in the social demography of British cities over the last two decades that are mapped spatially. The most significant shifts are in household form and are underpinned on the one hand by changes in social attitudes, and on the other by growing longevity. In 1994–5 in Great Britain more than a quarter of households consisted of one person living alone. This is almost double the proportion in 1961 (Central Statistical Office, 1996). This is in part the result of more older people living alone but also reflects the growing tendency of young people to live alone, particularly men. The number of men under pensionable age living alone is expected to be the largest group of one-person households by the year 2011. This has implications for city structures and planning since the consumption patterns of men without children in terms of urban services like transport may impose different requirements on urban space than families.

Currently, women over pensionable age constitute the largest group of single people at 12 per cent. There are significant planning issues that result including housing, transport and community care provision. Older people, and older women particularly, form the largest group in local authority housing – 26 per cent of people over 65 and 27 per cent over 80 are public tenants. Cuts in local authority housing will thus have an immediate impact on this group, whose other housing options are few. For the more than 60 per cent of older people who are home-owners there are different issues, such as poor quality stock which is in a state of disrepair and for which the owner may not have the money to fix or ameliorate. Thus, though there may be apparent housing security represented by statistical accounts of tenure, when these are cross tabulated with age and gender, pockets of housing poverty may exist in localities of seemingly adequate housing.

The growth in lone parent households is the most striking demo-graphic shift of the last two decades increasing from 8 per cent in 1971 to 22 per cent in 1991. This is a result of more younger women having children alone, an increase in divorce and separation, as well as chang-ing social attitudes. Yet this is an overwhelming gendered as well as spa-tially differentiated picture, where only 1 per cent of dependent children lived with a lone father in 1994–5. The proportion of lone parents is highest in the North West, where one-third of families with dependent children were lone parents. East Anglia had the lowest proportion at 14 per cent. There is also great variation within regions. For example, Greater London and other metropolitan areas have the highest proportions – in inner areas particularly – while Buckinghamshire and Surrey have the lowest number of single parents. Again, single parents are very dependent on local authorities for their housing, especially women. One year after divorce, where this took place between 1991 and 1993, and where the former matrimonial home was owner occupied, 11 per cent of women were renting from the social sector. They are also poor, with many women solely dependent on benefits for their incomes (Land, 1999).

Smaller household size is also a result of other trends, such as a greater number of marriages ending in divorce and people choosing to have fewer children. Where people live in non-nuclear family house-holds, their needs for social services and other public services differ. This is not to suggest that they are not dependent on various forms of social provision – they are – but access to resources and consumption patterns takes a different form. In traditional nuclear families many of the social and domestic needs of an individual are met within the home and are often provided by women. A single household may look elsewhere for these needs to be met. Though little work has been done in Britain in this area, the trends in many US cities show an increasing consumption of takeaways and precooked food by single people. This has implications in terms of the distribution of shops and retail outlets, the distribution of commercial and residential land uses and so on.

Social-spatial divisions are most clearly mapped on the employment/unemployment axis. The single most determinant cause of poverty is unemployment, from which other conditions such as homelessness, ill health and crime can arise. The important point here for the argument is that statistics of regional unemployment mask differences between and within households. Thus within one spatial community where unemployment is high, the impact is strongly differentiated. Pahl's (1984) study in the Isle of Sheppey illustrated the different resource gathering abilities of different household members and their access to self-provision of goods and services through informal sectors. Skill levels, local knowledges and contacts all have an effect. Thus unemployment can mean different things to different people. Some individuals may be able to find other forms of income, while for others there is no such option.

Race and gender represent significant cleavages as does age, while each of these varies spatially between cities in different parts of the UK. Overall, 38 per cent of white women and 72 per cent of white men work full time. When these figures are compared across ethnic groups some striking differences emerge: 49 per cent of African, Caribbean and other black men of non-mixed origin, 65 per cent of Indian men and 41 per cent of Pakistani/Bangladeshi men work full time. The racial differences among women are much less significant, except for the latter group. Thus 37 per cent of black women, 36 per cent of Indian women and only 12 per cent of Pakistani/Bangladeshi women work full time. Some of these differences arise from a variation in skill and education levels, others from discrimination by employers and others – particularly where gender is concerned – from differences in cultural expectations. Women are much more concentrated in part-time work: 29 per cent of white women and 15 per cent of black women, compared to 5 per cent and 8 per cent of men in these groups, work part time.

The UK has higher economic activity rates for women than Germany and France, but lower than Japan or the United States. Even where women are in full-time work, despite popular public assumptions that there is much greater equality than two decades ago, the gender gap in income has remained remarkably constant. This is partly a result of occupational segregation where women are concentrated in clerical, secretarial and service sector jobs, while men are more concentrated in managerial and administrative sectors as well as the industrial sector. Campaigns for greater gender equality have shifted these balances surprisingly little.

The gender gap in gross weekly earnings is also structured by age. The largest difference is for people in their forties where the gap is over £140 per week. Though the gap between men and women's average wages has remained fairly constant (roughly at two-thirds) since 1971 the gap between lowest and highest earners has widened. For men the gap between those in the top and bottom deciles was £203 in 1971 rising to £419 in 1995; for women the gap grew from £122 to £290 in the same period. Women still take major responsibility for caring for children and other dependants, which has a profound effect on their labour force participation.

Unemployment is also cross cut by gender, race and age. Eight per cent of white men and 5 per cent of white women compared to 21 per cent of black men and 14 per cent of black women were registered as unemployed in 1995. At the same time, economic activity rates among young men between 16 and 24 have fallen off from 81.8 in 1984 to 75.1 in 1994, reflecting their vulnerability to unemployment. Unemployment was highest in the North at just under 11 per cent and lowest in East Anglia at 7 per cent, but these figures are even more differentiated within cities. In Hackney in 1995, the rate was almost 30 per cent, in Newham it was almost 25 per cent and in Knowsley in Liverpool it was 19 per cent. Duration of unemployment varies. Men are more likely to be long-term unemployed than women, and the likelihood of long-term unemployment increases with age. Short-term unemployment is highest among 16–19 year olds with 40 per cent of women in 1995 being unemployed for less than three months.

The last part of the jigsaw to be filled in here is housing. It is well known that there is substantial regional variation in house prices in the UK. The average dwelling price in 1994 varied from £52 838 in Yorkshire and Humberside to £88 163 in Greater London with substantial variation within regions also. The form of tenure of a household is highly affected by age, gender, race and ethnicity, and household type. For example, 20 per cent of Indian households own outright, 64 per cent own with a mortgage and 7 per cent rent from the social sector, compared to 26, 41 and 21 per cent for white households. There is also striking ethnic differentiation of location, with two-thirds of Afro-Caribbean households compared to one-third of Asian Londoners living in the 14 boroughs that constitute the inner city (Cross and Waldinger, 1992, p. 159). Or, looking at the wider picture, 11.5 per cent of economically active white people live in Greater London or the industrial heartlands of the West Midlands compared to an equivalent figure of 46 per cent and 15 per cent for ethnic minorities (p. 158). The life cycle effect reveals a trend from private renting as the major form of tenure for younger households, particularly single men, to outright owner occupation for over half of households where the head is over 60. Homelessness statistics are difficult to evaluate since so much homelessness goes unreported or is concealed. Taking homeless households accepted into temporary accommodation as one measure, there has been a decrease in the number of households living in temporary accommodation from 58 000 in 1993 to 52 000 in 1994, of which over one-fifth are homeless as a result of the breakdown of a relationship with a partner. A disproportionate number of those households accepted as homeless in London during the last decade were female-headed and or ethnic minorities (London Housing Unit, 1989, pp. 52–4). How much the recent drop in the figures reflects changes in housing policy is difficult to assess. In inner city areas of London and other major provincial cities, the numbers of homeless single people are reported by voluntary agencies to be on the increase.

REFLECTIONS ON 'COMMUNITY' FOR CITIES IN TRANSITION

These statistics reflect the impact of global forces on cities which have been highly differentiated, with cities' success depending on their ability to find a place in the new urban hierarchy. It is very clear from this brief statistical sketch that where you live, whether you are a man or woman, old or young, black or white has an enormous impact in terms of your likely labour market participation, income and access to housing, among other things. It is not the purpose of this chapter to explain these differences which have been the subject of debate and analysis for many years. This chapter has set out to do several things. The first point is that the notion of simply polarized or dichotomized social-spatial divisions in cities does not take us far enough. What is needed instead is more textured analyses and research to explore how the different marginalities or forms of exclusion interrelate to concentrate disadvantage in order to construct policies for change. Cities have always been, and will always be, places of heterogeneity.

Second, the statistical picture illustrated how salient social, demographic and cultural differences are. Because most of the available statistics are presented at too aggregated a level, it is difficult to assess how different individuals within different households in areas of concentrated deprivation are negotiating disadvantage. Only more local research would be able to illuminate the key strategies that people follow. Bridge's work on social networks and class (1995, 1997) shows the importance of certain individuals' roles in a community as brokers between groups and into the wider community. In all communities, however defined, some individuals will have links to employment opportunities and other external resources within and outside the community, while others will not. Any simple mapping of social spatial divisions will not pick this up.

The third point raised in this chapter revolves around the question of differences and their status and meaning. Difference and diversity are crucially linked with polarization and divisions. In this sense, difference implies a hierarchy of power by which some are excluded and marginalized and others are not. But difference might also be constructed in a more positive vein. Individuals of different genders, age, race and ethnicity, sexuality and so on will usually value their specificity, and not necessarily want to be subsumed under some homogenized notion of community for whom certain urban policies, for example urban regeneration policies, are devised. Also, as has been pointed out, the disadvantage which accrues from any of these intersects in complex ways which are hidden in the broader picture. The issue then becomes, on the one hand, what are the crucial factors which marginalize and exclude a group or individual. On the other hand, how do we rethink notions of community, which recognize that difference is an integral part? To return to Marcuse's ideas – when are the walls a bad thing and when are they not? How far can a mutual recognition of others' identities go, and how far is difference an outcome of socio-economic fragmentation?

Part of the answer in looking at questions of difference, and the exclusions which result, lies in understanding where notions of threat derive from. Sibley attempts to do this in his work (1995). In his view, people are marginalized because they are feared and created as 'other'. Powerful groups 'purify' and dominate space to create fear of minorities and ultimately exclude them from having a voice. He argues that often in local conflicts in the city a community will represent itself as normal and is threatened by those who are perceived as different. Fears and anxieties are expressed in stereotypes which logically could be challenged by greater knowledge of, and interaction with, the unknown others (p. 29), though such a move could have limited success if done halfheartedly.

These ideas connect with Sennett's earlier (1971) work on the uses of disorder. Sennett rails against the suburban neighbourhood, socially homogeneous and enclosed. Such environments encourage the persistence of the myth of a purified community of neighbourliness and security (although divisions may lurk under the surface). It also perpetuates a form of parochialism based on a naive childlike psychology about other communities in other areas that helps to hold together the internal community myth. Sennett argues that the only way to break down these purified notions, the only way to develop full maturity, is to encounter other groups and situations. This happens in the inner city with its mixed communities in a form of politics of encounter. Indeed Sennett proposes a radical withdrawal of municipal support structures (bureaucracy, overall metropolitan planning, policing of local disputes) to heighten the encounter between and within groups. These anarchic survival communities avoid the isolation of their suburban counterparts. However, this is a politics of encounter that is bought at the expense of any civic responsibility.

The idea of community based on civic responsibility has been taken up by the political left and right. Communitarians like Etzioni call for a re-establishment of strong families and social responsibility in parenting as a catalyst to promote civic responsibility. These are the values of small-town America imported into the metropolis. However, the socio-demographic arrangements they favour (e.g. the nuclear family) deny difference in parenting as experienced in the inner city. On the other hand, those on the right have begun to focus on the notion of community to try to re-establish the moral order of the suburb. This notion draws on Chicago School human ecology which sees the heterogeneity of the inner city and its forms of social competition as a form of social disorganization. In contrast are the 'natural areas' of the suburbs where the social metabolism of the city is stabilized and a mutual moral order can develop. This is civic conservatism. Both left and right raise the potential for various forms of moral authoritarianism.

In postmodernist writing political liberalism and traditional ideas of community are seen as dangerous in that they both dissolve difference. Young in *Justice and the Politics of Difference* (1990) constructs an ideal of city life as a vision of social relations, as affirming group difference or as 'openness to unassimilated otherness' or a 'being together of strangers'. For Young the unpredictability and heterogeneity of the city are the ingredients for a sense of openness to others and mutual affirmation of difference. The difficulty of Young's position for the present argument is that, in order to promote a difference based on fluid subjectivities, she removes explicitly the other form of difference, namely socio-economic divisions. In order to establish the urban as a form of relationship in the unoppressive city she must remove material deprivation and unemployment to create a city of abundance. This is the opposite of Sennett's move to remove municipal support to produce survival communities.

The consequences of the intersection of political economy (and social fragmentation) and communities of feeling and solidarity might be seen most clearly when the two confront each other in communities subject to change. Marx argued that the community of people was easily under-mined by the community of money. Logan and Molotch (1987) saw the use value of neighbourhood (neighbourliness, affective relationships) being subject to threat from the exchange value of place. Smith (1996) sees the process of gentrification as an urban frontier, a frontier of capital, social division and discourse. The frontier of capital involves the movement of investment into hitherto devalorized neighbourhoods, which leads to a social division as many working-class residents are dis-placed. This process is supported by an ideological scripting of the city through civic boosterism and notions of revitalization. This is a discourse that writes out the displaced poor. Smith argues that with the recession and degentrification in the late 1980s in the USA this civic boosterism has been replaced by a neo-conservative urban politics of the revanchist city. This is a politics of revenge where those most marginalized by the reconfigured community of money in the city (the poor and homeless) are scapegoated because of their visibility (e.g. with such policies as zero tolerance to beggars). In this sense difference is used as an ideological weapon.

One possible resolution to the opposition between notions of com-munity and difference is to posit community as more fluid in social, temporal and spatial terms. Communities are contingent and dynamic. For instance, they may mean different things to different people at various stages of the lifecycle. In his study of gentrification in a north London neighbourhood Bridge (1995) used social network analysis to demonstrate that the lack of class action in the changing neighbour-hood could be understood by the fact that the neighbourhood was not the critical site of class association for working-class residents. Class connections had not dissipated, they were simply spread throughout the metropolitan area. Nevertheless there were some residents who felt the social contestation of space in the neighbourhood very keenly, especially older people and mothers with young children whose social networks at that time in their lives were concentrated on the neighbourhood.

What urban policy should not do is to treat community as some form of solidaristic whole. Usually community is used as if it is a homogeneous category. Community implies unity and the notion is increasingly deployed to evoke affective relationships, connection and continuity. At the same time, communities in practice are those who share a common heritage or set of concerns, a common self-identification or culture or set of norms, and are usually defined by differentiating themselves from others. When this is done as a process of exclusion or claiming power it is different from when this is done as a form of resistance or solidarity by those who are powerless, which brings us back to Marcuse's concerns.

In conclusion, there seem to be a number of strands which emerge from this chapter which deserve more detailed research and consideration in urban policy. These are that cities are increasingly complex and complicated places where simple divisions – core and periphery, rich and poor, blacks and whites and so on – tell only part of the story. What is important therefore is to analyse these differences to see where they are productive and where they simply represent concentrations of disadvantage. What is also important is to recognize that economic, social and cultural differences are persistent, and if notions of community and social justice are to be rethought and maintained in some form, then the tensions will need to be addressed. This means seeing individuals on their own, or individuals within households and communities as differently placed in terms of access to resources and opportunities depending on a range of crosscutting and interrelated factors such as race, age and gender. It also means taking on the symbolic exclusions in city spaces that Sibley discusses, as well as the more material and graphic exclusions of the gated suburbs in Davis's Los Angeles (1992).

References

J. Allen and D. Massey, *The Economy in Question* (London: Sage, 1988).

G. Bridge, 'Gentrification class and community: a social network approach', in A. Rogers and S. Vertoved (eds), *The Urban Context: Ethnicity, Social Networks and Situational Analysis* (Oxford: Berg, 1995).

G. Bridge, 'Mapping the terrain of space-time compression: power networks in everyday life', *Environment and Planning D: Society and Space*, 15 (1997) 611–18.

M. Castells, *The Rise of the Network Society* (Oxford: Blackwell, 1996).

Central Statistical Office, *Social Trends* 26 (London: HMSO, 1996).

M. Cross and R. Waldinger, 'Migrants, minorities and the ethnic division of labour', in S. Fainstein, I. Gordon and M. Harloe (eds), *Divided Cities* (Oxford: Blackwell, 1992).

M. Davis, *City of Quartz* (New York: Vintage, 1992).

S. Fainstein, I. Gordon and M. Harloe (eds), *Divided Cities* (Oxford: Blackwell, 1992).

H. Land, 'The changing world of work and families', in S. Watson and L. Doyal (eds), *Engendering Social Policy* (Buckingham: Open University Press, 1999).

J. R. Logan and H.L. Molotch, Urban Fortunes, the Political Economy of Place (Berkeley: University of California Press, 1987).

London Housing Unit, *One in Every Hundred* (London: London Research Centre, 1989).

P. Marcuse, 'Dual city: a muddy metaphor for a quartered city', *International Journal of Urban and Regional Research*, 13: 4 (1989) 697–708.

P. Marcuse, 'Not chaos but walls: postmodernism and the partitioned city', in S. Watson and K. Gibson (eds), *Postmodern Cities and Spaces* (Oxford: Blackwell, 1995).

J. Mollenkopf and M. Castells (eds), *Dual City: Restructuring New York* (New York: Russell Sage Foundation, 1991).

R. Pahl, *Divisions of Labour* (Oxford: Blackwell, 1984).

S. Sassen, 'Rebuilding the global city: economy, ethnicity and space', in A. King (ed.), *Re-Presenting the City* (London: Macmillan, 1996).

R. Sennett, *The Uses of Disorder: Identity and City Life* (New York: Knopf, 1971).

D. Sibley, *Geographies of Exclusion* (London: Routledge, 1995).

N. Smith, *The Urban Frontier* (Oxford: Blackwell, 1996).

S. Watson and K. Gibson (eds), *Postmodern Cities and Spaces* (Oxford: Blackwell, 1995).

I. Young, *Justice and the Politics of Difference* (Princeton, NJ: Princeton University Press, 1990).

8 Socio-Economic Exclusion and the Stability of the Urban Social Order

Henning Schridde

INTRODUCTION

In the past two decades, social and economic modernization processes have produced growing poverty and social exclusion in virtually all major European and American cities (Fainstein and Fainstein, 1985; Commission of the European Communities, 1992; Madden, 1996). For a long time western industrialized societies believed that poverty would become a thing of the past with increasing prosperity. Even now, the belief that rising economic growth could solve the problem of growing poverty and social exclusion is still dominant. Particularly in the 1980s, the European Community member states exhibited an apparent paradoxical trend. On the one hand, there was steady economic growth and rising prosperity in the member states and the US, and on the other hand, the number of poor among the population rose markedly. One popular theory in urban research claims that economic growth and rising prosperity generate poverty in society, polarization within urban society and the accumulation of private wealth and public poverty (see Sassen, 1996; Dangschat, 1995; Noller and Ronneberger, 1995; Ronneberger, 1994b; Jaschke, 1992). Big cities are fast becoming reservoirs for the homeless and penniless, foreigners, victims of family break-ups and other people needing care, where crime, gang warfare, aggression and violence are rife. As the former Lord Mayor of the City of Munich, Kronawitter, pointed out in his inaugural speech, more and more slums for the poor are being built, while the wealthy encapsulate themselves in safe residential areas with private security systems. In the face of this trend, the city itself is becoming a 'trouble spot' and the loser in a process of modernization which was forced upon it, because the profits from modernization will not pay for a compensatory social policy (Kronawitter, 1994; Voscherau, 1994).

'The costs were once considered the burden of the excluded; but the true costs are now becoming evident in the urban system. ... The many externalities resulting from inequalities hamper future economic growth' (Brink, 1996, p. 65). How is it possible for urban social policy to provide lasting security for the economic, social and political foundations of cities?

This chapter begins by discussing poverty and social exclusion. Then the new role of the city in the global economy is considered and the social transformation of cities is described. Finally, empirical findings on poverty and social exclusion in German cities are compared and Hanover is used as a case study. The last section will be dedicated to the contribution made by social, political and economic cohesion to the stabilization of the urban social order.

POVERTY AND SOCIO-ECONOMIC EXCLUSION

As Simmel so aptly put it, poverty describes a social relationship. And as Room pointed out, the interpretation of poverty and social exclusion are based on different social concepts. Using Esping-Andersen's typology of welfare state regimes (1990), Room distinguishes between the dominant liberal view of society in the Anglo-Saxon world which accepts the notions of disadvantage and poverty and the dominant continental tradition. This latter, predominantly French, tradition emphasizes (a) the significance of mutual rights and the need to include social groups in a society which comprises a moral and political community with a social democratic tradition, and (b) the importance of equal rights for citizens to underpin good social relations (Room, 1995a, 1995b).

Absolute and relative poverty

A distinction is made in poverty research between absolute poverty where physical subsistence is endangered and relative poverty.

Nowadays, it is generally accepted in Britain as well as in France and Germany that no assessment of what corresponds to poverty can be made without taking account of the general contemporary standard of living in the particular country and in the particular period under consideration (Wilson and Wilson, 1982, p. 74; Atkinson, 1975, p. 187; Huster, 1996, p. 22). According to the Commission of the European Communities, relative poverty is classed as follows: those with so little money that they are excluded from the way of life which is accepted as a minimum in the member state in which they live. The Commission has set a specific poverty threshold value, whereby households and individuals are classed as needy if they have under 50 per cent of the average net income per capita of the population. Income-related poverty prevents those affected from accessing the major cultural and social provisions in society. This relative income-related concept of poverty was expanded and enhanced to include the resource theory approach. This questions the total material resources which are available to the individual or household. In addition to income from work, this includes private and public means, as well as cash and transferable capital assets (Huster, 1996).

Poverty and problem groups in society

According to the many surveys that have been undertaken, the risk of becoming impoverished affects a few clearly identifiable groups in society, namely the unemployed, large families, the chronically sick and long-term care cases, plus elderly people and unskilled immigrants (Landua and Habich, 1994). These groups which are specifically poverty stricken are a mark of the changing social and economic structure of our time. Figure 8.1 shows the trends of various

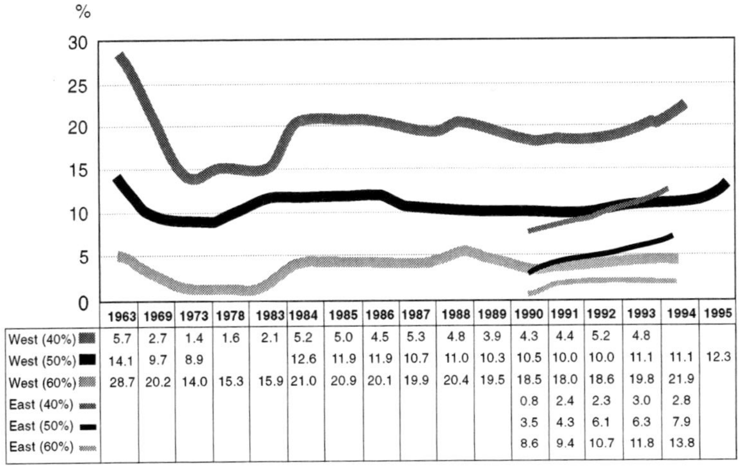

	1963	1969	1973	1978	1983	1984	1985	1986	1987	1988	1989	1990	1991	1992	1993	1994	1995
West (40%)	5.7	2.7	1.4	1.6	2.1	5.2	5.0	4.5	5.3	4.8	3.9	4.3	4.4	5.2	4.8		
West (50%)	14.1	9.7	8.9			12.6	11.9	11.9	10.7	11.0	10.3	10.5	10.0	10.0	11.1	11.1	12.3
West (60%)	28.7	20.2	14.0	15.3	15.9	21.0	20.9	20.1	19.9	20.4	19.5	18.5	18.0	18.6	19.8	21.9	
East (40%)												0.8	2.4	2.3	3.0	2.8	
East (50%)												3.5	4.3	6.1	6.3	7.9	
East (60%)												8.6	9.4	10.7	11.8	13.8	

Sources: Semrau (1990); Statistisches Bundesamt (1997)

Figure 8.1   Percentage of poor people in Germany 1963–95.

threshold limits for income-related poverty in West Germany between 1963 and 1995.

Up to and including the 1970s, poverty in Germany could be tackled effectively. When the early structural crises hit the economy, the poverty rate began to rise despite a range of government-funded measures introduced by the Federal Republic in attempts to counter the problem. In the 1980s the incidence of poverty remained stable at around 10 per cent. However, if the rise in the number of inhabitants in (West) Germany of over 4 million is taken into account, then the percentage figure represents an increase in the number of poor in absolute terms. During the 1990s, poverty in Germany began to rise again. Poverty in East Germany is fast approaching West German levels. In view of these trends, rising poverty looks set to continue in the future.

Poverty is a selective social risk. Not everybody is exposed to the risk of becoming poor to the same degree. If we return to the criterion of income-related poverty (under 50 per cent of the average net income), 27 per cent of the total jobless were classed as poor, 23 per cent of households of five or more, 33 per cent of single parents, 20 per cent of the immigrant population and 14 per cent of children (Statistisches Bundesamt, 1994). However, these figures tend to disguise huge regional differences. One example of this is child poverty. In many cities over 20 per cent of children live on social security and in some parts of cities this rate accounts for up to 50 per cent (Stadt Essen, 1993; Stadtteilbüro Malstatt, 1993). Any discussion of poverty and exclusion thereby necessarily involves groups facing major problems.

Dynamics of poverty

Dynamic poverty research has addressed the characteristics of the poor as well as the duration and continuity of poverty in recent years (Leibfried et al., 1995). The duration and outcome of poverty depend mainly on the causes of poverty and the chances of escaping it. Becoming poor is caused by factors such as increasing periods of unemployment and family background. The reasons for getting into poverty may also constitute possible ways of getting out again. For example, marrying again, starting work or eligibility for some other benefit, such as pensions, mark the end of a period of claiming social security benefit. Getting into and out of the poverty trap and the duration of poverty vary depending on the cause of poverty. Unemployment represents one of the main causes of poverty.

Over half of the unemployed have been claiming benefit for under one year, although studies also show that the unemployed with disabilities or the elderly unemployed normally spend a longer time in poverty than unemployed people without problems of this kind. Even in cases of families with a history of poverty, there are clear differences. Single parents tend to spend longer on social security than other groups. In Hamburg for example, single parents claim social security for an average of 3.5 years. The duration of poverty suggests a new dimension in terms of time in patterns of social inequality (Berger, 1994, p. 39). Destandardization of lifestyles leads to changing patterns in the duration and outcome of poverty. Figure 8.2 shows the duration of income-related poverty for West Germany from 1984 to 1992. Thirty per cent (under the 50 per cent scale) or almost half of the population (under the 60 per cent scale) are hit by poverty at some time in their lives, if only temporarily. Poverty extends right through the middle classes. By contrast, there are a small number of long-term poor whose chances of escaping poverty are low. As studies in the United States and Britain have shown, temporary poverty is in no way as harmless as it might sound. The short-term poor are more at risk of getting caught in the poverty trap again. Studies from the US confirm that 60 per cent of those who come off welfare claim state benefit again within two years

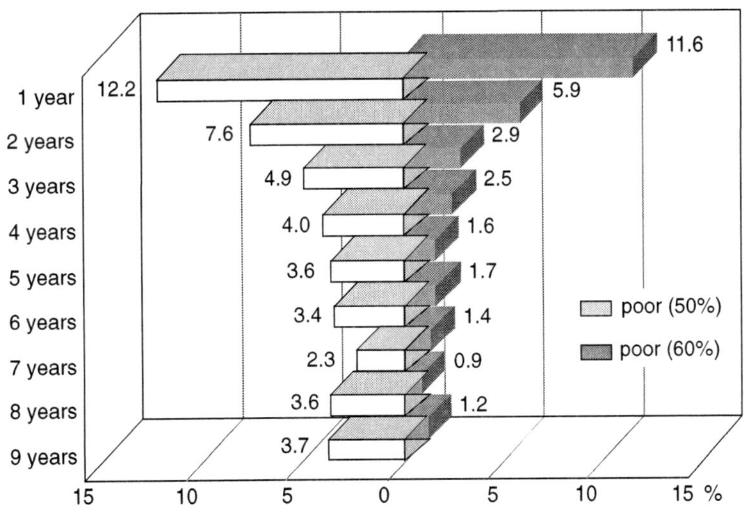

Source: Statistisches Bundesamt (1997)

Figure 8.2   Duration of poverty in West Germany 1984–92.

(see *Hannoversche Allgemeine Zeitung,* 7 January 1997). In Britain it has been reported that 29 per cent of those who manage to escape poverty go back into poverty within a year (Walker, 1997, p. 5). Even if they no longer require state support, this by no means represents the end of poverty. Numerous social security claimants remain in the lower income brackets after coming off benefit. In the United States, for example, 33 per cent are classed as 'working poor' one year after they stop claiming, and in Britain only 3 per cent of those who escape the bread line have an above average income one year later.

Despite shorter claim period trends in social security in the 1980s, this should not be interpreted as an improvement in the situation of social security claimants (Ludwig, Leisering and Buhr, 1996, p. 26). Both long- and short-term claims have increased, although the number and consequently the proportion of short-term claims have risen faster. Fluctuation among the poor has increased at the same rate as the rise in poverty. Due to the cumulative effect of long-term claims, the results of a cross-sectional study show that there are more long-term cases among the poor population (Busch-Geertscma and Ruhstrat, 1992, p. 367). This is why poverty reports from numerous cities also conclude that around 40–50 per cent of social security claimants have been claiming benefit for over five years. In addition, long-term cases are often concentrated in particular areas. Initial evaluations of recent social security statistics indicate that the duration of the average individual claim ranges from 71 to 10 months in the inner city areas of Hamburg (Erdmann, 1996, p. 236).

Biographical representation of poverty

Poverty also covers the perception of their circumstances by individuals themselves. Poverty and the continuity of poverty do not need to be experienced by those affected as social decline and marginalization or lead to deprivation and depression. The relationships are far more complex (Leibfried et al., 1995, pp. 107–31).

The consequences of social security claims and poverty must be seen in each individual setting. Leibfried therefore distinguishes between subjective stopgap claimants (53 per cent), failed stopgap claimants (10 per cent) and subjective long-term claimants (37 per cent). In his biographical representation of poverty, he distinguishes between the following:

- *Negative perception*. Social security claim is disguised by other events such as illness, poverty or unemployment.
- *Biographical perspective*. This group evaluates poverty by way of comparison with its respective peer group.
- *Biographical accounting*. Social security is countered by changes in personal circumstances. Social security can help in emergencies (homelessness), allow for a new start (divorce) or with the essential aims in life (single parents).
- *Global negative evaluation*. Social security claims are seen as a burden and excluding, whereby this response does not necessarily apply for long-term claims.

The biographical representation of poverty points out that individuals have different potential to overcome their situation, to escape from poverty or to come to terms with it.

Exclusion

In modern societies, differences can be seen between a large number of specialized independent rational, closed functional arrangements, whose systematic logic has a marked impact on the living conditions for individuals affected by these arrangements. As there is no common view on inclusion in society, it is determined by the individual functional systems. Modern societies are highly integrated in terms of exclusion zones so that by commercializing all areas of life and with the decline of the welfare state, exclusion within one functional system virtually automatically triggers exclusion from other functional systems (Brock and Junge, 1995, p. 179). Social exclusion therefore shifts the emphasis to relationships within society, or in other words, low social participation, lack of social integration and lack of power (Commission of the European Communities, 1993, p. 11; Room, 1995b; Buffoni, 1997, p. 115). The forms and levels of social exclusion can be identified in greater detail for each functional system (Peters, 1993; Münch, 1995; Schridde, 1995; Kronauer, 1997; Walker, 1997).

Economic exclusion

Since the 1970s, unemployment in Western Europe has risen to over 20 million. Over 8 million were unemployed for over one year (Huster, 1996). National labour market policy plays a substantial role as it provides assistance for reintegration or secures income.

In many countries, youth unemployment also represents a great problem. Many young people have no qualifications, as a result of which they are unable to gain access to income, wealth or social provision. As the education system still has a class related bias, vertical inequality structures are reproduced (Meier, 1995).

Stable or falling real income and polarization of income structures are further indicators of one of the dangers of economic exclusion. In addition, there are the increasing restrictions on government transfer payments so that exclusion from the economic sector is heightened by welfare service cutbacks.

Political exclusion

The power of the economy to destroy society has been tackled through the economic integration of general wealth, mass consumption and political integration of the welfare state. This integration is based on consensus about the legal role of the state. Today, this consensus is more at risk than ever before. It is not just that the ability to devise effective policy has declined as a consequence of globalization, but also that the socially excluded no longer have any hope that politics can change their situation.

In addition, there is the fact that the convergence trends in society seen in the 1980s have disappeared. Access to the elite ceased to be simply a question of achievements and qualifications, although the legitimacy of the elite suffered as a result (Vester et al., 1993, p. 46). 'The wealthy have a virtual monopoly over all political rights. The poor and disadvantaged will not find anyone in any of the main political parties who is ... willing to change this situation' (Galbraith, 1992, p. 136).

Last but not least, membership of minority ethnic groups can also lead to political exclusion. If up to 30 per cent of immigrants live in a city like Frankfurt am Main, then the issue of political rights of participation arises at the local level.

Cultural exclusion

Cultural exclusion means exclusion from what is generally held in common, from involvement in socially conventional practices, and from opportunities to learn about these practices. Questions of 'good taste' and 'character' represent cultural exclusion via the media.

Cultural exclusion is exclusion from opportunities to live in accordance with generally accepted standards of behaviour, to share similar goals in life and common values.

Social exclusion

Family, relations and neighbours represent traditional established networks which provide solidarity and can offer social and material support in difficult living conditions. They can be seen as a social and domestic milieu at the micro level. According to studies of structurally unequal living conditions and of the individuals affected, milieu-specific living environments (micro milieus) can provide both 'support' and a 'filter function' (Herlyn et al., 1991, p. 27). Changes in budget structures, demographic change, the erosion of established milieus have contributed to an increase in the phenomenon of social exclusion. The consequences include alienation, emotional deprivation, identity problems and self-defeatism. Social exclusion thereby consolidates poverty, demoralization and deprivation. The micro level of the domestic setting and the macro level of inner city areas therefore represent an important resource for social integration. The inner city area, particularly for the poor population, serves as a place of security, safe living, social linkages and social belonging (Herlyn et al., 1991, pp. 232–42).

Spatial exclusion in society

Poverty and social exclusion are becoming increasingly concentrated in big cities, especially in the poor areas known as 'trouble spots' or hyper-ghettos. There people face the prospect of being stuck in a vicious circle of poverty forever, where poverty is handed down from the parents to the next generation of children. A new urban underclass is emerging (Wilson, 1987; Alisch and Dangschat, 1993; Kristensen, 1995; Schneider-Sliwa, 1996; Madden, 1996). In the poor areas, life is not just an expression of poverty and social exclusion, but also leads to a higher risk of remaining poor (Farwick, 1996). Time-space social stratification is the frame within which inequalities of access to resources and life chances are contained today which are more acute than any which prevailed during the period of class-based industrial society (Herlyn et al., 1991, p. 107; Tobias and Boettner, 1992; Buffoni, 1997, p. 118). If you take the extent of social segregation as a measure of social distance, growing poverty and spatial exclusion of the poor represent a massive threat to social cohesion in the cities, according to European Commission findings (Commission of the European Communities, 1992). As urban policy cannot maintain order in its own exclusion zones, hyper-ghettos develop their own structures which may be completely separate from society.

GLOBAL ECONOMIC RESTRUCTURING AND THE SOCIAL TRANSFORMATION OF CITIES

Under conditions of economic, job and population growth, urban policy-makers were confronting similar problems almost everywhere up to the mid-1970s. The common policy of the cities was an urban growth policy designed to improve social integration and functional performance throughout the city. However, during the 1980s, this uniform pattern of development began to be eroded. In the German city system there have been signs of a two-way split. In the second half of the 1980s cities were upgraded as special areas to attract inward investment at the global level (Sassen, 1991; Knapp, 1995; Eade, 1997). Paradoxically, as spatial and political barriers to capital investment were removed, sensitivity to comparative advantage heightened in terms of urban differences (Noller, Prigge and Ronneberger, 1994, p. 17). Against this background city councils began to sell the special features of their city over their rivals via an 'entrepreneurial urban policy'.

The aim was to cater for global companies seeking new locations (Fromhold-Elsebith, 1995; Knapp, 1995; Mayer, 1996) to avoid declining into 'extended workbenches' like many old industrialized urban areas, or turning into marginalized urban areas (Krätke, 1996). Globalization of the economy has had far-reaching consequences for both cities and urban society. These are presented below in brief (see Sassen, 1991, 1996; Prigge, 1994; Ronneberger, 1994a, 1994b; Krätke, 1996).

- Concentration of government, decision-making, finance, marketing and control functions (headquarters economy) in the cities and simultaneous extensive geographical decentralization of products and supplies in the so-called developing countries.
- The metropolis is turning into a geographical intersection for production, finance and control in an increasingly transnational economic organization.

- World city hypothesis – the way in which the integration of a city into the global economic system determines its economic/social and spatial/structural development.
- Social restructuring of labour markets, growth of high-skilled and semi-skilled occupations, including precarious and flexible employment conditions, informal and formal economy, growing job migration.
- Increasing up-front investment by cities to attract relocating enterprises and growing demands of urban professionals for soft locational factors leading to conspicuous consumption by the new elite.
- New time organization of city society based on flexible working and production times (24-hour society).
- Elimination of low value, low yield use of space, replaced by high value and highly profitable headquarters economy.
- Competing use of urban space between professionals and poor population (gentrification).
- Growing social polarization of income and wage structures and increasing spatial polarization in society, creation of hyper-ghettos.
- Growth of violence, racism and crime.

Although the consequences of globalization and 'entrepreneurial urban policy' are clear, where all policy areas are designed to meet the target of economic prosperity, there is still a dominant traditional belief in growth in the cities. Growth policy is legitimized in the hope that the earlier common policy can be restored, and where this growth policy has already been severely hit, many cities are moving from a 'social net' strategy (secondary labour market, qualification programmes, expanding social infrastructure) to a policy of social damage limitation in order to protect the interests of the 'first' and 'second' city from the 'third' marginalized city (Rodenstein, 1987; Dangschat, 1994, p. 32). However, the policy of damage limitation in society is in imminent danger of being turned into a policy of social exclusion at federal level.

REBUILDING URBAN SOCIETY

Cities are places and engines of social and economic change. In the past they have shown themselves to be integrating machines. Today, on the other hand, the centrifugal forces of modern society are making an impact on cities and thereby bringing about a more heterogeneous urban society. Changes in labour markets prompted by globalization are producing new career models, recruitment patterns, job environments and a whole new set of values (Noller and Ronneberger, 1995). Careers with a high proportion of cultural capital investment (education) which demand more flexibility, mobility, creativity, decision-making ability and team spirit are dominant. 'The new class of service providers requires career oriented, well educated people who are under great pressure to perform in their free time as well. This produces attitudes which can be described as conspicuous consumption, i.e. hedonism, individuality, flexibility and lack of solidarity' (Dangschat, 1995, p. 52). Inner cities are being gentrified and rebuilt into areas of competing and distinctive lifestyles. The gentrifiers are transforming entire areas with their patterns of consumption and housing demands (Herbst, 1992; Noller and Ronneberger, 1995, p. 84; Franzmann, 1996; Helbrecht, 1996).

Social restructuring necessitates the breakdown of the traditional milieu. Even the traditional middle classes (petit bourgeoisie) are being crowded out and feel threatened by the conspicuous consumption, distinctive lifestyles and dominance of the urban professionals in both material and symbolic terms (Ronneberger, 1994a, p. 192). The middle classes respond with fatalism, political disaffection or, in some cases, even racism, exclusion of the weak from society and demarcation of boundaries. Some sections of the middle classes view fringe groups as an inevitable stage in the metropolitanization process, and mystify and legitimize their exclusion as part of the natural process of selection. In this, they are supported by an urban policy which requires scapegoats to bridge the local/global contradictions and which aims to integrate the social contrasts of a split society through cultural differences in lifestyles (Freyberg, 1992; Jaschke, 1992; Prigge, 1994, p. 55; Ronneberger, 1994a, pp. 189, 196). The transnational class, the vanishing middle class and the urban underclass reflect the more fragmented social structure in modern urban society. This pluralistic way of life and individualistic behaviour has also affected the poor communities. Indeed, the risks of the modern career built on individualization are in part a cause of that growing poverty and social exclusion (Berger, 1994). Following the transformation in the labour markets, changing family and demographic structures, the varying levels of cultural and social capital, decline in the welfare state systems and deregulation policy of the 1980s, there has been a massive increase in the causes of poverty and the number of people at risk (Bordieu, 1991; Berger, 1994). Poverty has many facets (Leisering,

Character	Modernized 14% → 20%	Partly modernized 38% → 45%	Traditional 46% → 35%
Upper class **22% → 19%**	Alternative milieu 4% → 2%	Technocratic/ liberal milieu 9% → 9%	Conservative elitist milieu 9% → 8%
Middle class **58% → 59%**	Hedonistic milieu 10% → 13%	Upwardly mobile milieu 20% → 24%	Petit bourgeois milieu 28% → 22%
Lower class **18% → 22%**	New workers milieu 0% → 5%	Non-traditional milieu 9% → 12%	Traditional workers milieu 9% → 5%

Sources: Vester et al. 1993 p. 16.

Figure 8.3   Social milieus in a pluralistic class-based society 1982–91.

1993). It does not necessarily have to be a permanent feature of a marginalized or socially excluded fringe group.

On the contrary, mixing vertical social class structures with horizontal structures of social inequality leads to social risks bringing about the development of fringe groups, and tends to extend into the broad 'middle of the road' groups in society (Chassée et al., 1992, p. 7; Leibfried et al., 1995). However, according to one hypothesis, recruitment patterns for long-term poverty are limited to a few milieus in society.

In spite of the apparent dismantling of social barriers, divisions form in a pluralistic class-based society along the lines of risk of poverty, conditions for getting into and escaping poverty, biographical representation and duration of poverty (see Figure 8.3).

The proportions of the population in these milieus vary in different cities, and the main focus of local urban policies can also vary. The global and the local confront one another in the different environments and social milieus. Social transformation and urban social cohesion depend essentially on the compensatory nature and culture of the social milieu, i.e. the integrative force of the social milieu (Vester et al., 1993, p. 25). Although these considerations are purely hypothetical in character, against a background of analysis of urban conflict and social change they constitute valid empirical evidence. Urban conflict is not just produced by objective, conflicting areas of interest. It can also be viewed as a part of the social exclusion process and of the battle for the integration of particular lifestyles in society (Hitzler, 1994).

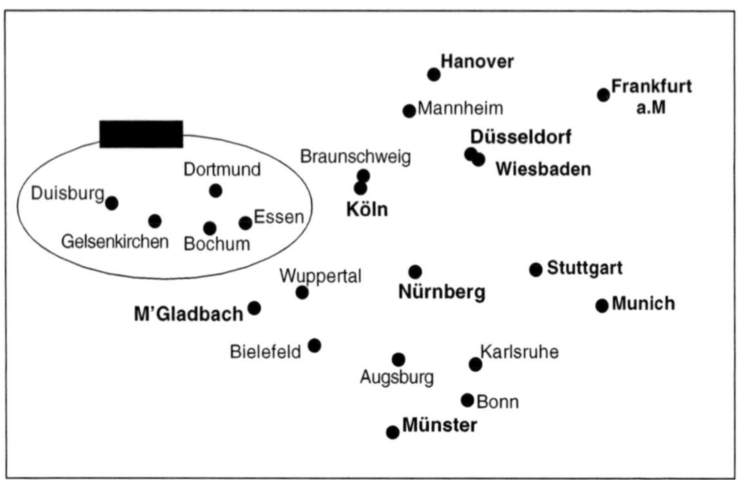

Figure 8.4 Multi-dimensional scale analysis of major German cities based on social, economic and fiscal variables.

POVERTY AND SOCIAL EXCLUSION IN MAJOR GERMAN CITIES

Since the 1980s, all major German cities have experienced growing poverty and social exclusion in the wake of social and economic modernization incentives (Breckner et al., 1989; Schridde, 1995; Dangschat, 1996). Figure 8.4 portrays a multi-dimensional scale analysis drawn up on the basis of social, economic and fiscal variables in order to obtain a general picture of the similarities and differences between major German cities.

Old industrial cities were the first to be hit by rising poverty trends following structural unemployment.

Using the north/south economic divisions, the numbers of unemployed and social security claimants rose in the cities in the Ruhr. Poverty in the cities has turned into urban poverty, and socioeconomic exclusion in the cities has become urban exclusion and marginalization (Lee, 1989). For a long time prospering cities, such as Munich and Frankfurt, did not seem to have been affected by poverty, although the numbers of unemployed and benefit claimants rose there too. Given their economic prosperity, they continued to believe that they could afford to pursue a common policy. Now that they have recognized that the welfare state is overburdened and the centrifugal

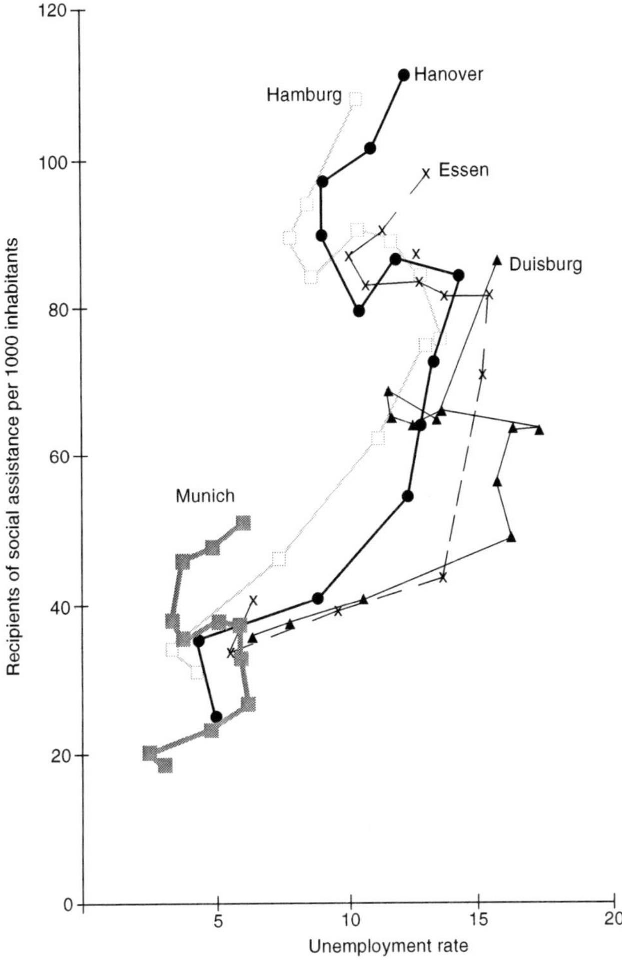

Figure 8.5 Social assistance density and unemployment rate 1978–95.

forces of the global economy are overtaxing their cities and making them lose out in the modernization process, they have also begun to complain about the decline of urban society (Kronawitter, 1994). In Figure 8.5 unemployment trends and social security needs between 1978 and 1995 for a number of major cities are represented as intersecting coordinates in graph form.

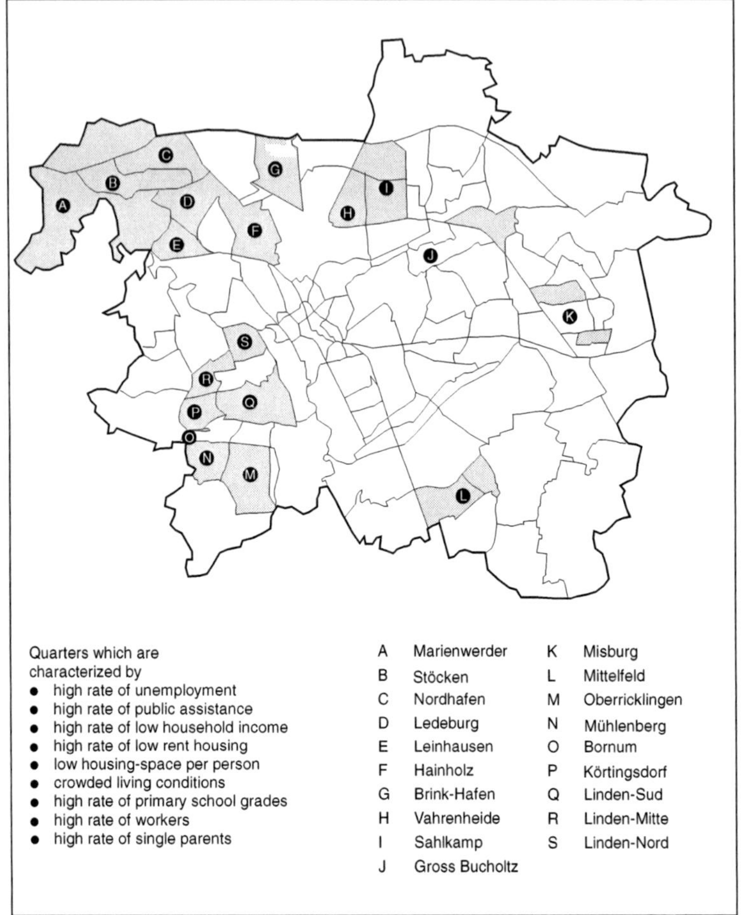

Figure 8.6   Disadvantaged urban areas in Hanover.

Unemployment rates and the demand for social assistance density are shown to be on the increase for all cities. Hanover and Hamburg have the joint highest demands for social assistance. Furthermore, there are different characteristics between the different cities over time which can be traced back to the differing social and economic structures and forms of socio-political intervention (Schridde, 1995). What implications does this have for spatial characteristics within a city? Spatial structures will be discussed, using Hanover as an example. Figure 8.6 represents the results of a factor analysis using a range of structural attributes.

With this type of model it is possible to determine the cumulative effect of variables such as unemployment, social security needs, poor living conditions, low level skills and school education in various parts of the city. Those with extremely negative characteristics can be classed as poor areas. Thus, Hanover is split into a disadvantaged north-west and a privileged south-east part. The following areas reported extreme results: Vahrenheide, Sahlkamp, Linden, Mühlenberg and Mittelfeld. In Vahrenheide, for example, there is a high proportion of rented homes (64 per cent). There are also concentrations of social security needs of up to 40 per cent and an unemployment rate in individual groups of up to 30 per cent (Landeshauptstadt Hanover, 1993). In many families, claiming social security is a normal part of life. In Mühlenberg, 55 per cent of all families are on social security and in Vahrenheide the figure is 38 per cent. In these urban areas, there are concentrations of single parents, of whom 65 per cent in Mühlenberg are claiming social security.

Even if attempts are made not to stigmatize such areas as trouble spots, the phenomena of lawlessness and violence can be observed. Local retailers in Vahrenheide complain about youth crime. Shop theft is carried out by gangs of youths (*Hannoversche Allgemeine Zeitung*, 14 May 1994). There are also conflicts between the local gangs, some of which are truly multi-ethnic, and new residents such as refugees and asylum seekers (*Hannoversche Allgemeine Zeitung*, 8 March 1995; Michalzik, 1993; Kilb, 1993).

Objective structural analysis can reveal only half of the poverty and social exclusion. The filter and support function of the local social setting is just as important in any analysis. In this context it shows that there are different poor settings in Vahrenheide and Linden. Despite the same structural situation in principle, 56 per cent of the population felt unsafe at night in their area in Vahrenheide, whereas in Linden only 24 per cent felt the same way. The evaluation of their own urban area confirmed this trend. Linden got a grade of 2.3 from its residents and Vahrenheide got 2.8.[1] Disintegration processes therefore affect subjective emotive feelings of safety as well as identification with one's own area. In addition, voting levels (see Figure 8.7), which were also included as an indicator of political exclusion, show that the people in Linden were more socially integrated than the people of Vahrenheide. Voting analysis reveals that the dominant Social Democratic Party is losing increasing numbers of votes in

     Henning Schridde

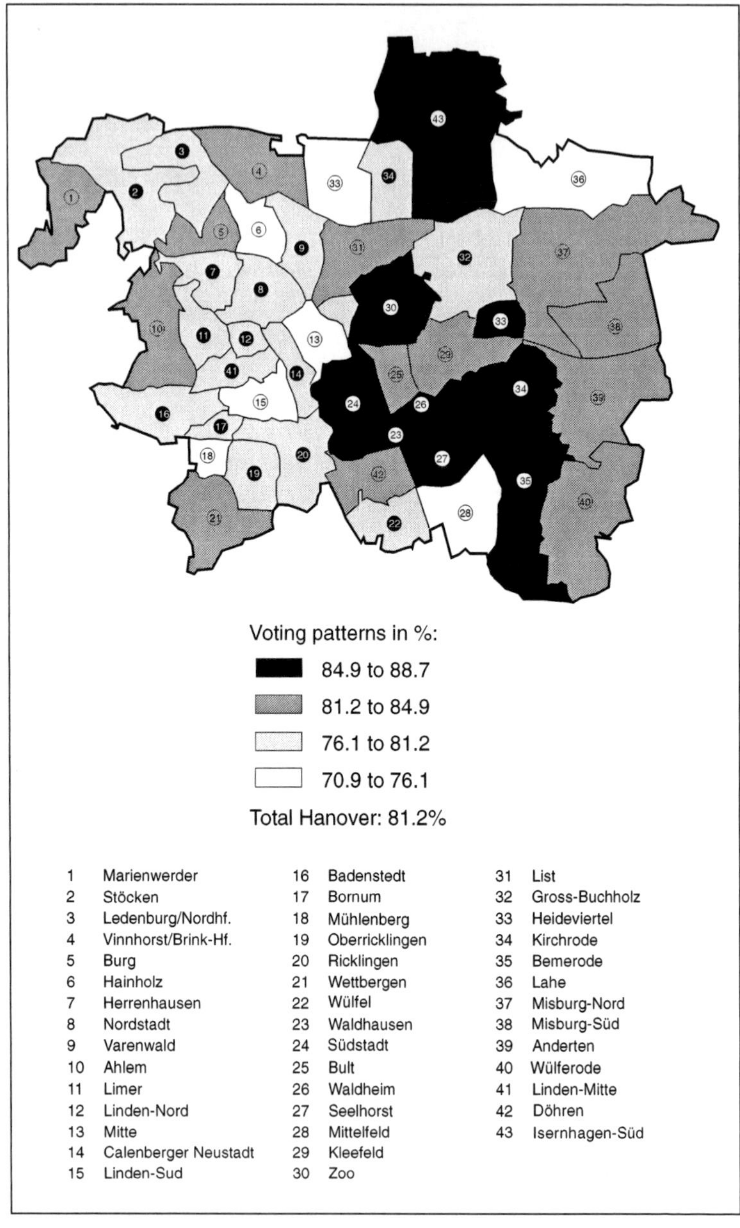

Figure 8.7   Voting patterns in Hanover 1994.

these urban areas, though the political shifts show up another clear distinction. In Linden the Bündnis90/Green Party has profited most from the rising number of abstentions, whereas in Vahrenheide the Republicans have gained ground (Hermann, 1996, p. 60).

How much of a burden people in poor areas consider their disadvantage to be depends primarily on the micro-milieu they experience with its 'filter function' between structurally unequal living conditions and the subjective concerns of those affected (Herlyn et al., 1991; Hermann, 1996, p. 67). In Linden, in a former working-class area with mixed functions, social neighbourhood relations are still intact, with coexisting integrated settings between the former working-class community, the student population and the ethnic communities which help individuals to find their way and feel secure. These structures also enable social capital to be transformed into economic capital, e.g. by working on the side and with temporary jobs. Yet, in Vahrenheide, a new monofunctional housing estate on the urban fringe with a high proportion of council housing, these structures do not exist. This is one reason why there are signs that this area is on a downward spiral (Wilson, 1987; Kristensen, 1995, p. 148; Krätke, 1996, p. 186).

URBAN SOCIAL ORDER – STABILIZATION OR BREAKDOWN?

The growing problem of poverty and social exclusion in cities appears to be unbroken with no end in sight at the moment and no way out of this situation. Although the optimum way of fighting poverty and social exclusion would be uniform targeted measures by the European Community, nation states and urban authorities, this would require a complex multilevel policy design. The political context of the EC, nation state and subnational urban authorities is not yet ready for this. In fact, there is still a good deal of contradiction in their activities. So far, cities have been left largely to their own devices in tackling the problems of poverty and social exclusion.

Urban authorities now have a range of options on how to approach the problem of poverty. To date, in poverty analysis, the dominant approach has been the so called 'pathogenic analysis', a term which was taken from health psychology which concentrates on pinpointing rising poverty and social problem groups (Blanke and Schridde, 1994). It culminates in the assumption that more and more hyper-ghettos and an urban underclass are emerging in big cities. An analysis of this kind does not extend beyond a new type of 'impoverishment theory'. Using the example of the differences between the urban areas in Hanover and figures for the entire city (Schridde, 1995), it is the local social context which brings out these particular structural 'problem' developments that may lead to poverty and socio-economic exclusion. The interconnected processes between labour markets, housing markets, social policy and urban domestic settings play a key role in the pattern of responses (Läpple, 1996, p. 131).

In the current phase, socio-economic exclusion is interpreted as a threat to social cohesion and the urban social order (Commission of the European Communities, 1992), although no explicit causal relationship has yet been identified between socio-economic exclusion and stability of the urban social order.

It can be argued in theory that urban society could be integrated by having a strategy of exclusion of the poor, perhaps by defining an exclusion zone. This would then be a society which was no longer willing to maintain order in its exclusion zone (Luhmann, 1996). It would therefore hardly be surprising if independent forms of social, economic and political order developed in hyper-ghettos as the site of entrenched exclusion. They might take the form of quasi-feudal patterns in a compartmentalized discriminating society. Lawless areas is a term which is frequently used by conservative thinkers in Germany. This is not an unreasonable description. The legitimacy of the conventional political and social order may be lost in such places. Exclusion requires legitimacy. Yet it seems that these specific legitimacy standards could be rendered invalid by the erection of barriers to access (social convergence) (Brock and Junge, 1995). The universal basic principles of urban social order could therefore be breaking down.

However, it might be more practical to argue that a blinkered approach in urban policy towards a citadel economy may have some attraction for the city elders, particularly for those who see themselves in global cities (Friedman and Wolff, 1982). It might be economical and social, but would also be counterproductive because it would foolishly squander the potential for stabilizing urban society. Sassen and Satler (1992) studied the pressure on low-cost room space in inner city working-class areas in New York by estate agents and gentrification. They were able to demonstrate that old economic structures in working-class areas were clearly economically viable, even if in the short term higher tax income could have been raised for the city through high value use. It also showed that a new type of reurbanization could be started by immigrants and the growing number of single parents, which could lead to the revitalization of public life and the local community and thereby to an increase in the integrative forces in the area.

In economic terms, it was sensible of the city to keep this area for the sake of the urban economy, because it covered the demand for budgeted services and thereby strengthened the urban economy substantially. In social terms, it was sensible because it provided resources for the bare necessities of life and integration (OECD, 1996, p. 113).

The study by Läpple et al. (1994) on future prospects for the economy in Hamburg came to similar conclusions. Assuming a distinction between basic and non-basic industries, he identified a range of subeconomies with different traditions and linkages in global, national and local competitive and interrelating contexts. One of the largest subeconomies was local businesses. Sustaining urban development in a global world cannot therefore be achieved by responding to the rapidly changing location preferences of global operations, but by recognizing the need to embed firms in urban production and innovative settings to maintain social and political cohesion in urban society (Läpple, 1996). Socio-economic and spatial exclusion not only endangers the existence of locally oriented commercial operations, but also adversely affects the urban economy as a whole and the urban social order in particular.

Urban policy is still Fordist in many ways. Big problems need big solutions, was Ford's motto. Urban policy should learn from the economy. It is rather the small, decentralized and very often uncoordinated innovations that contribute to the stabilization of the urban social order. Environmental intervention and a local area based urban policy of restocking would make a great contribution towards the stabilization of the urban social order. The European Commission has formulated a similar statement to this effect. Urban issues should be tackled in an integrated way, supporting business creation, improving infrastructure and the physical environment.

Cities are the site and cause of poverty and social exclusion. Even if there is no doubt that the national and European level should be jointly responsible for eradicating poverty and social exclusion, the cities are still left to cope with these problems on their own to a large extent. Many cities still fail to see the need to promote economic, social and political cohesion within the urban social order. In times of uncertainty about what will happen in the future, many of the city fathers tend to keep to what is tried and tested. However, their global

market orientation is exacerbating the problems which they are trying
to solve. Urban cohesion is a functional requirement for the survival
of the city. On the other hand, exclusive orientation towards a citadel
economy will destroy the city, which will only survive as a 'cathedral in
the desert' where the high priests of capital and their local governors
rule over the common rank and file.

Note

1.   The evaluation of urban areas in terms of quality of life and living stan-
      dards are based on a scale of 1 to 5, where 1 corresponds to extremely
      good and 5 represents poor quality of life and living standards
      (Landeshauptstadt Hannover, 1995).

References

M. Alisch and J. Dangschat, 'Räumliche Konzentration von Armut in
      Hamburg [Spatial concentration of poverty in Hamburg]', *Nachrichtenblatt
      zur Stadt- und Regionalsoziologie* [*Newssheet on Urban and Regional
      Sociology*], 1 (1993) 40–51.
H.-J. Andreß, G. Lipsmeier and K. Salentin, 'Soziale Isolation und mangelnde
      Unterstützung im unteren Einkommensbereich? [Social isolation and lack
      of support in low income brackets?]', *ZfS*, 4 (1995) 300–15.
A.B. Atkinson, *The Economics of Inequality* (Oxford, 1975).
P.A. Berger, 'Individualisierung und Armut [Individualization and poverty]',
      in M. Zwick, *Einmal arm, immer arm?* [*Once Poor, Always Poor?*]
      (Frankfurt am Main/New York, 1994) pp. 21–46.
B. Blanke and H. Schridde, 'Verfall der Stadtgesellschaft? Perspektiven
      kommunaler Sozialpolitik [Decline of urban society? Prospects for
      local authority social policy]', *Soziale Sicherheit* [*Social Security*]', 7 (1994)
      254–9.
M. Bommes and A. Scherr, 'Exklusionsvermeidung, Inklusionsvermittlung
      und/oder Exklusionsverwaltung [Avoiding exclusion, fostering inclusion
      and/or managing exclusion]', *Neue Praxis* [*New Practice*], 2 (1996) 107–23.
P. Bordieu, 'Physischer, sozialer und angeeigneter Raum [Physical, social and
      acquired space]', in M. Wentz, *Stadt-Räume* [*Urban Spaces*] (Frankfurt am
      Main, 1991) pp. 25–34.
I. Breckner et al., *Armut in Reichtum* [*Poverty in the Midst of Affluence*]
      (Bochum, 1989).
S. Brink, 'Social renewal and livable environments', in OECD, *Housing and
      Social Integration* (Paris, 1996) pp. 65–146.
D. Brock and M. Junge, 'Die Theorie gesellschaftlicher Modernisierung und
      das Problem gesellschaftlicher Integration [The theory of social modern-
      ization and the problem of social integration]', *ZfS*, 3 (1995) 165–82.

L. Buffoni, 'Rethinking poverty in globalized conditions', in J. Eade (ed.), *Living in the Global City: Globalization as a Local Process* (London/ New York, 1997).

V. Busch-Geertscma and E.-U. Ruhstrat, 'Kein Schattendasein für Langzeitarme! Wider die Verharmlosung von Langzeitarmut im Zusammenhang mit der "dynamischen" Armutsforschung [Don't hide the long-term poor! Against trivialization of long-term unemployment in dynamic poverty research]', *NDV*, 11 (1992) 366–70.

K.A. Chassée et al., 'Randgruppen und Modernisierung [Fringe groups and modernization]', in K.A. Chassée, A. Drygalla and A. Eggert-Schmid-Noerr, *Analysen zu Randgruppen und zur Randgruppenarbeit [Fringe Groups and their Activities]* (Bielefeld, 1992) pp. 7–28.

Commission of the European Communities, 'Die soziale Entwicklung in den Städten [Social development in cities]', *Soziales Europa*, Beiheft 1 [*Social Europe*, Supplement 1] (1992).

Commission of the European Communities, 'Für ein solidarisches Europa: der Kampf gegen die soziale Ausgrenzung [Towards solidarity in Europe: fighting social exclusion]', *Soziales Europa*, Beiheft 4 [*Social Europe*, Supplement 4] (1993).

J.S. Dangschat, 'Strukturpolitik versus Stadtteilpolitik. Welche Probleme lassen sich auf der Ebene städtische Quartiere bearbeiten und lösen? [Structural policy versus inner city area policy: which problems can be handled and solved at the urban level?]', *Standpunkt: social 1 [Journal for Social Workers]*, special issue, *Stadtentwicklung und soziale Politik [Urban Development and Social Policy]* (1994) 27–36.

J.S. Dangschat, '"Stadt" als Ort und Ursache von Armut und sozialer Ausgrenzung [The "city" as the site and cause of poverty and social-exclusion]', in *Aus Politik und Zeitgeschichte [Politics and History]*, B31–2 (1995) 50–62.

J.S. Dangschat, 'Zur Armutsentwicklung in deutschen Städten [On the growth of poverty in German cities]', in Akademie für Raumforschung und Landesplanung [Academy for Spatial Research and Regional Planning] (eds), *Agglomerationsräume in Deutschland. Ansichten, Einsichten, Aussichten [Large Cities in Germany: Views, Insights and Prospects]* (Hanover, 1996) pp. 51–76.

F. Dubet and D. Lapeyronnie, *Im Aus der Vorstädte. Der Zerfall der demokratischen Gesellschaft [In the Outback of the Outskirts: The Decline of Democratic Society]* (Stuttgart, 1994).

J. Eade (ed.), *Living in the Global City: Globalization as a Local Process* (London/New York, 1997).

T. Erdmann, 'Bezugsdauer von Sozialhilfe 1994 [Social security claim periods 1994]', in *Hamburg in Zahlen [Figures for Hamburg]*, 8 (1996) 234–6.

G. Esping-Andersen, *The Three Worlds of Welfare Capitalism* (Cambridge, 1990).

N.J. Fainstein and S.S. Fainstein, 'Die Umstrukturierung der amerikanischen Stadt, in vergleichender Sicht [Restructuring in the American city: a comparative perspective]', in J. Krämer and R. Neef (eds), *Krise und Konflikte in der Großstadt im entwickelten Kapitalismus [Crisis and Conflict in Major Cities under Late Capitalism]* (Basel, 1985) pp. 88–112.

A. Farwick, *Armut in der Stadt – Prozesse und Mechanismen der räumlichen Konzentration von Sozialhilfeempfängern* [*Poverty in the city: processes and mechanisms affecting the spatial concentration of social security claimants*], ZWE Arbeit und Region, Arbeitspapier [Central Economic Unit: Labour and Regions, Working Paper] No. 20 (Bremen, 1996).

G. Franzmann, *Gentrification. Theorie und Forschungsergebnisse* [*Gentrification: Theory and Research Findings*] (Opladen, 1996) pp. 229–60.

T. von Freyberg, 'Städtische Modernisierung und soziale Polarisierung. Anmerkungen zur Armutentwicklung in Frankfurt/Main [Urban modernization and social polarization: notes on poverty growth in Frankfurt am Main]', *Widersprüche* [*Contradictions*], 44 (1992) 51–70.

J. Friedman, 'Ein Jahrzehnt world-city Forschung [A decade of world city research]', in H. Hitz et al. (eds), *Capitales Fatales. Urbanisierung und Politik in den Finanzmetropolen Frankfurt und Zurich* [*Doomed Cities: Urbanization and Politics in the Financial Centres – Frankfurt and Zurich*] (Zurich, 1995) pp. 22–44.

J. Friedman and G. Wolff, 'World city formation: an agenda for research and action', *International Journal of Urban and Regional Research*, 6 (1982) 309–44.

M. Fromhold-Elsebith, 'Das "kreative Milieu" als Motor regional-wirtschaftlicher Entwicklung [The "creative milieu" as the motor of regional economic development]', *GZ*, 1 (1995) 30–47.

J.K. Galbraith, 'Herrschaft der Zufriedenen. Die Kapitulation der Demokratie vor der Armut [The culture of contentment: the collapse of democracy in the face of poverty]', *Der Spiegel*, 36 (1992).

W. Glatzer and W. Hübinger, 'Lebenslagen und Armut [Social status and poverty]', in D. Döring and E.-V. Hanesch (eds), *Armut im Wohlstand* [*Poverty in the Midst of Affluence*] (Frankfurt am Main, 1990) pp. 31–55.

R. Greca and P. Erath (eds), *Regionalisierung sozialer Dienste in Deutschland* [*Regionalization of Social Services in Germany*] (Eichstätt, 1995).

H. Häußermann and W. Siebel, *Neue Urbanität* [*New Urbanity*] (Frankfurt am Main, 1987).

H. Häußermann and W. Siebel, 'Die Politik der Festivalisierung und die Festivalisierung der Politik. Große Ereignisse in der Stadtpolitik [Politics of "festivalization" and the "festivalization" of politics: great events in urban policy]', in H. Häußermann and W. Siebel (eds), *Festivalisierung der Stadtpolitik* [*'Festivalisation' of Urban Policy*] (Opladen, 1993) pp. 7–31.

M. Heiner, 'Aufbau und Nutzung politischer Netzwerke in der Gemeinwesenarbeit [Setting up and using policy networks in community work]', in M. Bitzan and T. Klöck (eds), *Jahrbuch Gemeinwesenarbeit 5. Politikstrategien – Wendungen und Perspektiven* [*Community Yearbook 5. Policy Strategies: Changes and Prospects*] (Munich, 1994) pp. 90–116.

I. Helbrecht, 'Die Wiederkehr der Innenstädte. Zur Rolle von Kultur, Kapital und Konsum in der Gentrification [Revival of the inner cities: the role of culture, capital and consumption in the gentrification process]', *GZ*, 1 (1996) 1–15.

A.N. Herbst, 'Banker, Broker, Stadtneurotiker und Postkultur [Bankers, brokers, urban neurotics and the postmodern mentality]', *Frankfurter Rundschau*, 10 October 1992.

U. Herlyn et al., *Armut und Milieu. Benachteiligte Bewohner in großstädtischen Quartieren* [*Poverty and Milieu: Disadvantaged Residents in Inner City Areas*] (Basel, 1991).

T. Hermann, 'Faß ohne Boden? Soziale Ungleichheit und Prozesse sozialer Integration und Ausgrenzung in Hannover [Bottomless pit? Social inequality and processes of social integration and exclusion in Hanover]', H. Schmalstieg (ed.), *Zukunftfähiges Hannover* [*Towards a Secure Future for Hanover*] (Hanover, 1996) pp. 53–72.

R. Hitzler, 'Radikalisierte Praktiken der sozialen Distinktion. Zur Politisierung des Lebens in der Stadt [Radicalized forms of social difference: on the politicization of life in the city]', in J. Dangschat and J. Blasius, *Lebensstile in den Städten. Konzepte und Methoden* [*Lifestyles in the City: Concepts and Methods*] (Opladen, 1994) pp. 47–58.

R. Höft-Dzemski, 'Zur Einkommensposition von Haushalten von Sozialhilfeempfängern in den Jahren 1972–1992 Teil 1 [Income of social security claimant households between 1972 and 1992 Part 1]', *NDV*, 11 (1994a) 405–9.

R. Höft-Dzemski, 'Zur Einkommensposition von Haushalten von Sozialhilfeempfängern in den Jahren 1972–1992 Teil 2 [Income of social security claimant households between 1972 and 1992 Part 2]', *NDV*, 11 (1994b) 441–4.

E.-U. Huster, *Armut in Europa* [*Poverty in Europe*] (Opladen, 1996).

H.-G. Jaschke, 'Neue Armut und Stadtentwicklung. Welche Rolle spielt "Armut" in der neueren politischen und wirtschaftlichen Stadtdebatte? [New poverty and urban development: what role does "poverty" play in the new political and economic urban debate?]', *Widersprüche* [*Contradictions*], 44 (1992) 9–20.

V. Kaske, 'Europas Kommunen und der Kampf gegen soziale Ausgrenzung [Europe's local authorities and the battle against social exclusion]', *NDV*, 5 (1994) 192–5.

R. Kilb, 'Zerteilte Stadtregion – Zerissene Lebenswelten Jugendlicher in benachteiligten Wohngebieten. Beispiel Frankfurt/M. [Fragmented urban regions: the torn lives of young people in disadvantaged residential areas in Frankfurt am Main]', *Dt. Jugend* [*German Youth*], 2 (1993) 69–78.

W. Knapp, 'Global – Lokal [Global vs. local]', *Raumforschung und Raumordnung* [*Spatial Research and Spatial Order*], 4 (1995) 294–304.

S. Krätke, *Stadt, Raum, Ökonomie* [*City, Space and Economy*] (Basel, 1996).

H. Kristensen, 'Social exclusion and spatial stress: the connections', in G. Room (ed.), *Beyond the Threshold: The Measurement and Analysis of Social Exclusion* (Bristol, 1995) pp. 146–57.

M. Kronauer, '"Soziale Ausgrenzung" und "Urban underclass". Annäherung an neue Formen gesellschaftlicher Spaltung' (Ms) ["Social Exclusion" and the "Urban Underclass": Theory of New Forms of Social Divisions (Manuscript)], *Leviathan* (1997).

G. Kronawitter (ed.), *Rettet unsere Städte jetzt!* [*Save Our Cities Now!*] Manifest der Oberbürgermeister, Düsseldorf [The Lord Mayors' Manifesto, Düsseldorf] (1994).

D. Läpple, 'Ökonomische Perspektiven der Städte [Economic prospects for cities]', *Die alte Stadt* [*The Old City*] 2 (1996) pp. 128–40.

D. Läpple, H. Deecke and T. Krüger, *Strukturentwicklung und Zukunftsperspektiven der Hamburger Wirtschaft unter räumlichen Gesichtspunkten* [*Structural Development and Future Prospects for the Hamburg Economy in Spatial Terms*], Gutachten für die Stadtentwicklungsbehörde der Freien und Hansestadt Hamburg [Expert Report for the Planning Department of the City of Hamburg] (Hamburg, 1994).

Landeshauptstadt Hannover, *Sozialbericht 1993. Zur Lage der Kinder, Jugendlichen und Familien in Hannover* [1993 social report on the situation of children, youth and families in Hannover], Schriftenreihe zur kommunalen Sozial-, Jugend- und Gesundheitspolitik 13 [Local Authority Social, Youth and Health Policy Series 13] (1993).

Landeshauptstadt Hannover, *Repräsentativerhebung 1994 zu kommunalen und sozialen Fragen* [1994 survey of local authority and social issues]', Schriften zur Stadtentwicklung Nr 61 LH Hannover [Urban Development Records No. 61, State Capital of Hanover] (1995).

D. Landua and R. Habich, 'Problemgruppen der Sozialpolitik im vereinten Deutschland [Problem groups for social policy in unified Germany]', *Aus Politik und Zeitgeschichte* [*Politics and History*], B3 (1994) 14.

R. Lee, 'Urban transformation: from problems in to problems of the city', in D. Herbert and D. Smith (eds), *Social Problems and the City* (Oxford, 1989) pp. 60–78.

S. Leibfried et al., *Zeit der Armut* [*Times of Poverty*] (Frankfurt am Main, 1995).

L. Leisering, 'Armut hat viele Gesichter. Vom Nutzen dynamischer Armutsforschung [Poverty has many faces: the use of dynamic poverty research]', *NDV*, 8 (1993) 297–305.

M. Ludwig, L. Leisering and P. Buhr, 'Armut verstehen. Betrachtungen vor dem Hintergrund der Bremer Langzeitstudie [Understanding poverty: observations in the light of the Bremen long-term study]', *Aus Politik und Zeitgeschichte* [*Politics and History*], B31–2 (1996) 24–34.

W. Ludwig-Mayerhofer, 'Was heißt und gibt es kumulative Arbeitslosigkeit? Untersuchungen zu Arbeitslosigkeitsverläufen über 10 Jahre [Is there such a thing as cumulative unemployment?, If so, what does it mean? Studies in unemployment patterns over ten years]', in W. Zapf, J. Schupp and R. Habich (eds), *Lebenslagen im Wandel: Sozialberichterstattung im Längsschnitt* [*Transformation of Social Status: A Longitudinal Study*] (Frankfurt am Main, 1996) pp. 211–39.

N. Luhmann, *Politische Theorie im Wohlfahrtsstaat* [*Political Theory in the Welfare State*] (Munich/Vienna, 1981).

N. Luhmann, 'Inklusion und Exklusion [Inclusion and exclusion]', in N. Luhmann, *Soziologische Aufklärung* [*Sociological Information*] (Opladen, 1996) pp. 237–64.

A. McGregor and M. McConnachie, 'Social exclusion, urban regeneration and economic reintegration', *Urban Studies*, 32: 10 (1995) 1587–600.

J.F. Madden, 'Changes in distribution of poverty across and within US metropolitan areas, 1979–1989', *Urban Studies*, 33: 9 (1996) 1581–600.

M. Mayer, 'Postfordistische Stadtpolitik [Post-Fordist urban policy]', *ZS. Für Wirtschaftsgeographie* [Journal of Economic Geography], 1–2 (1996) 20–7.

U. Meier, 'Die Herkunft bestimmt immer noch die Lebenschancen [Origin still determines opportunities in life]', *FR*, 107, 9 May 1995.

P. Michalzik, '"Das sind kleine Monster". Wie Sozialarbeiter und Polizisten im Ruhrgebiet auf die zunehmende Gewaltbereitschaft und die wachsende Brutalität der Kinder reagieren ["They are little monsters". How social workers and the police in the Ruhr respond to growing violence and brutality of children]', *Südddeutsche Zeitung*, 2–3 January 1993.

R. Münch, 'Elemente einer Theorie der Integration moderner Gesellschaften [Elements of a theory of integration for modern societies]', in J. Berl, *Soziolog*, 1 (1995) pp. 5–24.

T. Münch, 'Arme Stadt – Reiche Stadt [Poor city – rich city]', *AKP*, 6 (1991) 43–4.

P. Noller and K. Ronneberger, *Die neue Dienstleistungsstadt [The New City as a Service Provider]* (Frankfurt am Main, 1995).

P. Noller, W. Prigge and K. Ronneberger, 'Zur Theorie der Globalisierung [On globalization theory]', in P. Noller, W. Prigge and K. Ronneberger, *Stadt-Welt. Über die Globalisierung städtischer Milieus [World Cities: On the Globalization of Urban Settings]* (Frankfurt am Main, 1994) pp. 13–21.

OECD, *Strategies for Housing and Social Integration in Cities* (Paris, 1996).

B. Peters, *Die Integration moderner Gesellschaften [Integration of Modern Societies]* (Frankfurt am Main, 1993).

W. Prigge, 'Urbi et orbi. Zur Epistemologie des Städtischen [Cities and the world: epistemology of the urban]', in P. Noller, W. Prigge and K. Ronneberger, *Stadt-Welt. Über die Globalisierung städtischer Milieus [World Cities: On the Globalization of Urban Settings]* (Frankfurt am Main, 1994) pp. 63–71.

M. Rodenstein, 'Durchstaatlichung der Städte? [State-run cities?]', in W. Prigge (ed.), *Die Materialität des Städtischen [The Material Nature of Cities]* (Basel, 1987).

K. Ronneberger, 'Zitadellenökonomie und soziale Transformation der Stadt [The citadel economy of the ruling class and the social transformation of the city]', in P. Noller, W. Prigge and K. Ronneberger, *Stadt-Welt. Über die Globalisierung städtischer Milieus [World Cities: On the Globalization of Urban Settings]* (Frankfurt am Main, 1994a) pp. 180–97.

K. Ronneberger, 'Die neuen Städter. Zum Auftstieg einer neuen Subkultur [New urbanites: an emerging subculture]', in P. Noller, W. Prigge and K. Ronneberger, *Stadt-Welt. Über die Globalisierung städtischer Milieus [World Cities: On the Globalization of Urban Settings]* (Frankfurt am Main, 1994b) pp. 249–57.

G. Room, 'Poverty in Europe: competing paradigms of analysis', *Policy and Politics*, 23: 2 (1995a) 103–13.

G. Room, 'Poverty and social exclusion: the new European agenda for policy and research', in G. Room (ed.), *Beyond the Threshold: The Measurement and Analysis of Social Exclusion* (Bristol, 1995b).

S. Sassen, *The Global City: New York, Tokyo, London* (Princeton, NJ, 1991).

S. Sassen, *Metropolen des Weltmarktes [Global Market Centres]* (Frankfurt am Main, 1996).

S. Sassen and G. Satler, 'Manhattan's 14th Street – ein Billigmarkt für Minderheiten/Raumnutzungen der Arbeiterklasse in der Metropole des Finanzkapitals [Manhattan's 14th Street: a cut-price market for minorities. Use of space by the working classes in the finance capital of the world]', in

H.-G. Helms, *Die Stadt als Gabentisch* [*The City as a Display of Gifts*] (Leipzig, 1992) pp. 91–108.

R. Schneider-Sliwa, '"Hyper-Ghettos" in amerikanischen Großstädten. Lebensräume und Konstruktionsprinzip der urban underclass [Hyperghettos in major American cities: spatial living conditions and the structure of the urban underclass]', *GZ*, 1 (1996) 27–42.

H. Schridde, *Neue sozialpolitische Tendenzen in deutschen Großstädten* [*New Socio-Political Trends in Major German Cities*] (Düsseldorf, 1995).

H. Schridde, 'Von der Arbeitsmarkt zur Armutspolitik, Wandel lokaler Arbeitsmarktpolitik in den 90er Jahren [From labour market policy to policy on poverty: transformation in local labour market policy in the nineties]', in B. Schäfer and G. Wewer, *Die Stadt in Deutschland* [*The City in Germany*] (Opladen, 1996) pp. 123–42.

U.-K. Schuleri-Hartje, 'Neue Armut – Handlungsansätze der Kommunen [New poverty – local authority responses]', *DifU-Materialien*, 3 (1995).

P. Semrau, 'Entwicklung der Einkommensarmut [Growth in income poverty]', in D. Dörling and E.-V. Hanesch (eds), *Armut in Wohlstand* [*Poverty in the Midst of Affluence*] (Frankfurt am Main, 1990).

R. Servian, *Theorising Empowerment: Individual Power and Community Care* (Bristol, 1996).

Stadt Essen, *Ansätze neue sozialer Kommunalpolitik* [*New Approaches to Social Policy at the Local Level*], Informationen und Berichte zur Stadtentwicklung Nr 74, Essen, Amt für Entwicklungsplanung, Statistik, Stadtforschung und Wahlen [Information and Reports on Urban Development No. 74, Essen, Office for Development Planning, Statistics, Urban Research and Elections] (1993).

Stadt Essen, *Integratives Entwicklungskonzept für Essen-Katernberg – einen Stadtteil mit besonderem Erneuerungsbedarf* [*An Integrated Plan for the Development of Essen-Katerberg: An Inner City Area in Special Need of Urban Renewal*] (1995).

Stadtentwicklungsbehörde (STEB) der Freien und Hansestadt Hamburg, [Hamburg City Planning Department], *Armutsbekämpfung in Hamburg*, 5. Auflage [*Fighting Poverty in Hamburg*], 5th edn (Hamburg, 1996).

Stadtteilbüro Malstatt, *Von der Not im Wohlstand arm zu sein* [*The Misery of Being Poor in Times of Prosperity*] (Saarbrücken, 1993).

Statistisches Bundesamt (ed.), *Datenreport 1994. Zahlen und Fakten über die Bundesrepublik Deutschland* [*1994 Report: Facts and Figures on the Federal Republic of Germany*] (Bonn, 1994).

Statistisches Bundesamt (ed.), *Datenreport 1997. Zahlen und Fakten über die Bundesrepublik Deutschland* [*1997 Report: Facts and Figures on the Federal Republic of Germany*] (Bonn, 1997).

D. Sudjic, 'The slicker city', *The Observer*, 9 February 1995, 25.

G. Thieme and H.D. Laux, 'Soziale und ethnische Konflikte im Restrukturierungsprozeß. Die Unruhen vom Frühjahr 1992 in Los Angeles [Social and ethnic conflicts in the renewal process: the Los Angeles riots in spring 1992]', *Erdkunde* [*Geography*], 4 (1995) 315–34.

G. Tobias and J. Boettner, 'Wenn die Kohle für die Kohlen knapp wird [When there is no more money to go round]', *Sozial Extra* [*Social Extra*], 4 (1992) 8–11.

M. Vester et al., *Soziale Milieus im gesellschaftlichen Wandel* [*Social Milieus in a Changing Society*] (Cologne, 1993).

H. Voscherau, 'Die Großstadt als sozialer Brennpunkt – am Beispiel Hamburg [The city as a trouble spot: the case of Hamburg]', in G. Kronawitter (ed.), *Rettet unsere Städte jetzt!* (*Save our Cities Now!*) (1994) pp. 77–106.

R. Walker, 'Poverty and social exclusion in Europe', in A. Walker and C. Walker (eds), *Britain Divided: The Growth of Social Exclusion in the 1980s and 1990s* (London, 1997).

K. Wermker, 'Haushaltsdefizit, Einwohnerverlust, Arbeitsplatzabbau. Konsequenzen für die soziale Infrastruktur [Budget deficit, declining local population and job cuts: consequences for the social infrastructure]', *Bauwelt* [*Building World*], 24 (1988) 1012–16.

B.J. Whelan and C.T. Whelan, 'In what sense is poverty multi-dimensional?', in G. Room (ed.), *Beyond the Threshold: The Measurement and Analysis of Social Exclusion* (Bristol, 1995) pp. 29–48.

S. Willeke and A. Fink, 'Abschied vom Wohlstand [The end of prosperity]', *Die Zeit*, 23, 31 May 1996, 9–1.

T. Wilson and D.J. Wilson, *The Political Economy of the Welfare State* (London, 1982).

W.J. Wilson, *The Truly Disadvantaged. The Inner City, The Underclass and Public Policy* (Chicago, 1987).

9 Industrial Past and Urban Future in the Ruhr

Walter Siebel

If one asks people in Europe what they immediately associate with the term urbanity, there is little by way of hesitation. Urbanity means crowded streets, 24-hour shopping and the traditional character of the European city. The only place where no easy answer can be found is in Germany. The Allied bombers, West German investors and East German planners have left very little of the original, historical character of the European city intact. This is one reason why Germans go to Italy or London to experience urbanity, unless they are town planners, in which case, they are currently trying to reconstruct the nineteenth century, as can be seen in Berlin.

There is no doubt that the image of the urban city one sees is a backward-looking one. It is the European city of the Middle Ages up to the nineteenth century, the city of pre-industrial society. This image contains three basic elements – the enormous difference between public buildings in the centre and the outskirts, the contrast between urban and rural life and the close-knit mix of functions and social groups in the residential areas. By the nineteenth century this structure had begun to crumble. Modern industrial society separated living, working, recreation and travel functions and allocated them different times and places. The contrast between the high-rise city and the flat rural landscape was lost in the mass of the urban sprawl.

From the moment one glances away from the remaining pre-industrial civic structures, the modern character of the city is visible everywhere right out to the hinterland around the big cities. That is where the modern city can be found, especially in the former industrial regions which never had a medieval or feudal city centre, e.g. in the northern part of the Ruhr.

In such areas, one can see everything a city needs in terms of living, working, travel and recreation, according to the Athens Charter. Yet, there is still one thing missing – there is no sign of an urban city. Everything that fits in with the image of a European city is missing – a central core, urban/rural contrast and a mix. This is urbanized countryside without a real city.

Plate 9.1   Thyssen-Miederich: a view of the Ruhr.

Only 150 years ago, the Ruhr region was still a sparsely populated marshy lowland where there was no community with a population of more than 500. In the middle of the last century it began to be taken over and occupied by industry and Prussia treated the area like a colony. For example, the inhabitants were deliberately denied rights to local self-government and higher education. In the brief period of sixty years up to the beginning of the First World War, this sparsely populated meadow land was transformed into an enormous machine for producing coal and steel.

In the Ruhr communities did not develop around a castle, town hall, church or market as happened with the traditional European city. They were centred around coalmines or steelworks. Now that the heavy industry which originally created and characterized the region is disappearing, a lot more than just the economic base is being lost. The heart of the community has also been destroyed, not just in physical terms, but also in terms of its social, political and cultural core.

The factory was at the heart of the community. It was a place of domination and exploitation, as well as the seat of power and an object of pride for the working community.

Plate 9.2   A steel plant.

All that is left today is an enormous, gaping hole. It represents one of the most difficult urban renewal tasks, namely to fill the empty space both literally and in abstract terms with a new, distinctive urban quality. If the region does not succeed in developing this distinctive urban quality, it will never be able to compete in the long term. How might such a quality be achieved?

Not by forcing the region to adopt across the board the centralized structure of the pre-industrial European city at this late stage. Projecting the image of a pre-industrial European city over modern community structures would, at best, produce a cheap version of urbanity, like Disneyworld. However, the wish to revive the character of the city from a bygone age does bring out one important perspective, that of history.

The fact that the image of the urban city is often attached to the remains of a bygone age underlines the historical dimension of urbanity. Urbanity embodies the presence of past events in the daily life of

                    Walter Siebel

Plate 9.3   A power plant.

the city dweller. In an urban city, there are stories to tell about the squares, the buildings, the streets. An urban city develops as part of a historical process, as a shared memory which is reflected in the buildings, streets and squares. By their very nature, new things do not have a past. It takes time for areas of a city to develop urban qualities.

The Ruhr has not had a history of its own. Now that the industrial society which created and exploited the region is disappearing, the Ruhr has, for the first time, acquired a history of its own and thus it can develop its own special urban identity through its history. Monuments to industry are beginning to emerge.

The world is currently experiencing a period of rapid historical change, particularly in the industrial areas which were founded in the nineteenth century as a result of the development of industrial society,

Plate 9.4 Prosper III coalmine in 1930.

Plate 9.5 Prosper III coalmine site in 1996.

around the old bourgeois cities and seats of court. For example, traditional industry has declined in places like Lyon, Manchester and Berlin. Docks, slaughterhouses and industrial plants are turning into wastelands. The task of dealing with this obsolete infrastructure is particularly problematic in traditional industrial areas like the Ruhr, because there are no pre-industrial city centres to provide the basis for shared memories.

Urban spaces develop gradually and continue to undergo change as a result of the ageing process of a city. And a city ages when the purpose for which it was originally built no longer exists. Now that industrial society is abandoning its own purpose-built community structures, cities are experiencing a period of rapid social change, whereby they are aging more rapidly and are making room for new kinds of urban spaces to develop. This applies in the former German Democratic Republic and in the Ruhr, indeed everywhere in the urban areas of big cities.

Various approaches have been suggested for dealing with the heritage of industrial society. One example is of an urban renewal programme for the Ruhr at the International Building Exhibition at Emscher Park (IBA). The approach which is in the end adopted for these remaining features of industrial society will determine the future urban quality and identity of the old industrial regions.

At first, the reaction of many in the region was to demand that the industrial plants which were no longer needed should be bulldozed. This reaction is very understandable. First, an industrial region like the Ruhr usually has few links with its past. These regions have made their mark in the modern age because they grew up with modernism. Therefore, the past is bad for their image and stands in the way of anything new. Second, industrial plants can become derelict very quickly. This is one reason why their upkeep is so expensive. Third, and very important, empty factory buildings remind people of the lowest point in their working lives, when they learnt that their job was no longer worth anything and their qualifications were obsolete.

The desire to suppress the past is easy to understand on both economic and psychological grounds. Yet, when everything is demolished, all that is left is empty space which is not empty just in the physical sense. There is also a loss of identity. The first priority of the IBA was to suspend the demolition and so gain time to rethink the future of the buildings. The second task was to learn to look at the extant features of bygone industrial society from a different angle.

One of the most spectacular projects at the IBA in Emscher Park was the preservation and conversion of the gas tank at Oberhausen. It

Plate 9.6   Gas tank at Oberhausen: exterior view.

is said to be the largest gas tank in continental Europe, a massive eyesore from the outside, but inside it is like a timewarp.

The room is 110 metres high and measures 67 metres in diameter. Apart from a few maintenance workers, nobody has ever had the opportunity to see this room as it was originally built to store gas. Now the IBA is trying to stage events to give the general public a chance to see this room from a new angle. Cultural events have been staged and an exhibition mounted of the history of industrial society entitled 'Fire and Flames'. It was the most successful exhibition in West Germany in 1995, in part due to the splendid room in which it was located.

Learning to see from a different angle does not just mean looking at something from a different perspective; it also means changing the way one evaluates what one sees. Only by confronting society today with the industrial past, can one begin to change aesthetic values. This aesthetic process of confrontation with the heritage of the industrial past can begin in earnest only now that industrial society is in decline. The castles along the Rhine could be seen as objects of romantic aestheticism only when the knights were no longer the overlords. As long as merchants feared that the knights would force them to pay their dues, they had no time for any romantic aesthetic appreciation of castles. In fact, as a general rule, in times of crisis and social upheaval, such as when

Plate 9.7   Gas tank at Oberhausen: interior view.

globalization dethroned the steel barons or revolution ousted the monarchy, new opportunities for the use of space develop. Such opportunities thrive on the conflict between the original obsolete use of the space and ideas about new uses which could be developed. It is not the aesthetic appreciation of the structural decay which is the governing factor, but the downfall of the powerful. The spaces tell the tale of domination and exploitation, but the new users are no longer in thrall to the old masters. From a historical perspective, a show of force or control of the workforce is as nothing. The historical perspective offers opportunities for developing a new urbanity. However, one problem is that these spaces are all too frequently redeveloped by town planners because they have a horror of empty spaces. This horror cannot be based solely on the argument for environmental recycling!

Plate 9.8   Zollverein XII coalmine, now a museum.

A stay of execution offers time to reconsider. A change in the way one evaluates what one sees is vital, if one is to succeed in the task of finding sound future uses for these features of the past. As already argued, one element of the urban quality of the city is the constant reminder of the past in the everyday life of a city dweller. In order to ensure that old buildings and other features are really part of the everyday life of a city dweller, they must also have some practical use. These practical uses may well include the creation of museums. Yet this cannot be the sole answer. As they are places of work, the most obvious solution would be to convert them to a new economic use with a secure future. The IBA builds only on industrial wasteland, whether it be for homes, parks or places of work.

Plate 9.9   Part of the interior of Zollverein XII coalmine, converted into office space.

Establishing museums would serve to keep memories of industrial society alive. To convert these buildings to some other use would keep the economic future of the region alive. But is it enough to try to turn the surviving structures of industrial society into something that offers a well based new identity for the region?

Past knowledge is an integral part of any identity. But there are also hopes and dreams about the future; and knowledge of the present also plays a vital part in the creation of a well founded identity. With a sound knowledge of the present, it is possible to strike a balance between past life and future hopes, as well as between the different roles people play as part of a family, in the labour force, as a citizen, or even as a football player or tourist. The ultimate test of personal identity is maintaining the precarious balance between the contradictions in the various roles one has to adopt, the good and bad experiences in life and knowledge of future opportunities and risks.

This can also apply to the identity of a region. It includes more than just past knowledge and future dreams. One can escape into the future just as well as into the past, by choosing to avoid addressing the issues of today. At the moment this is happening in the Ruhr in

Plate 9.10   Industrial wasteland.

the current climate of structural change with all the associated economic, social, political and environmental problems. It is the case that monuments to industry mean contaminated land, unusable buildings and a steady process of decay and dereliction. Thus, there is a third type of use, namely, leaving everything to decay and thereby creating no-go areas.

Mines were once places full of dirt, chaos, dangerous working conditions and exploitation. An industrial wasteland as a prohibited area where buildings are left to decay may be a better way of confronting the past than information boards attached to large, clean machines in aesthetically pleasing monuments to the past.

If one wants to keep the heritage of industrial society alive as part of the daily life of the inhabitants of such areas by using vivid reminders of the past, all three approaches are needed – the museum as a permanent reminder, modern economic use and the decaying pile of contaminated waste.

Only when all three approaches are brought together for one purpose can these sites of a bygone industrial age contribute to an urban identity which is truly unique to the old industrial regions.

Part III

Global Concerns and Local Strategies

10 Local City Structures under Pressure to Change

Herbert Schubert

ON THE STATUS OF THE GLOBALIZATION PROCESS

The term 'globalization' has really come into its own in recent years, although the concept of a centrifugal broadening of our horizons on a world scale is not new. Wallerstein (1974, 1979, 1983) first described how capitalism would develop as a historic global system in a series of publications back in the 1970s. In his interpretation, the global system is a configuration of central, semi-peripheral and peripheral states. It is thereby described as one unit with a single division of labour and many different cultural systems (1979, pp. 31–67). However, in the 1990s, the process of development of the division of labour has intensified.

Originally, internationalism was an invention of Social Democrat labour leaders to counter nationalistic capitalist warmongers. In the meantime, internationalism has swapped sides. The global system is becoming characterized less by the political stance of nation states, and more by the global economic configuration of 40 000 international businesses. The new International is a capitalist organization which is putting the screws on nation states worldwide, for example with only low tax havens showing a profit. Through this process, workers' wage levels are also kept artificially low because workers in every nation are being played off against one another. After the breakup of the Communist bloc in Eastern Europe, the global march of capitalism gained fresh impetus and is now threatening the functional capability of nation states and their democratic stability. The rapid rate of change and gradual redistribution of power and wealth is crippling established social structures (Martin and Schumann, 1996).

Year on year, more and more people are losing their jobs and facing an uncertain future in society in Western Europe and specifically in Germany. The term 'one-fifth society' is common currency. It means one-fifth of the population of working age should be enough to keep the global economy booming in the next millennium. For the bottom 80 per cent, the bread and circuses approach may become reality. To prevent mass social rejection in Western society, world politicians are supporting a strategy of keeping the mass of the population quiet with a mixture of entertainment and a good diet.[1]

EFFECTS ON URBAN RESIDENTIAL AREAS

The global race for maximum efficiency and minimum wages is not just having profound social repercussions. As well as changes in interdependence between labour markets and work processes, traffic flows and consumption patterns are having a direct impact on urban areas (Harvey, 1990). With multinational concerns also intensifying the rivalry between urban regions, the pressure is on to secure the competitiveness of the urban economic base. Consequently, the cities are the places where globalization is visible and tangible in physical terms. There are three main areas of activity involved (Dangschat, 1996):

- restructuring of regional economic processes;
- changing local structures and local policy;
- polarization and pluralization in urban society.

Restructuring regional economic organization is normally reflected in changes in employment figures, sectoral structure, labour market regulation, new technology and new forms of production organization. Changes in local policy orientation are seen in new urban development strategies concentrating on development of the economic base. In order to strengthen the location, urban images are created to attract new investment, company relocations and city tourists en masse. Characteristic attractions include postmodernist architecture, symbolic revamping of public spaces and development of an entertainment infrastructure for multilingual and highly mobile sectors of the population. These represent a new type of person – the cosmopolitan city dweller as the new urban elite (Engelsdorp Gastelaars, 1988, pp. 38–42). This elite can be described as:

- career-driven, not family-oriented;
- prefers circle with broad interactive network and no local base linked to relatives and neighbours;

- engaged in a wide area of activity outside the home and region;
- prefers to keep a distance from own locality;
- interested in specialist events and services in city centres.

Häußermann and Siebel (1987) call them the 'new urbanites' who have freed themselves from the 'constraints of family life'. As single people, for example, they are free to pursue their own independence, lifestyle, self-determination, dynamism and individuality.

One particular characteristic of socio-cultural pluralization in different lifestyles exhibiting conspicuous leisure patterns and consumer expectations can be the breakdown of traditional ties. Individuals have freed themselves from the typical constraints and characteristic identity of belonging to a class, home and family, and religion. This has been accompanied by a steady rise in individual potential capabilities and development opportunities which are the results of modernization, such as higher qualifications in education from generation to generation, sexual equality, rising prosperity, more leisure time and increasing mobility.

When an individual is freed from a variety of cultural, social and economic ties, such as the traditional prescribed roles in life, this process is known as 'individualization'. The rigid set of rules laid down in the past have lost their control function. When individual decisions are no longer determined by superior binding sets of rules, this process inevitably leads to pluralization in forms of behaviour and ways of life.

In everyday life, all areas of experience are determined by individual freedom to make decisions. Attitudes and patterns of behaviour in terms of work, family, leisure and consumption have produced pluralist complexity. Only recently has variety been evaluated in qualitative terms in new lifestyle research. People with similar outlooks on life and a similar way of life tend to meet in certain social milieus (Hradil, 1987). They have similar living conditions and personal preferences based on common lifestyles (Schulze, 1992). On the basis of similar achievements in life and similar patterns of behaviour in terms of work, leisure activities and consumption, a common milieu emerges.

In the new milieus which have superseded the vertical hierarchical class model in German society, pleasure-seeking age groups with distinctive, complementary styles are predominant. Consequently, young and old people are no longer necessarily fundamentally linked by way of social class or as relatives. There is a marked tendency to separate into sections of lifestyle groups which are to a great extent cut off from one another.

In urban centres, unrelated people living together is especially predominant in the new milieus. Milieus which follow traditional family and generation patterns are very neighbourhood-oriented and locally based (Spiegel, 1983, pp. 83–97). Where there is no close family in the milieu, people focus on the socio-cultural position of their age group, are more mobile and tend to identify more with non-local structures of consumption and entertainment opportunities. This is linked to compartmentalization in public life and a further loss of significance for smaller local structures (Schubert, 1996, pp. 73–88).

The polarization of urban society does not now mean the confrontation between wealth and absolute poverty which existed in the nineteenth century when there was a dire lack of food and clothing. Nowadays, cities have a problem of relative poverty which describes the social situation of the worse off by comparison with the well off. Relative poverty consists of two aspects: 'benefit entitlement' and 'having enough money to live on'. With 'income-related poverty', the availability of financial resources is the key to acquiring the essentials in life, whereas with entitlement, the supply of essentials is guaranteed. These essentials include entitlement to social security benefit, housing allowance, subsidized leisure activities, health care and integration in the social security system.

The development of poverty in cities is comparable to an iceberg, where only a very small part is visible above water. Consequently, the public display of poverty in city centre shopping areas only represents a minute fraction of the real problem, while the real fight against poverty rages beneath this public display of poverty. Around one-tenth of the population in German cities can maintain a normal standard of living only with outside help to supplement their income, i.e. via social security benefit. Normally, unemployment is responsible for this situation. In addition to poverty which is addressed by social security benefits, there is also 'the grey area of poverty'. The grey area means people who are entitled to social security, but who do not claim it, so they live on incomes below the level for benefit entitlement (the unofficial figures in the social security statistics). All in all, the poor in many cities in Germany account for somewhere between one-fifth and one-quarter of the population.

The term polarization describes the physical split between rich and poor in urban centres. There are clear divisions in nearly all large cities in Germany between the well off and less well off urban areas.

There are three aspects to this split which are closely linked in urban poverty (Alisch and Dangschat, 1993):

- economic inequality in income, property and position in the labour market;
- social discrimination in education, health, benefit entitlement and the housing market;
- cultural segregation in terms of ethnic origin, religion, civilized patterns of behaviour and normative orientation.

The impact on the physical structure in major cities can be illustrated via a three-part scenario (Häußermann and Siebel, 1987; Froessler and Selle, 1989):

- The 'primary sector' is represented by self-contained, aesthetically pleasing urban architecture in internationally competitive economic centres – such as the well known international highlights, i.e. city tourism, airports, exhibition centres, congress halls, cultural and consumer institutions of international acclaim, offices in prime locations, branches of international organizations and residential areas for highly qualified staff whose careers and incomes are determined by the international labour market.
- The 'secondary sector' of the city covers ordinary places of work, residential areas and middle-class areas of activity, as well as including central institutions like universities, courts, regional administration and middle-class business.
- The 'tertiary sector' covers poor and marginalized fringe areas with no growth or modernization potential, like council estates, slums and industrial wasteland, areas for the unemployed, foreigners, immigrants suffering discrimination, drug addicts, outsiders and the poor.

Unmodernized inner city areas with a high density of housing and high-rise buildings are typical locations for the poor in the 'tertiary sector'. A strong mix of users provides a favourable framework for a social mix, and poor sectors of the population then tend to integrate relatively well. In addition, on the outskirts of cities, there are areas with relatively low-density housing and high-rise buildings. This applies specifically to the large housing estates of the 1960s and 1970s. However, they have hardly any shops or private service providers or local authority infrastructure. Due to the acute polarization and relatively high numbers of council housing, these areas are often publicly stigmatized as deprived areas.

On the other hand, there are the typical wealthy or well off areas of the city. These are mostly turn of the century residential areas close to the city centre with a high standard of modernization, a high proportion of owner occupiers and detached family houses in the few rural oases and top locations which the city still has to offer.

One important factor influencing this situation is turbulence due to relocation (Heusener and Schubert, 1995). The city operates like an 'immersion heater'. While the new generation in the form of young, new residents flows in, other people move away. Well-off families and established professionals look for quality green-belt locations. This process culminates in a form of 'slow polarization'. There is a strong trend for family households in both upper and middle income groups to favour suburbanization (Landeshaupstadt, 1993). Many choose locations around urban cores on financial grounds or to improve their standard of living or move to the high value rural areas at the edge of the conurbations.

As a result of this pattern of choice on where to live, growing suburbanization is putting great pressure on many urban cores and increases the potential of polarization and poverty. This is particularly so as households on lower incomes remain in the inner cities, not least as they are dependent on benefit or rented flats. Immigrant families from minority ethnic groups are usually to be found in the poor population.

LOCAL STRUCTURES UNDER PRESSURE TO CHANGE

The term 'local' is generally used in relation to a place. There is a difference between the symbolic attachment to a place people know and the link to a place in terms of local authority boundaries within which people live. In the nineteenth century, the reform of the Prussian social order granted citizens the right to participate in the government of their city and institutionalized the independent authority of local authorities. Ever since, the local authority responsible for a particular area, such as a city or rural community, provides the infrastructure to support residential areas.

In Germany, most local communities are parts of rural districts. A rural district and its local communities share the work of carrying out local authority duties. Only major urban centres are autonomous and have district-wide responsibilities. The infrastructure services deserve special mention. They range from the road network, electricity and gas supplies, water supply, sewage and waste disposal, to building and upkeep of schools, educational and welfare care establishments, cultural and social facilities.

In the design of the modern estate, people do relate only to the small area near their home because cities and local communities have different kinds of centres. Not all infrastructure services are provided in every location. In a central location, there is normally a local concentration of infrastructure facilities offering goods and services over a limited market area. This illustrates the supply function which a central location has as a major, medium or minor centre for neighbourhoods or for those areas without a centre in the surrounding countryside. There are also small-scale sectoral links, as the population in non-central locations demands what is offered in the central locations in the catchment area, such as work, trades, services or culture (Akademie für Raumforschung und Landesplanung, 1995).

Against this background, the term 'local' has been extended to cover a wider area in terms of the neighbouring locations or local networks providing structural links. These are regions where their cultural context represents home, area of activity and landscape. The residential area and area of activity of an individual is the space he or she covers via the various locations in the execution of his/her activities. This means that each individual could draw a star-shaped diagram of the routes taken and the locations of his/her activities and in the centre is the home. This spatial pattern helps residents make mental maps of what they perceive as mental images about connected places. The core of these spatial functions is the home because of the symbolic attachment for the residents. The basis is familiarity since childhood or long-term residence and is linked to a particular cultural and social, local and regional structure.

The quality of the landscape and architecture are converted into symbols of attachment to a place in the mental maps of the population and are thereby overshadowed by live networks of local and regional associations.

In the wake of globalization, micro structures of residential environments and urban areas no longer determine what is local; now it is the turn of the gargantuan sprawl of urban settlements. Micro spatial units are becoming superfluous, including the human measure of what can be reached on foot and what is on the horizon for the underprivileged, such as children and old people. This reflects the erosion of differentiated local structures in cities. These local structures become nothing more than living and sleeping places and access roads for traffic.

CITIES PERSONIFIED AND CAST IN STONE

There is a theory that this change in urban areas is linked to historical changes about how people imagined the human body functions. Each civilized epoch created some kind of 'body image' of their urban communal life either consciously or subconsciously. These models of human interaction in the city were related to discoveries about our body functions (Sennett, 1995).

In the Christian world in medieval times the heart was the point of orientation in the city. From this model came the integrating shape in the architecture of the squares, as we know them from Italian cities. Like a stage at the theatre, the traditional marketplace or piazza crosslinks the urban interactive network (Karrer, 1995; Dellemann and Günter, 1972). The city of stone as a local supply centre developed out of the human concept of the heart in the body.

The discovery of circulation of the blood by Harvey in the seventeenth century generated a new model for the modern age. With the system of arteries and veins came the idea of growing traffic in circulation. The city thereby lost its integrated form. Separate routes and symbols were derived from this concept of the human body. The public was domesticized by this process. Urban contact between people was privatized and they withdrew into their houses. Consequently, the piazza or local centre was forced into the background in everyday life.

Now we are standing on the threshold of the postmodern city. The new model of urban life is derived from notions of genetic/biochemical and neurobiological communications. There are already a few forms of this vision of the city in existence. The model of the 'telematic' city is being introduced.[2] The city is seen as a huge technical infrastructure network which is linked to all the other cities in the world. From this concept follows the idea of liquefying spatial structural patterns. For communications, superfast data transfer now counts for as much as direct interpersonal contact.

Accelerating the rate of data transfer without physical interaction means that we no longer need the local or human measure of direct visibility or walking distance.

LOSS OF IMPORTANCE OF LOCAL URBAN SPACE

In the transition to the communications era (Lutz, 1986), new responsibilities are already being placed upon urban centres. As the institutions supporting the cultural and economic process of differentiation, they will become vital to economic growth (Jacobs, 1984), especially as global economic development is not just based on multinational trade channels and links, but also on the cultural force of cities as the focal points in the global economic system (Huber, 1993). New IT and telecommunications technology has initiated rapid innovation. Social subsectors, such as culture, lifestyles, value orientation, law, politics, economy and science are progressing to a new level of complexity. Restructuring of social, political and economic relations is taking place. Cities are thereby losing their independent status and being integrated into broader structures. In the communications era, it is not the space that is disappearing, but the individual small-scale location is losing its status in the expansion of space (Franck, 1995, pp. 301–15).

With this transition to the communications era, the traditional concept of the city as a social and cultural network made up of several public areas of interest and of urban areas is losing its shape. The city in the age of communications is turning into a 'postmodernist Babylon'. Paradoxically, social ties and direct communication are declining in the face of a range of pluralist lifestyles. Even systems of social linkage in the cities are beginning to disappear as local structures are being swept away in the wake of broader structures in global society.

This can be described as the 'micro/macro paradox of the communications era'. For example, it is a well known fact that young single men can actively communicate with people in the most far flung corners of the globe via the World Wide Web on the Internet and still have no comparable direct links to their neighbourhood or residential environment. This paradox of isolated mass communications is producing socio-cultural development problems for cities. They are faced with the emerging paradox of 'separation and closeness' or 'absence and presence' (Beck, 1995, pp. 32–56).

City motorways have damaged, destroyed and transformed public urban space. By way of comparison, deep weals will be made by the 'data superhighways' in the public sectors of urban centres. Since information can be obtained and generated at will, when, where and how you want on these superhighways, people can 'free themselves from space, material and time'.

This will give the independence of the modern individual a further push. An army of self-employed mobile workers will characterize new production, industrial and service systems in the millennium (Vebacom, 1995). Social isolation has been identified as the greatest problem in this emerging society of teleworkers. People are not normally suited to the independence of telematics. It is difficult to make up for the lack of social contact at work in the private sphere because teleworkers can scarcely make distinctions between work and private life, let alone keep them separate (Monas, 1994, pp. 7–11).

This trend will strengthen competition in the city so that public use will be forced back even further into the private sector. As land resources become scarcer, transport and economic/technical matters will dominate other uses. So, the future of classical features of urban areas is in the balance. When sales of expensive building land in urban centres are based purely on fiscal grounds, the architecture of the service economy with their monofunctional office locations will minimize opportunities for complex mixed use and contribute towards further segregation and desolation in the cities.

LOSS OF SPATIAL LINKS

During the urbanization process over the past 150 years, regional mobility and widescale migration have gained in importance. By contrast, traditional local communities have lost their ability to overcome life's risks as they occur (de Swaan, 1993). With the transformation of the social networks due to modernization and mobility, the geographical radius for interactive links will also change (Floeting and Henckel, 1993).

In early times, daily life was closely linked to the narrow boundaries of traditional residential areas. Within these local boundaries, the neighbourhood and relatives living locally or in the region represented the most important categories in terms of social ties. In industrial society these restrictive physical boundaries were overcome. With modernization came more opportunities, with the result that social ties became more varied and physical boundaries moved beyond the local area. In the age of communications, the importance of physical distance has continued to increase with the development of transport and communications technologies. As a result, the geographical range is increasing all the time.

The term 'network' symbolizes a system of human relations. People and participants are represented as nodes for the purpose of this image, whereby each one is directly or indirectly linked to all the other nodes.

The links represent interaction and the intervals between nodes or links may be part of a loose or tightknit network. The idea behind this image is that people can only achieve their goals in active collaboration with others. Instead of a hierarchical class model with few active elements, everyone is active and dependent on one another.

Social networks are the primary means of forming the main links between the individual and wider social entities (Schenk, 1984). They link individuals to intermediary organizations, urban centres and social systems. Members of a society are integrated into society via 'personal networks'. In the current socio-ecological environment, social networks are classed as part of the social infrastructure (Schubert, 1995). With their informal infrastructure, private interactive networks are highly integrating and provide both instrumental and emotional support. Buzzwords, such as reliability, sustainability, loyalty, belonging, joint action, solidarity and help, characterize their wide range of functions. Social support organizations provide local or regional services via the formal infrastructure where required for immediate basic support which cannot be provided via informal interactive networks. However, no longer is enough done. This theme was first taken up in research on the quality of life and in age-related research (Schubert, 1990a, 1990b, 1992, 1994) because social ties are extremely important for a healthy life as people grow older.

As part of the process of modernization, the urban network framework has changed considerably. From isolated closed local network models, a global model is now available to the public on a supra-regional scale. Extensive interactive networks linking several locations or even conurbations via telecommunications and rapid transport systems have become a matter of pride. Consequently, both physical and social forms have been transformed where interactive social networks have been set up and nurtured. Traditional physical and social areas are moving further into the background and new ones are taking their place (Pappi and Melbeck, 1988, pp. 223–50). Traditional areas, such as local squares or public institutions, and traditional social networks, such as relatives and neighbours, are being pushed aside as more and more personal networks link the major cities. Now, new spaces, such as the workplace and commercial leisure facilities, as well as new social fields, such as work colleagues and friends, are playing an increasing role in personal network links.

This 'delocalization' trend in social networks could cause extreme problems for cities as they begin to lose their endogenous driving force. In the 'endogenous potential' model, local living environments are not just seen as areas of economic use, but also as places for cultural and political development. If they are no longer self-supporting, capitalized economic, social, cultural and political forces in the cities will no longer be manageable or sustainable. Therefore, urban centres need structures consisting of small local parts because they are the only places where endogenous potential can be activated with locally based players. These include small and medium sized firms, households, regional workers' organizations and associations, decision-making bodies at regional/state level, local authority institutions and key staff in local community organizations (Perucci and Potter, 1989).

PROMOTING LOCAL IDENTITY AS THE FUTURE RESPONSIBILITY OF THE CITIES

Therefore, one of the socio-cultural responsibilities of cities is to promote local identity so that both the population in general and the economically active can identify with the small-scale systems in their particular locations. Strengthening the feeling of belonging among social and economic actors is an important requirement for building up local communications networks and thereby for the (re)construction of the socio-cultural base.

- First, there are innovative ideas for infrastructure which promote new links and compensate for missing links. Nowadays, these ideas cannot be based purely on an abstract supply concept; they must actively support interactive networks for segregated and compartmentalized sectors of the urban population. Public sector services promoting social and cultural work include nursery schools, schools, leisure facilities, cultural meeting places, district lending libraries and other local community services. These must be measured in terms of whether they will strengthen networks in local areas. Above all, urban based bodies must provide public forums for those who are unable to participate in the commercial world due to their disadvantaged status.

- Second, these strategies need to include new housebuilding methods, especially for council housing. Building contractors should provide models for new community housing and estate construction. Also, housing associations should involve future residents more in development planning to support new local networks.
- Third, the promotion of clubs near residential areas is another priority. These associations consist of groups of people who meet to pursue common interests, first and foremost. Traditionally, new residents of multi-ethnic origin, and of different generations all integrate via these associations. Club life becomes one of the main forms of informal public life in the area. As each generation has its own interests, the variety and broad spectrum of interests is continually expanding. They may range from the latest sport to alternative hobbies and current subcultural interests. Groups of people from new areas who cannot organize themselves need therefore to be attracted by the range of local authority infrastructure facilities on offer. Facilities need to reflect changing interests and also need to be made more accessible to ensure that the locally based nodes of networks of different interests remain intact.
- Fourth, if people feel useless and bored, they soon lose interest in joint action and social ties when their residential areas begin to lose their identity as a place of residence (Sennett, 1996). Loyalty to the place which is the centre of their life declines when the local surroundings offer few opportunities to compensate for the losses suffered from the global economy and the extended range of experience gained from television and the media. As the whole world becomes the horizon in terms of a sense of identity, all feeling for the immediate local surroundings is lost. This is where local institutions need to step in and counteract with a strategy of miniaturizing areas of experience. Where else can we experience nature, culture, celebrations and other events face to face, if not on our doorstep? Urban planning is therefore facing a series of particularly tough challenges. It must re-miniaturize and pedestrianize public space. The dense concentration of urban space, pubs, playgrounds and marketplaces needs to be developed to provide a new identity. Urban development and construction needs to develop new recognizable means of identification and a strong mix of activities. Beck called this 'gradual polygamy for the urban district' (1995, p. 47).

Architecture in public areas will soon be back in demand, as soon as people have experienced an overkill of virtual reality in global cyber space. Then the socio-cultural hunger (which is bound to return soon) for coherence, real variety and common ground as well as public life in urban areas will return. We need to act now with planning principles to help ensure that home, work and support services are located close together with mixed-use functions, opportunities, sustainable education, cultural life and infrastructure services within community life, recreation areas and meeting places outside the home. Last but not least, there should be ample scope for creativity in the immediate local area for neighbours to meet and for residents to shape their own living conditions.

Notes

1.   Statement by US politician Zbigniew Brzezinski, during a conference organized by the Gorbachev Foundation on globalization issues on 27 May 1995 at the Fairmont Hotel, San Francisco.
2.   One example is the 'Info-city' model by Vebacom in North Rhine-Westphalia.

References

Akademie für Raumforschung und Landesplanung, *Handwörterbuch der Raumordnung* [Spatial Research and Regional Planning Academy, *Concise Dictionary of Regional Planning*] (Hanover, 1995).

M. Alisch and J.S. Dangschat, *Die solidarische Stadt – Ursachen von Armut und Strategien für einen sozialen Ausgleich* [*Solidarity in the City – Causes of Poverty and Strategies for Social Compensation*] (Darmstadt, 1993).

U. Beck, 'Risiko Stadt? Architektur in der reflexiven Moderne [Cities at risk? Architecture of reflexive modernity]', in U. Schwarz (ed.), *Risiko Stadt? Perspektiven der Urbanität* [*Cities at Risk? Prospects for Urbanity*] (Hamburg, 1995).

J.S. Dangschat, 'Lokale Probleme globaler Herausforderungen in deutschen Städten [The local dimension of global challenges in German cities]', in B. Schäfers and G. Wewer (eds), *Die Stadt in Deutschland. Soziale, politische und kulturelle Lebenswelt* [*The City in Germany: Social, Political and Cultural Living Environment*] (Opladen, 1996) pp. 31–60.

P. Dellemann and R. Günter, *Kommunikation, Sozioökonomie, Städtebau. Eine Stadtbeobachtungsmethode zur Beurteilung der Lebensqualität* [*Communications, Socio-economics and Urban Architecture: An Urban Observation Model for Assessing Quality of Life*] (Bonn, 1972).

A. de Swaan, *Der sorgende Staat, Wohlfahrt, Gesundheit und Bildung in Europa und den USA der Neuzeit* [*The Caring State. Welfare, Health and Education in Europe and the US in Modern Times*] (Frankfurt am Main/New York, 1993).

R. v. Engelsdorp Gastelaars, 'Revitalising the city and the formation of metropolitan culture: rivalry between capital cities in the attraction of new urban elites', in A. de Swaan et al., *Capital Cities as Achievement* (Amsterdam, 1988) pp. 38–42.

H. Floeting and D. Henckel, 'Lean Production, Telematik, just-in-time. Stadträumliche Wirkungen neuer Produktions- und Logistikkonzepte [Lean production, telematics, just-in-time: impact of new concepts of production and logistics on urban areas]', *Stadtbauwelt* [*Urban Building Environment*] 120 (1993) 2623–9.

G. Franck, 'Der innervierte Raum. Zum Einfluß der Telematik auf Stadt und Umwelt [Innervated space: the influence of telematics on the city and the environment]' in U. Schwarz (ed.), *Risiko Stadt? Perspektiven der Urbanität* [*Cities at risk? Prospects for Urbanity*] (Hamburg, 1995) pp. 301–15.

R. Froessler and K. Selle, *Die Erneuerung der 'Dritten Stadt'* [*Renewal of the Divided City*], Werkstattbericht 26 der AG Bestandsverbesserung [Workshop Report 26, Housing Improvement Corporation], Dortmund (Hanover, 1989).

D. Harvey, *The Condition of Postmodernity* (Oxford, 1990).

H. Häußermann and W. Siebel, *Neue Urbanität* [*New Urbanity*] (Frankfurt am Main, 1987).

K. Heusener and H. Schubert, *Regionalreport zur Entwicklung der Wohnungs- und Baulandmärkte in Niedersachsen bis 2010* [*Regional Report on Housing and Real Estate Market Trends in Lower Saxony to 2010*] (Hanover, 1995).

S. Hradil, *Sozialstrukturanalyse in einer fortgeschrittenen Gesellschaft* [*Social Structure Analysis in an Advanced Society*] (Opladen, 1987).

J. Huber, *Regionalentwicklung in der Kommunikationsgesellschaft* [*Regional Development in Society in the Communications Era*] (Opladen, 1993).

J. Jacobs, *Cities and the Wealth of Nations* (New York, 1984).

M. Karrer, *Die Piazza. Frauen und Männer in einem süditalienischen Dorf* [*The Piazza: Men and Women in a Village in Southern Italy*] (Frankfurt am Main, 1995).

Landeshauptstadt Hanover, *Sozialbericht 1993. Zur Lage der Kinder, Jugendlichen und Familien* [*1993 Social Report: the Situation of Children, Young People and Families*], Schriftenreihe des Gesundheits-, Jugend- und Sozialdezernats, Band 13 [Serial publication, Health, Youth and Social Department, State Capital of Hanover, Vol. 13] (Hanover, 1993).

C. Lutz, 'Die Kommunikationsgesellschaft [Society in the communications era]', *Serial publication Gottlieb Duttweiler Institut, Rücklikom/Zurich*, Vol. 45 (1986).

H.-P. Martin and H. Schumann, *Die Globaliserungsfalle. Der Angriff auf Demokratie und Wohlstand* [The Globalization Trap: The Attack on Democracy and Wealth] (Reinbek, near Hamburg, 1996).

D. Monas, 'Home, Sweet Home', *Ericsson Connexion*, 9 (1994) 7–11.

F-.U. Pappi and C. Melbeck, 'Die sozialen Beziehungen städtischer Bevölkerungen [Social relationships in the urban population]', *Kölner*

Zeitschrift für Soziologie und Sozialpsychologie [*Cologne Journal of Sociology and Social Psychology*] (Special Edition 29, 1988) 223–50.

R. Perucci and H.R. Potter, *Networks of Power: Organizational Actors at the National, Corporate and Community Level* (New York, 1989).

M. Schenk, *Soziale Netzwerke und Kommunikation* [*Social Networks and Communications*] (Tübingen, 1984).

H. Schubert,'Wohnsituation und Hilfenetze im Alter [Living conditions and support networks in old age]', *Zeitschrift für Gerontologie* [*Journal of Gerontology*], 23 (1990a) 12–22.

H. Schubert 'Das Altern der westeuropäischen Staatsgesellschaften. Über Bevölkerungsentwicklungen während des abendländischen Zivilisationsprozesses [Ageing societies in Western Europe: population trends in the developing Western world]', in H. Korte (ed.), *Gesellschaftliche Prozesse und individuelle Praxis. Bochumer Vorlesungen zu Norbert Elias' Zivilisationstheorie* [*Social Processes and Individual Practice: Bochum Lecture Series on Norbert Elias's Theory of Civilization*] (Frankfurt am Main, 1990b) pp. 86–128.

H. Schubert, *Hilfenetze älterer Menschen. Ergebnisse einer egozentrierten Netzwerkanalyse im ländlichen Raum* [*Support Networks for the Elderly: Findings from the Analysis of Individual Networks in Rural Areas*], Institut für Entwicklungsplanung und Strukturforschung [Institute for Development Planning and Research] (Hanover, 1992).

H. Schubert, 'Hilfenetze älterer Menschen. Zur Bedeutung von räumlichen Entfernungen und sozialen Beziehungen für Hilfe im Alter [Support networks for the elderly: the significance of physical distance and social relationships in old age]', *Geographische Zeitschrift* [*Geographic Journal*], 82 (1994), 226–38.

H. Schubert, 'Stichwort "Soziale Infrastruktur" [Keyword: "Social infrastructure"]', in Akademie für Raumforschung und Landesplanung Hannover [Academy for Spatial Research and Regional Planning, Hanover] (eds), *Handwörterbuch der Raumordnung* [*Concise Dictionary of Spatial Management*] (1995) pp. 847–51.

H. Schubert, 'Zur Zukunft der soziokulturellen Netzwerke in den Städten [The future of socio-cultural networks in cities]', in H. Schmalstieg (ed.), *Zukunftsfähiges Hannover – Wege zur nachhaltigen Entwicklung einer Großstadt-Region* [The Future for Hanover: Achieving Sustainable Development in a Major City Region] (Hanover, 1996) pp. 73–88.

G. Schulze, *Die Erlebnisgesellschaft: Kultursoziologie der Gegenwart* [*Entertainment-oriented Society: Contemporary Cultural Sociology*] (Frankfurt am Main/New York, 1992).

R. Sennett, *Fleisch und Stein* [*Flesh and Stone*] (Berlin, 1995).

S. Sennett, 'Etwas faul in der Stadt [There's something wrong in the city]', *Die Zeit*, 5 (1996) 47.

E. Spiegel, 'Die Stadt als soziales Gefüge [The city as a social structure]', in Akademie für Raumforschung und Landesplanung [Academy for Spatial Research and Regional Planning] (eds), *Grundriß der Stadtplanung, Hannover* [*Urban Planning Compendium, Hanover*] (1983) pp. 83–97.

Vebacom, *Info City. Ein Europäisches Projekt für das 21. Jahrhundert* [*Info City. A European Project for the Millennium*] (Düsseldorf, 1995).

I. Wallerstein, *The Modern World System: Capitalist Agriculture and the Origins of the European World Economy in the Sixteenth Century* (New York, 1974).

I. Wallerstein, 'Aufstieg und künftiger Niedergang des kapitalistischen Weltsystems. Zur Grundlegung vergleichender Analyse [The rise and future fall of global capitalism: principles for comparative analysis]', in D. Senghaas (ed.), *Global Capitalist Economy* (Frankfurt am Main, 1979) pp. 31–67.

I. Wallerstein, *Historical Capitalism* (London, 1983).

11 European Union Policies and Funds – the Role of Urban Government in England

Randall Smith

Randall Smith

CONTEXT

What are the traditional forms of international activity that can be found in the cities and towns of Britain? The most high-profile activities are likely to be in the fields of sport and entertainment, particularly football and popular music, such as the Liverpool sound or, more recently, triphop, the Bristol sound. Less high profile but important for their impact on the local economy and the local labour market are transnational corporations. They may be sectoral in focus – electronics is a good example (Lawton, 1996) – or conglomerates.

Large, but not transnational, firms in a particular locality may well have strong export markets, as may the bigger law firms and management consultants. City centre (as opposed to high street) banks and other financial institutions make an important but not very visible contribution to the international profile of an urban area. For smaller firms, the local chamber of commerce provides a range of export services. By way of contrast, the core activities of locally and regionally based trade unions have not in general included an international dimension.

Universities have traditionally formed part of a global community through research collaboration and the interchange of ideas by means of participation in the meetings of international learned societies and through being among the early users of the Internet. Like the activities of commerce and business, these international linkages have not typically had a high local profile.

More visible have been the activities of local authorities through twinning arrangements with towns and cities in other countries. Educational exchanges, mainly at secondary level, have been widely developed. Fairly or unfairly, twinning has tended to be seen as an opportunity for foreign junketing by political leaders at the expense of the local ratepayer. An increasing concern for the well-being of the local economy, which developed in British local government during the 1980s, led to greater emphasis on the economic development function of local authorities. It took the form of foreign inward investment strategies including the place marketing of towns and cities, and required an international capacity to attract mobile capital (Young and Mills, 1993).

Lastly, and for a limited number of British local authorities, there has been the opportunity to engage in global debate about the role and future of local government under the auspices of the International Union of Local Authorities (founded 1919), the Council of European Municipalities and Regions (founded 1956) and the Congress of Local and Regional Authorities of Europe, itself part of the Council of Europe (established in 1949). Perhaps one of the most important products of the latter has been the Charter for Local Self-Government, which governments of national states have been invited to sign in recognition of the independent constitutional status of sub-national government. The May 1997 UK Labour government over-turned its predecessor's opposition to the Charter and agreed in principle to sign up.

These traditional international activities – exporting of goods and services, twinning, the sports and entertainment industries, blue skies research – were in place before the UK joined the European Community at the beginning of 1973. The local impact of EC policies, practices and procedures was discerned only gradually. In urban areas the influence of the common agricultural policy was reflected, perhaps opaquely, in the price of many goods. Larger businesses began to see increased opportunities for trade in countries near the UK, but declining industries, such as coal and steel, found themselves subject to retrenchment. Universities began to benefit from the EC's research and development programme, but the UK Research and Higher Education European Office was not established in Brussels by the Research Councils until 1984.

In the local authority world, the technical functions of environmental health and trading standards were among the services most strongly affected by EC directives in the early years. Although the former School for Advanced Urban Studies at the University of Bristol ran its first event in its policy-oriented seminar programme on Local Government and EEC Funds as early as January 1978, it was not until well into the 1980s that some local authorities began to develop strategies for influencing EC policy, particularly financial instruments such as the structural funds. Birmingham was the first British local authority to have a presence in Brussels (1984), closely followed by Strathclyde (John, 1995). However, it was with the reform of the structural funds which took effect in 1988 against a backcloth of cuts in public expenditure in Britain that EC money as a serious source of revenue led some local authorities to develop international practices with a particular focus on the European Community.

MULTILEVEL GOVERNANCE

Against this broad background of the international dimension of activity in British urban areas, this chapter focuses specifically on the role of subnational government (local government in the centralized unitary state of Britain) in the supranational arena of the European Union. Where does subnational government fit into the policy process? How significant are other subnational agencies?

For well over thirty years, academics have argued about the way the European Community functions. Two contrasting models are those of intergovernmentalism and federalism. The former emphasizes the collaboration between nation state members of the Community but no loss of political control – a *Europe des patries*. The latter suggests a partial loss of political control, or national sovereignty (Nugent, 1996) such that institutions at the supranational level have developed powers and competences which have a direct impact on the popula-tions of the nation states making up the Community, including links with subnational systems of government. One characterization of this model is the *Europe des régions*.

In the late 1950s these nation states numbered six and the pre-eminence of first-world economies remained unchallenged. The picture is very different forty years on. Member states currently total 15 and further enlargement is on the cards. The command economies of central and eastern Europe have collapsed and the former Soviet Union is in disarray. The USA is currently the dominant world power but for how long is anyone's guess. The globalization of the economy is now a commonplace and the turnover of large transnational com-panies comfortably exceeds the annual budget of many independent nation states.

The arguments of the intergovernmentalists and the federalists may or may not have been plausible in the 1960s. They both seem over-simple today. To strengthen the economic base of the European Community, policies have been formally agreed by the governments of the member states. Some have been implemented such as the less controversial of the proposals to bring about a single market by the removal of internal barriers to trade. Others are in immediate prospect such as economic and monetary union. Economic integration policies of this kind have dramatically changed the role of nation state governments. Not only has economic interdependence become transparent but key players now include supranational institutions such as the European Commission or the European Court of Justice. This is not to argue that nation state governments will wither away. The behaviour of the Spanish government in the Council of Ministers' meetings and other settings over the reforms of the structural funds for the 2000–6 period demonstrates how unlikely that is. However, it is remarked that member state governments have lost their monopoly powers. Neither the intergovernmentalist nor the federalist arguments reflect the current complexity of the European Community.

Analysts such as Hooghe (1995) and Marks (1993) argue that member state governments are not becoming obsolete but, nevertheless, European Community bodies do have an independent influence on the policy process. What has developed is a pattern of multilevel governance. 'The emerging picture is that of a polity with multiple, interlocked areas for political contest. The European level is one of them, where state executives, but also European institutions and a widening array of mobilized interests contend' (Hooghe, 1995, p. 176).

The question can thus be posed whether the array of mobilized interests includes or excludes subnational governmental entities, such as the *Länder* in Germany or local authorities in the UK. The systems of subnational government vary greatly between the member states of the European Community. Where there is a (quasi) federal system, representatives from regional level can be found negotiating on behalf of the national interest at Council of Ministers meetings. This is the case with Belgium and Germany, and potentially with Austria and Spain. The UK, by way of contrast, is a highly centralized unitary state, whose subnational system of governance is subject to the powers, even the whims of, central government, as the sorry story of the last quarter century demonstrates. Does the notion of multilevel governance embrace the activities and interests of UK local government in relation to European Community policies?

This question can be answered positively if it can be shown that representatives of UK local government are full members of networks that address EC policy concerns. The jury is still out as far as the recently constituted Committee of the Regions is concerned (Loughlin, 1996). In the last decade, many UK local authorities have invested in a Brussels office, more than from any other member state. A November 1995 survey by Martin Fairclough, a researcher in the office of Bristol's member of the European Parliament, Ian White, identified 26 offices supported either entirely or in part by local authorities in Britain. Their main functions were intelligence gathering to inform EU strategies and funding applications from the home base and provision of support for visiting delegations, but two-thirds of them also engaged in promoting the interests of their local areas to Commission officials and also to representatives of the UK central government based in Brussels. The broad intentions have been to ensure that discussions on shifts in policy direction were informed by regional or local as well as national considerations. These motivations for establishing an office in Brussels have been characterized by Marks, Nielsen, Ray and Salk (1996) as information exchange, resource pull and regional distinctiveness.

Lobbying in Brussels is a major industry, particularly by the business community (Mazey and Richardson, 1993; Greenwood, 1997). However, local government has played its part. Much lobbying has a specific objective in mind. In 1988, the local authority headed Coalfields Communities Campaign led a transnational effort to bring in special measures focusing on the needs of mining areas. In August 1989 the European Commission approved a proposal to establish a special programme (a Community Initiative) for the mining industry along the lines of the programmes for the steel and shipbuilding industries, and guidelines were published early in 1990. The Coalfields Communities Campaign claimed it was 'the principal architect' of the initiative (for the detailed story, see McAleavey, 1993).

Despite this kind of success, negotiations on major issues like the reform of the structural funds in general excluded the voice of British local government, even though the national level of local government (the local authority associations) did have an opportunity to put their views forward on the future of the structural funds to UK central government. The key players in the 1988 negotiations on the reforms came from member state governments and the European Commission. There was no major mobilization of subnational interests, as far as the UK was concerned. Expressing a view to UK central government was light years away from participating in the negotiations at the Copenhagen and Brussels summit meetings in December 1987 and February 1988.

The 1988 reforms at one level suggested that some kind of network could be required. Article 4.1 stated that 'Community operations ... shall be established through close consultation between the Commission, the Member State concerned and the competent authorities designated by the latter at national, regional, local or other level, with each party acting as a partner in pursuit of a common goal'. Partnership was one of the four principles underpinning the operations of the reformed funds along with concentration (targeting the funds to best effect), programming (pooling projects together for funding and processing purposes) and additionality (ensuring that the EC funds added to and did not replace domestic investment). The effect of the statement on partnership was somewhat spoilt in the preamble to the regulation which referred to close association between partners 'where appropriate', thereby leaving member state governments with a large degree of discretion.

The next revision of the structural funds, which took effect from the beginning of 1994, began in 1992. The Edinburgh summit in December 1992 saw agreement on the financial package for the European Community for the 1994–9 period. Based on this agreement, the Commission formally published its proposals for revising the structural funds regulations in March 1993. One of the elements in the proposals was further strengthening of the principle of partnership. The UK local authority sector argued that, with its democratic mandate, it should have a special role which should be explicitly recognized in the revised regulations. The response of the UK government at a bilateral meeting with local authority representatives was acceptance that local authorities should be recognized as a tier of government but it would be difficult to negotiate an appropriate form of words for inclusion in the regulations. The Council of Ministers adopted the revised regulations governing the structural funds in July 1993. The process of negotiation did not suggest either a partnership or a policy network involving subnational partners.

The same point can be made about the role of UK local government in the debate about the next reform of the structural funds to take effect after 1999. This followed intergovernmental agreement on the Amsterdam Treaty and was embedded in broader issues such as the overall financial framework, enlargement, defence and foreign policy issues and the overhaul of the institutions of the European Union. While the national level of UK local government was again active in lobbying both in relation to specific aspects of the Treaty, such as a clause on anti-discrimination and in arguing for any reform of the structural funds to take account of the interests of disadvantaged areas, it did not have any part to play in the formal negotiations.

The multilevel governance thesis is not fatally undermined by the hitherto weak role of UK subnational agencies in the policy-making process. The proponents of this thesis are as, if not more, interested in demonstrating the sharing of powers between national and supranational level.

> There are two sets of reasons why government leaders may wish to shift decision-making to the supranational level: the political benefits may outweigh the costs of losing political control or there may be intrinsic benefits having to do with shifting responsibility for unpopular decisions or insulating decision-making from domestic pressures. ... Multi-level governance does not confront the sovereignty of states directly. Instead of being explicitly challenged, states in the European Union are being melded gently into a multilevel polity by their leaders and the actions of numerous subnational and supranational actors.
>
> (Marks, Hooghe and Blank, 1996, pp. 348–9, 371)

Jeffery (1996), however, would argue that the link between the subnational and supranational levels is unlikely to flourish. 'There is no evidence ... of an SNA (subnational authority) capability of sustaining direct access channels to European-level institutions which bypass central governments. There is also little evidence that SNAs desire or aim to establish enduring central state bypass channels' (p. 209).

THE INFLUENCE OF SUBNATIONAL AGENCIES

So where do UK subnational actors have an influence? One plausible answer is in the application of the rules governing the structural funds. If networks in relation to the funds can be identified in the UK, they are linked to the implementation of policies that have been formally agreed, particularly through membership of monitoring committees. A study by Burton and Smith (1996) concluded that the 1989–93 national monitoring committee concerned with ESF-supported programmes to combat long-term unemployment (Objective 3) and to integrate young people into the labour market (Objective 4) did not go much beyond token consultation by UK central government with subnational agencies and non-governmental organizations. However, the latter two interests did find the presence of Commission officials on the monitoring committee helpful. They could reiterate concerns about the allocative mechanisms used by UK central government and they could point out that lack of progress in developing a monitoring system meant that the quality of training about which they were suspicious, especially of central government schemes, could not be assessed. The greater visibility of Commission officials increased the quality and frequency of informal contact between subnational and supranational interests. Technical expertise became more available to overburdened Commission officials. It may be at this level of technical advice that subnational interests may have their greatest influence on EU policy-making. As far as UK local government is concerned this is particularly the case with environmental and consumer protection issues. Regulatory systems may be more open to the views of subnational actors than are resource allocation systems.

Overall, the cumbersome and centralizing consequences of having a national committee for monitoring Objective 3 and 4 programmes resulted in an adversarial and competitive culture which undermined the prospect of genuine partnership, even though the UK 1994–9 Objective 3 plan to combat unemployment and to integrate young people into the labour market formally stated that the members of the partnership were 'clearly consulted on matters of preparation, focusing, monitoring and assessment of operations' (para. 7.1, p. 77). Over the years the local authority sector has been plugging the suggestion that the monitoring process for these ESF-supported programmes should be regionalized along the lines of the monitoring committees set up after the 1988 reforms covering areas eligible for European Regional Development Fund (ERDF) monies as well as ESF support (Objective 2 areas in industrial decline and Objective 5b areas of rural disadvantages). Burton and Smith (1996) examined the role of the 1989–93 monitoring committee in the West Midlands region of England. While being careful not to generalize from this single case study, they argued that the requirement to produce a regional plan led to closer involvement of local authorities in the region in this process compared with the part they played in developing the national plan for Objectives 3 and 4.

The planning debate at the regional level was taking place through interagency collaboration, and the main players were civil servants from the West Midlands regional office of central government, Commission officials and those local authority officials leading on the development of subregional programmes, which were in part based on pre-existing initiatives. (In the late 1980s, other regional and local players tended to be associated with a particular capital project rather than with the overall development of a regional plan.) Because of the close involvement of the local authority interests in subregional programmes and because they were in many cases the expert lead implementing agency, together with having a representative democratic legitimacy, the links between the subnational level and the national and supranational interests were complex. While the regional office of central government both chaired and serviced the monitoring committees, much of the 'real' discussion took place outside these formal settings in the day-to-day contact between officials from the Commission, central and local government and other interested parties. One experienced local government European Officer claimed: 'There is no problem in picking up the phone and getting views on a project ... DG XVI want to play an equal role to the secretariat (made up of civil servants servicing the monitoring committee) in giving the green light to projects.' 'The partnership principle and the establishment of regional monitoring committees blur state boundaries by providing subnational actors with a forum for closer communication with each other and with national and EU authorities' (Bradley, 1997, p. 46).

For the 1993 revision of the structural funds regulations, the Commission (or at least a senior official in DG XVI) positively encouraged local authorities to come together to draw up their own regional development strategies rather than rely on the regional office civil servants to do the drafting (McCarthy and Burch, 1994). In the UK these strategies had no official status, though central government officials agreed that they would be taken into account in the preparation of the official documentation for Brussels. In the West Midlands, the job was taken forward by the West Midlands Regional Forum of Local Authorities, who participated in monitoring committee discussions from January 1993. The new integrated Government Office for the West Midlands, which was formally established in April 1994, was prepared not only to make use of the Regional Forum's strategy document but also co-opted the key local authority staff who put it together to help draft the formal regional plan, known as the single programming document.

What might one conclude about the multilevel governance thesis based on experience in the UK, a centralized unitary state? If one drew solely upon the UK 1989–93 national monitoring committee addressing Objective 3 and 4 concerns, one might conclude that multilevel governance was a misnomer. A more appropriate term might be bilevel governance. Subnational agencies have not been involved in the major policy negotiations on the structural funds regulations.

Although local government in the UK is a creature of central government and has no independent part to play in negotiations to secure the national interest, the picture is, nevertheless, a little more complex for those regions which include within their boundaries Objective 2 or 5b areas. Local government, to repeat, was not involved in the negotiations about structural funds reform, yet the part played by West Midlands local government officials, alongside civil servants in formal and informal meetings with the Commission to discuss regional strategy priorities is an engagement which goes beyond the operational implementation activities of addressing issues of under-spend, timetable slippage and virement. Sometimes common practices were agreed between UK central and local government officials before a meeting with the Commission. Sometimes an alliance was established between the Commission and the subnational levels to influence the agenda on matters such as regional planning priorities. Here, the operation of multilevel governance can be discerned, if it is defined as the transfer of power from state executives to either the subnational or supranational levels or both.

The fieldwork for the case study in the West Midlands was under-taken in 1995 and covered the 1989–93 structural funds period. Have subsequent events in the 1994–9 period made the operation of multi-level governance more or less discernible? The broad answer is 'perhaps'. First, much of the operation of the European Social Fund has been regionalized, providing more opportunity for local players to affect the policy implementation process. Second, the European secretariat in the central government's regional office in the West Midlands is heavily staffed by secondees from local agencies to such an extent that they are taking on line management responsibilities. Third, official delegations from the West Midlands region now regularly include representatives from agencies other than central government. Fourth, the West Midlands office in Brussels is now supported by all the local authorities in the region.

Greater involvement at the policy implementation level is at best only an indirect reflection of multilevel governance. 'In a centralized state with a flexible, uncodified constitution, multilevel governance remains informal' (Bradley, 1997, p. 56). If the experience of the effectiveness of day-to-day operations is influencing central government in its stance on the next round of structural reforms, then it can be argued that local agencies are influencing, if not participating in, the policy debate in a way that is different from the activity of lobbying. The voice of UK local government in the lobbying process has, meanwhile, been heard more clearly, partly through the activities of the Committee of the Regions and the important influence of the UK Local Government International Bureau in the deliberations of the Council of European Municipalities and Regions. Nearly all of the UK is represented in one way or another by offices in Brussels, including a major investment by the West Midlands Region. All this adds up to a more robust local government presence in the corridors of the institutions of the EU, but the formal position remains that subnational agencies in the UK do not officially participate in policy-making negotiations on issues such as the reform of the structural funds.

The proponents of the multilevel governance thesis need to look to other member states, probably those with a federal structure, to find more convincing evidence of multilevel rather than bilevel governance. Hooghe (1996a) argues that 'regions and local authorities increasingly participate in European policy-making' (p. 121) and seeks to convince the reader of the salience of the multilevel governance thesis involving subnational agencies. In their chapter on the UK in the book edited by Hooghe (1996b), Bache, George and Rhodes are less than convincing in their support for this argument through their emphasis on the con-tinuing strength of UK central government in the EU policy-making process. 'Political resources, based on the right to make policy and decide on the framework for policy implementation, are strongly concentrated in the hands of central government' (p. 318).

The conclusion is that UK central government remains the sole negotiator in major debates about the future of EU policies, such as the reform of the structural funds. The presence, however, of a range of UK subnational interests in Brussels has led central government, through its own representation in Brussels, to listen to and brief local government representatives more regularly than used to be the case, if only to avoid undermining the UK government's negotiating position. One member of the staff of UKREP has specific responsibility to liaise with regional offices.

The part played by UK subnational government in the EU policy arena has increased, and Commission officials are willing to listen to the arguments of collectivities of subnational authorities, but whether this amounts to multilevel governance is open to doubt. More import-ant for UK local government is the part they have played in shaping regional plans, such that they have become recognized as true if not equal partners in the policy implementation and management process at the regional level. The argument for multilevel governance in the UK context is more persuasive if the focus is on policy initiation negotiations between central government and the Commission. This, however, is bilevel rather than multilevel governance. As Hooghe (1996a) herself points out: 'The intermeshed character of European decision-making makes it inevitable that Commission officials and national civil servants often find themselves in the same policy networks' (p. 92).

References

I. Bache, S. George and R.A.W. Rhodes, 'The European Union, cohesion policy and subnational authorities in the United Kingdom', in L. Hooghe (ed.), *Cohesion Policy and European Integration: Building Multi-Level Governance* (Oxford: Clarendon Press, 1996) chapter 9.

L. Bradley, *Regional Offices: Reclaiming the Regional Space*, master's thesis (Bruges: Department of Politics, College of Europe, 1997).

P. Burton and R. Smith, 'United Kingdom', in H. Heinelt and R. Smith (eds), *Policy Networks and European Structural Funds* (Aldershot: Avebury, 1996) pp. 73–119.

J. Greenwood, *Representing Interests in the European Union* (London: Macmillan, 1997).

L. Hooghe, 'Subnational mobilization in the European Union', *West European Politics*, 18: 3, July (1995) 175–98.

L. Hooghe, 'Building a Europe with the regions: the changing role of the European Commission', in L. Hooghe (ed.), *Cohesion Policy and European Integration: Building Multi-Level Governance* (Oxford: Clarendon Press, 1996a) chapter 3.

L. Hooghe, *Cohesion Policy and European Integration: Building Multi-Level Governance* (Oxford: Clarendon Press, 1996b).

C. Jeffery, 'Conclusions: subnational authorities and "European domestic policy"', *Regional and Federal Studies*, 6: 2, Summer (1996) 204–19.

P. John, *A Base in Brussels: A Good Investment for Local Authorities?*, Special Report No. 2 (London: Local Government International Bureau, 1995).

T. Lawton, 'Industrial policy partners: explaining the european level firm/Commission interplay for electronics', *Policy and Politics* 24: 4, October (1996) 425–36.

J. Loughlin, 'Representing Regions in Europe: the Committee of the Regions', *Regional and Federal Studies*, 6: 2, Summer (1996) 147–65.

P. McAleavey, 'The politics of european regional development policy: additionality in the Scottish coalfields', *Regional Politics and Policy*, 3: 2, Summer (1993) 88–107.

A. McCarthy and M. Burch, 'European regional development strategies: the responses of two northern regions', *Local Government Policy Making*, 20: 5, May (1994) 31–8.

G. Marks, 'Structural policy and multi-level governance in the EC', in A. Cafruny and G. Rosenthal (eds), *The State of the European Community II: The Maastricht Debates and Beyond* (Boulder, Colo.: Lynne Rienner, 1993) pp. 391–410.

G. Marks, L. Hooghe and K. Blank, 'European integration from the 1980s: state-centric v. multi-level governance', *Journal of Common Market Studies*, 34: 7, September (1996) 341–78.

G. Marks, F. Nielsen, L. Ray and J. Salk, 'Competencies, cracks and conflicts: regional mobilization in the European Union', in G. Marks, F.W. Scharpf, P.C. Schmitter and W. Streeck, *Governance in the European Union* (London: Sage, 1996) chapter 3.

S. Mazey and J. Richardson, *Lobbying in the European Community* (Oxford: Oxford University Press, 1993).

N. Nugent, 'Sovereignty and Britain's membership of the European Union', *Public*, 11: 2, Summer (1996) 3–18.

K. Young and L. Mills, *A Portrait of Change* (Luton: Local Government Management Board, 1993).

12 Defining Innovative Potential in City Regions

Arno Brandt

INTRODUCTION

Which direction should urban centres and metropolitan regions seek to develop in, in order to guarantee their future survival and success in the twenty-first century? This chapter addresses the basic factors governing the economic future of urban regions, and, more specifically, the conditions for developing innovative potential in regional business. The bottom line is that metropolitan regions, cost-intensive locations as they are, can only maintain and expand within the global economy if, firstly, innovative commercial activities are developed, and secondly, there is a close connection between the innovative potential of businesses in the region and that of the region itself. The more receptive regions are to innovative processes, the more favourable the business environment will be for successful 'production in the 21st century' (Lutz, Hartmann and Hirsch-Kreinsen, 1996).

In this context, innovation covers not only technological but also institutional and social developments. Innovative networking in relation both to intercompany cooperation and to a close interplay between commercial and non-commercial R&D institutions forms the basis for technological, institutional and social innovation, all of which are vital to the future of metropolitan regions. Thus the growing future impact of globalization will not in the least result in a loss of importance for the regional level; rather, it will strengthen the role of the regions as fields of activity.

GLOBALIZATION AND REGIONALIZATION

Virtually no other subject has attracted as much attention in economic policy debate in recent years as globalization. Even if we assume the term globalization does indeed describe an economic phenomenon that really exists, the inflationary way in which the term is being used makes one highly sceptical as to whether it will really serve as an explanation for all our current economic and social problems. It will certainly not suffice as legitimization for neoliberal processes of change, as justification for which the supposed constraints of the global market are invoked, and which are at least temporarily associated with growing social inequality and increasing interregional and intraregional disparities. Krugman (1994, 1996) has made a valuable contribution to exploding this 'myth of globalization' in his recent publications.

Nevertheless, the fact that a movement towards an increasingly global economy is in progress can hardly be denied. Globalization can initially be defined as a process whereby markets and production in different countries are becoming more and more dependent on one another (see OECD, 1995; UNCTAD, 1995; BIZ and IMF, various years). Such a change in the constellation of the world economy is particularly reflected in the following three indicators:

- World production or real world economic product increased at an average annual rate of approximately 3 per cent in the 1980s. Up to the mid-1980s world trade, i.e. the real value of worldwide exports, increased at a slightly faster pace of 3.5 per cent on average. However, between 1986 and 1993 exports grew by 5.5 per cent, which was almost double the figure for production. Currently, trade is growing more than twice as fast as production. The gap between the growth in global production and that in world trade is therefore widening all the time.
- In 1995 US$ 315 billion was spent on direct investment worldwide. This record value was up 40 per cent on the previous year. Between 1980 and 1994 the total value of direct investments increased almost sixfold to US$ 2700 billion, and therefore rose more than twice as fast as world trade. Although the majority of direct investment is still between industralized nations, the proportion involving developing and threshold countries has increased substantially from 18 per cent in 1990 to 28 per cent in 1995.
- At the end of 1995 the value of transactions on the international financial markets amounted to around US$ 38 billion, thus corresponding to six times the total value of international trade in goods and services. This explosive growth in market volumes can be attributed primarily to derivative financial instruments. Trade in derivatives has developed a powerful momentum of its own in recent years, since they can be used not only to hedge exchange rate risks but also to incur risks deliberately and trade them.

Consequently, in recent years activity in the markets for financial and real assets and for commodities has experienced a marked acceleration, with the growth in international financial market transactions outstripping that in real capital movements and the latter in turn outperforming trade in goods and services. To ignore the process of globalization under these circumstances would be like refusing to acknowledge the discovery of America.

And yet globalization means more than just the internationalization of economic processes of exchange. 'Globalization is based on an entirely new configuration of space and time' (Schmid, 1996). In particular, with the new information and communications technologies the networking of businesses and locations is possible beyond national borders, which represents a great leap forward in the qualitative dimension of economic development. New forms of functional division of labour, networked structures and changes in the pattern of demarcation between companies are reactions to the growing pressure of competition and to the increasing environmental uncertainties brought about by the progressive globalization of markets:

- Competitive pressure from globalization may impel companies to be more thorough than they had previously been in their efforts to optimize the relationship between corporate mission, the degree of vertical integration and the competitive environment. As a result of this process, many businesses have decided to concentrate on their core competences, which means that they need to establish new partnerships in order to ensure the availability of the complementary expertise they require. 'In order to be able to develop the combination of core competenences and complementary expertise required to implement its competitive strategy, the corporation is often compelled to rely on cooperation and strategic alliances with other companies' (Picot, Reichwald and Wiegand, 1996).
- As a result of the growing environmental uncertainty, which faces companies with the threat of their particular investments suddenly becoming valueless, it is worthwhile for companies to share risk, even to some extent in the field of their core competences, and to cooperate with other operators in the market.
- The growing pressure of competition is forcing companies to step up their innovative efforts, and this often demands linkages between previously distinct areas of technology (Schutz-Wild and

Lutz, 1997). Cooperation between businesses which had previously had quite different technological orientations therefore becomes a strategic success factor.

- Cost optimization strategies by manufacturers along the entire added value chain (systematic rationalization) are compelling direct suppliers to operate as systems suppliers. This competence can often be acquired by the relevant equipment suppliers only through horizontal cooperation agreements.

As a result of these varied responses to changing market conditions, many businesses are tending to forge close links with other legally and commercially independent businesses. These links are normally long term by their very nature, in order to prevent or minimize the risk of any potential exploitation of dependencies by the respective interests in the market. Only under such conditions are the parties involved prepared to contribute certain assets, such as specific human resources and special software solutions, and share their individual expertise. Basically, these types of network are founded on mutual trust in order to minimize the likelihood of opportunistic behaviour and to make elaborate control mechanisms unnecessary.

Thus these relatively new network structures cannot be reduced to their technical dimension, but also appear to be highly sensitive social phenomena which are strongly dependent on their historical, infrastructural, socio-cultural and political contexts. In this connection there are two main arguments that can be advanced in support of the proposition that the importance of the regional level is enhanced under conditions of globalization. Firstly, these increasingly specialized companies rely on an abundant supply of external services and infrastructure facilities (Kern, 1994). Training, R&D, communications and information, as well as soft locational factors in the regional environment of companies, are therefore playing an increasing role in competitiveness. Secondly, the level of trust required for the purpose of concluding cooperation agreements cannot be automatically assumed. Rather – to express it in terms of transaction cost theory – it depends on the kind of 'transaction atmosphere' that exists, which encompasses not only the technological and legal but also, and in particular, the social conditions required for the coordination of transactions (Williamson, 1985, 1991). The greater the climate of trust, the more likely it is that partnership as a form of coordination can establish itself as a viable alternative to power and hierarchy.

At this point, it seems appropriate to mention the theory of the innovative milieu, as it is perfectly consistent with the transaction cost theory approach.

> A milieu can be described as a specific constellation of economic, social, political and cultural players who have developed specific forms of communication and interaction. A particular role in this is assigned to the concept of 'trust', by which is meant relations of mutual goodwill between business competitors which at the same time are engaged in cooperation. A milieu provides the companies with dynamic stimuli, and the interaction of the companies reproduces this milieu. (Häußermann, 1995).

Basically this innovative milieu approach assumes that competitive businesses are more reliant on innovative networks now than in the past and that the innovative milieu represents the regionalized dimension of an innovative network (Sternberg, 1995).

To no small extent, the fact that goodwill relationships cannot easily be established with modern methods of technical communication underlines the particular importance of the region for the concept of trust. In the foreseeable future, face-to-face contact will remain essential for establishing, reviewing and extending goodwill relationships. Although the use of modern IT and communications technology may theoretically increase the possibility of doing without face-to-face contact, it is still a long way from eliminating it completely (Beckmann, Brandt and Kastning, 1996). From these arguments relating to the nature of business communications, we may conclude that in a world of networked economies with global processes of exchange, it is nevertheless still economically worthwhile to maintain a high level of locational proximity between partners involved in cooperation. Furthermore, it may be supposed that in view of the existing advantages of agglomeration, the nodes of the modern networked economy will be concentrated in metropolitan areas.

INTRAREGIONAL OR INTERREGIONAL NETWORKING?

From the above consideration, the most logical conclusion appears at first sight to be that successful regions excel precisely because they have large numbers of innovative companies which are more or less closely networked with each other on an intraregional basis, and also quite closely networked to other regional institutions with complementary competences, such as regional R&D establishments. However, it is not quite as simple as that. Even if it is assumed that regional cooperation is highly significant, the following assumptions are also worth noting:

- The competitiveness of regional companies will grow in line with their success in supraregional and international competition. To this extent, intraregional networks form the backbone supporting interregional alliances.
- With the growing pace of globalization, SMEs in particular will increasingly have to face supraregional and international competition and will consequently also enter into interregional alliances in order to secure their markets.
- In many cases new alliances are based on personal contacts, and interregional partnerships often develop as a result of former employees, whose role in establishing cooperation is often decisive, now being employed with companies and institutions in supraregional locations.

For these reasons the relationship between intraregional and interregional cooperation therefore remains a contradictory one. A high degree of networking between regional companies themselves does not exclude strong cooperative links to supraregional institutions with complementary competences and vice versa.

In my view, the preliminary findings of a research project by the German Research Association on the technological change and regional development in Europe, which addresses intra- and interregional networking among SMEs in particular regions of Germany, also point to a tendency for things to move in this direction. The regions initially compared were economic areas of Baden in the state of Baden-Württemberg, the state of Saxony and the research triangle of Hanover, Braunschweig and Göttingen in Lower Saxony. The preliminary findings of the research project led by Professor Ludwig Schätzl of the Economic Geography Department of the University of Hanover basically revealed the following (Sternberg, 1997):

- Among SMEs with network links to other interests in the market, innovative companies are clearly overrepresented as compared to non-innovative companies.

- Of all the potential groups of external coooperation partners, the one that innovative companies cooperate with most is that of research establishments within their own regions.
- Among the regions compared, the region of Baden, which is considered in Germany to be particularly innovative, is the one with the highest proportion of intraregional networking. Whereas about half of the innovative SMEs in the region cooperate with companies within the state of Baden-Württemberg, the equivalent figure for the research triangle of Hanover, Braunschweig and Göttingen – relating to cooperation with companies within the state of Lower Saxony – amounts to only about one-third.
- Although the proportion of SMEs with network links to R&D institutions varies only slightly between the comparative regions, Baden has the lowest proportion of intraregional cooperation links between companies and research institutions.

Overall, these results suggest that there can be no question of a dichotomy in which either intra- or interregional networks can be identified as determining the economic success of regional businesses. Rather, intra- and interregional cooperation tend to have a reciprocal relationship. Partnerships which work well within the region can therefore improve the chances of successful interregional networking. Consequently, activities by regional players aimed at improving conditions for the development of innovative networks or innovative milieus are justifiable. Against this background, it is essential from a regional economic perspective for the development potential of regional partnerships to be examined more closely.

THE BUTCHER, THE BAKER ...

Some time ago Reich (1994) reported that strategies of crisis management in response to structural change generally fall into two categories, which he called the butcher strategy and the baker strategy.

The butcher increases his profitability by cutting out everything that is superfluous. The baker improves his by adding value to the individual ingredients. In other words, the baker strategy means investing in the skills of the employees by providing both in-house and external training. As a result, companies acquire key staff with the necessary authority to make decisions or improve the production process to boost sales.

Applied to the regional business environment, this would mean investing more in intelligent ways of improving regional innovative potential rather than lowering locational costs to the levels of the Far East. There is a great deal to support the theory that 'cheap locations' are not equipped to manufacture leading-edge products (Brake, 1995). Advanced infrastructure, highly developed training and scientific environments and high quality soft locational factors do not normally show any great correlation with low locational costs. The concentration of the most modern production and service activities in conurbations is an indication that these relatively expensive but also very high quality locational factors may be necessary preconditions for economic activity. Cooperative links between the potential initiators of innovation, which require a high level of trust, do not flourish in an atmosphere of social and cultural conflict, but require underlying conditions which promote the establishment of social contacts, support cooperative bargaining methods and foster the development of corporate cultures which favour consensus and mutual trust.

In order to forestall any misconception that the interests of the employees do not play any part in these conditions, it should be noted that such a 'transaction atmosphere' also favours the development of industrial relations of a kind that are beneficial in dealing with complex work processes. For processes of this kind which require great care, creativity and the use of specific knowledge shared between a number of employees, long-term cooperation is advantageous due to the high cost of replacing lost employees (Nutzinger and Eger, 1997). A 'voice mechanism', which the German model of labour relations is based on, requires a fundamental consensus and a minimum level of social harmony. Such social arrangements do not tend to flourish in areas of social conflict.

We are now left with the question of the extent to which innovative networks or milieus are susceptible to political shaping or control. In addition to the tasks of ensuring a closely knit network of facilities for promoting innovation, transfer of knowledge and cooperative links in the regional economy, of maintaining a supply of well trained manpower with a varied range of qualifications, of providing high quality facilities for initial and further training and links to efficient communications and transportation systems, and, in the field of soft locational factors, of providing quality living and housing conditions, there are above all two areas that are important. The first is the matter of networking innovative companies with firms and institutions which are able to offer complementary competences. Second, increased efforts need to be made to bring existing non-commercial R&D staff in the region together with potential commercial users. Such promotional activities ought to be accompanied by additional measures to develop internal innovative capabilities within the business, as innovative companies show an above average inclination to enter into cooperative arrangements.

Such programmes can only be realized where suitable projects can be found which invite identification and afford enough potential to attract innovative players within a region. Promoting cooperation in terms of establishing network structures can only ever be project-oriented. At least with specific projects there is a chance that different players with different competences will be brought together and that additional problem-solving expertise will emerge as a result of collective learning processes. As a result, new synergies are released which are vital for innovation.

In a different context, Matzner (1997) has commented that the promotion of partnerships needs to be directed. As potential cooperation partners do not necessarily recognize the advantage of closer cooperation from the outset, as in the much quoted example of the prison walls dilemma, it is the task of the responsible political authorities to set up positive sum games.

With the approach of EXPO 2000, Hanover has a unique opportunity to exploit this World Exposition as a 'laboratory of the future' in its own regional environment, and thereby provide additional incentives for all kinds of forms of cooperation and unusual innovative efforts. In his outstanding analysis of special regional activities within limited periods of time, Siebel (1992) noted that traditional World Expositions based on the rationale of the Eiffel Tower or cathedral models created substantial problems and risks for regional development. This is another reason why it is necessary for the World Exposition in Hanover to be conceived as a 'new type of EXPO'. Following this line of thought, it is vital that the EXPO project should be linked to a strategy of mobilizing regional players and resources. Not only the EXPO project entitled 'The City and Region as Exhibits', which involves regional model solutions to problems relating to the EXPO theme of 'Humankind, Nature, Technology' being shown in settings away from exhibition grounds, but also numerous areas of as yet unmet regional need in the fields of energy, transport, the environment and communications technology offer a wealth of opportunities for the promotion of project-based networks. Many businesses and academic institutions in the Hanover region possess special competences in presenting solutions to these specifically regional areas of need, which at the same time are areas of great potential for the future. Combining these competences could release forces of innovation which would afford the businesses in the region in particular new market opportunities. However, many of the players whose activities are relevant to regional policy would have to change their attitudes before an aggressive innovation strategy of this kind could be initiated. To this extent, there is still reason to fear that in terms of economic stimulation EXPO 2000 will go down in history as a chapter of wasted opportunities.

CONCLUSION

In Germany at least, promoting innovative networks is not considered a natural part of the repertoire of activities of local authority and regional policy-makers. According to a survey by the German Institute for Urban Studies (DIFU) only one-fifth of the cities questioned had set up networks or networking concepts 'in any form' (Hollbach-Grömig, 1996). The promotion of networking is clearly still in its infancy and there are still very many unknown quantities. Whereas traditional concepts of economic incentives are currently experiencing a revival in many areas, networking and milieu approaches are in many instances not being practised widely enough, even where the material conditions appear to be favourable. The reasons behind this include both the intangible nature of the new concepts and the fact that any success is only perceptible in the long term. The fact that the relatively new regional economic theories relating to innovative networks and milieus have still not been empirically tried and tested may also play a part. With the extension of the German Research Association study referred to above to a total of eleven European regions, including metropolitan areas such as Vienna, Stockholm and Barcelona, this empirical shortfall will soon be substantially reduced. There will nevertheless always be an element of risk attached to any determined networking policy. 'If you do something new, you cannot be sure that it will be better. But if you want to do something better, you have to do something new' (Georg Christoph Lichtenberg).

References

K. Beckmann, A. Brandt and C. Kastning, 'Multimedia in der Hannover Region – Informations- und Kommunikationstechnologien Standortfaktor [Multimedia in the Hanover region – IT and communications technologies as investment conditions]', *Beiträge zur regionalen Entwicklung [Contributions to Regional Development]* 56 (1996).

BIZ [Bank for International Settlements], various years.

K. Brake, 'Auf den Weg in die Dienstleistungsgesellschaft – Städte ohne Industrie [Towards a society of service providers – cities without industry]', in DIFU [German Institute for Urban Studies], *Produzierendes Gewerbe in der Stadt [Manufacturing Enterprise in the City]* (Berlin, 1995).

H. Häußerman, *Die ökonomische Entwicklung der Großstädte [Economic Development of Large Cities]*, Lecture given on 16 June 1995, Hanover (unpublished).

B. Hollbach-Grömig, *Kommunale Wirtschaftsförderung in den 90er Jahren [Promotion of Economic Development at Local Level in the Nineties]* (Berlin, 1996).

International Monetary Fund (IMF), *International Financial Statistics*, various years.

H. Kern, 'Globalisierung und Regionalisierung [Globalization and regionalization]', in W. Krumbein (ed.), *Ökonomische und politische Netzwerke in der Region [Economic and Political Networks in the Regions]* (Münster and Hamburg, 1994) pp. 141–52.

P. Krugman, *Peddling Prosperity* (New York, 1994).

P. Krugman, 'Wettbewerbsfahigkeit, Eine gefahrliche Wahnvorstellung [Competitiveness – a dangerous illusion]', in *Jahrbuch Arbeit und Technik 1996 [1996 Labour and Technology Yearbook]* (Bonn, 1996) pp. 37–49.

B. Lutz, M. Hartmann and H. Hirsch-Kreinsen (eds), *Produzieren im 21. Jahrundert. Herausforderungen für die deutsche Industrie [Production in the 21st Century: Challenges for German Industry]* (Frankfurt and New York, 1996).

E. Matzner, 'Inszenierung von Positiv-Summen-Spielen als primäre Aufgabe der Politik [Positive sum games as a principal task of policy]', *Gewerkschaftliche Monatshefte [Union Monthly Bulletins]*, 4 (1997) 232–8.

H. Nutzinger and T. Eger, 'Arbeitsmarkt zwischen Abwanderung und Widerspruch' [Labour market between exit and voice], *FAZ*, 5 April 1997.

Organization for Economic Cooperation and Development (OECD), 'International direct Investments', in *Statistics Yearbook* (1995).

A. Picot, R. Reichwald and R.T. Wiegand, *Die grenzenlose Unternehmung – Information, Organization und Management [Enterprise Without Frontiers – Information, Organization and Management]*, 2nd edn (Wiesbaden, 1996).

R. Reich, 'Backen statt Schlachten [Baking not butchering]', *Die Zeit*, 8 February 1994.

C Schmid, 'Urbane Region und Territorialverhältnis – zur Regulation des Urbanisierungsprozesses [Urban region and territorial relations – regulation of the urbanization process]', in M. Bruch and H.-P. Krebs (eds), *Unternehmen Globus [Global Enterprise]* (Münster, 1996) pp. 224–53.

L. Schutz-Wild and B. Lutz, *Industrie vor dem Quantensprung – Eine Zukunft für die Produktion in Deutschland* [*Industry Before the Quantum Leap: A Future for Production in Germany*] (Berlin, 1997).

W. Siebel, 'Die Internationale Bauausstellung Emscher-Park – Eine Strategie zur ökonomischen, ökologischen und sozialen Erneuerung alter Industrieregionen [International construction exhibition at Emscher Park: a strategy for economic, environmental and social renewal of old industrial regions]', in H. Häussermann (ed.), *Ökonomie und Politik in alten Industrieregionen Europas* [*Economy and Policy in the Old Industrial Regions in Europe*] (Basel, Boston and Berlin, 1992) pp. 214–31.

R. Sternberg, *Technologiepolitik und High-Tech-Regionen – Ein internationaler Vergleich* [Technology Policy and High-Tech Regions: An International Comparison] (Münster and Hamburg, 1995).

R. Sternberg, *Intraregional vs Interregional Linkages between R&D Institutions and Innovative SMEs: Empirical Results from Recent Surveys in German Regions*, unpublished manuscript (Cologne, 1997).

United Nations Conference on Trade and Development (UNCTAD), *World Investment Report* (1995).

O.E. Williamson, *The Economic Institutions of Capitalism* (New York and London, 1985).

O.E. Williamson, 'Comparative economic organization: the analysis of discrete structural alternatives', *Administrative Science Quarterly*, 36 (1991) 269–96.

13 Local Capacity in Bristol – Tentative Steps towards Institutional Thickness

Nick Oatley and Christine Lambert

INTRODUCTION

The first part of this chapter discusses the concept of local institutional capacity. Local institutional capacity generally refers to the ability or power of localities to shape or create a successful future for themselves, and to adapt to the increasing rate of change in markets and in government policy regimes. It therefore relates closely to discussions of the relative competitiveness of localities in an increasingly internationalized economy, where competitiveness is seen to be related to the economic, environmental and locational attributes of places and to their political and administrative capacity to compete. In the second part of the chapter we chart the evolution of local capacity in Bristol, looking particularly at recent attempts to create/enhance institutional capacity through the development of partnership, collaboration and consensus building, efforts made necessary by the diminution of old powers and competencies in local government, the uncertain future of some key local economic sectors and policy innovation by central government.

Interest in local capacity has grown in the context of increasing awareness of the importance of the impact of international economic processes on local areas. This encompasses the growth of processes of international economic integration and the transnational mobility of capital consequent on the development of information technology, and the development of transnational government and trading blocs within which economic activity is increasingly footloose. Alongside this is the growing significance of inter-local competition for mobile investment and state funding and a growth of interest in the factors that allow localities to exercise economic and political leverage in order to capture and sustain growth. In addition, the growth of new economic sectors (producer services such as finance, business services and research and development and consumer industries such as tourism and leisure) make new demands on an urban environment:

> What is at issue is not simply access to markets, inputs or labour supply. Rather it is factors such as access to key decision-makers, up-to-the-minute information, specialized services, an accommodating regulatory environment, underpinned by a quality of life that facilitates the recruitment of skilled and highly mobile professionals.
>
> (Cheshire and Gordon, 1996)

Rather than seeing cities and local areas as helpless victims of a globalizing economic order, this sort of analysis emphasizes that localities are in a position to influence their own destinies.

DEFINING CAPACITY AT THE LOCAL LEVEL

The factors that help to shape and constrain the capacity of localities to adapt to a changing external economic and political environment are diverse. In the literature on the relative competitiveness of different cities and success of local economic development strategies, factors operating at a number of different levels are discussed.

First, there is a set of factors that operates at the international, national and regional level and that attributes cities to specific niches or nodes within the overall urban hierarchy and shapes wider forces of growth and decline (Fainstein, 1990). Second, these factors are mediated by national political responses to restructuring that shape the kinds of policies it is possible for localities to pursue. Government policies with respect to urban and regional development, to subnational government structures and local government powers and resources will set limits and create differential potential for 'local proactivity'. Third, there are factors specific to particular places – the local social and economic structure, the range of political interests and the relations between them, and the actions they take – that also help to determine the strategies developed to adapt to economic and political change.

The first set of factors includes shifting patterns of investment and disinvestment that result in new patterns of uneven development. Sharp decline in manufacturing investment throughout western developed countries has been accompanied by service sector growth, though regions and cities experiencing the worst consequences of industrial decline have not necessarily been those to benefit from the growth of new industries, revealed in the 1980s in widening regional economic disparities.

In relation to the second set of factors, the UK has experienced the decline of national policies to direct and manage regional economic development, and a growing emphasis on spatially targeted urban regeneration initiatives. In the period since 1979 private sector led regeneration has been emphasized, with local authorities displaced from a central role and initiatives focusing on physical infrastructure and property development. However, in the most recent round of urban policy innovation, local authorities have been given a strategic coordinating role, albeit one which requires collaboration with business and community sectors in devising and delivering urban regeneration strategies. More broadly, local government budgets have been reduced and competencies and powers have been transferred to other public, semi-public or private agencies. Formal regional and subregional structures are weakly developed in the British context, and the latest round of local government reform if anything contributes to institutional fragmentation and undermines the capacity for strategic economic development. Hence in the British context the capacity of local government to promote local economic and social development has been substantially reduced, and the mismatch of administrative boundaries and functional economic areas undermines the ability to develop coherent responses to economic restructuring. Hence local governments are increasingly pushed into strategic alliances with neighbouring authorities and with the private and community sectors to overcome the contemporary fragmentation of much urban governance.

Inter-urban competition has been given an additional boost in the UK by the emergence of a new phase of competitive urban policy (Stewart, 1996). Through initiatives such as City Challenge, the Single Regeneration Budget (SRB) and Capital Challenge central government has explicitly put funding for regeneration and economic development activities up for a competitive bidding process. To succeed in the new competition for public funding, localities must put forward proposals designed to improve their structural competitiveness. Moreover, funding is conditional on localities putting in place institutional structures that bring the business and community sectors within the policy-making and implementation process and which give the impression, at least, of consensus among the relevant actors.

Following the recognition that real power to reshape urban areas now lies beyond local government, capacity is increasingly seen as exercised or articulated through inter-organizational relationships.

This reflects a new set of ideas that assert the significance of local factors that enable adjustment (or not) to wider processes of economic, political and social change and the increased salience of linkages and networks between stakeholders. Hence there has been research examining the motivations and activities of different local institutions and relations between them, alternatively conceptualized as: leadership (Judd and Parkinson, 1990), growth coalitions (Harding, 1991), policy regimes (DiGaetano and Klemanski, 1993), local modes of regulation (Mayer, 1994), institutional thickness (Amin and Thrift, 1994) and collective action (Cheshire and Gordon, 1996), all expressing the idea that successful localities display certain characteristics in terms of local institutional arrangements.

There is a good deal of overlap in these accounts of changing forms of urban governance. For Judd and Parkinson, leadership capacity is defined in terms of 'the range, stability and durability of local mechanisms and alliances which have been developed that allow a city to respond proactively to external economic pressures'. Successful cities are those where local elites can project a coherent image for the locality and exploit national resources of money, legislation and political support. Amin and Thrift (1994) seek to identify the key factors which 'allow certain places to retain a high degree of local economic "integrity"'. They highlight the degree of institutional thickness in a locality, referring to the number and diversity of institutions (firms, business organizations, trade associations, local authorities, development agencies, marketing organizations, etc.), the level of interaction between them, coalitions that serve to socialize costs and control rogue behaviour, and the development of a shared agenda for economic development. For Cheshire and Gordon (1996) collective action to promote territorial competitiveness is enhanced where a small number of authorities represent a functional economic region, in which there is complementarity of interests and a strong sense of cultural and/or political identity that can override local factional interests.

In regime theory, the configuration of local power structures and pattern of governance is linked to the wider economic context – which sets the conditions for local strategy development and the national political context – establishing the parameters for local governance (DiGaetano and Klemanski, 1993). Thus the character of regimes and their primary purpose changes over time and from place to place. A common feature of regime research is the emergence of energetic growth coalitions in the late 1980s in response to shifts in the economic and political context. More optimistically, there is a belief that the new (post-Fordist) local governance creates the potential for a significant redistribution of political power to groups (minority groups, women, environmental interests) that have traditionally been excluded from the centres of decision-making (Mayer, 1994).

Thus contemporary discussions of capacity start with the assumption that the effectiveness of local action depends on the cooperation of a wide range of governmental and non-governmental agencies between which there is a high level of interaction, often institutionalized in various forms of partnership. The purpose of such alliances is: to establish consensus and a shared vision for the development of a locality; to mobilize skills, expertise and resources to enhance competitiveness; to engage in networking and lobbying in relevant markets and political arenas; to exercise clear and effective leadership while maintaining flexibility; and to deliver on plans.

However, as Amin and Thrift (1994) point out there is no functional linkage between institutional thickness and economic development. Some successful localities may not display the characteristics of institutional thickness, while some that do continue to decline economically, highlighting the role of wider economic and political factors in shaping the fate of particular localities. Furthermore, there is no guarantee that the benefits of growth will be equally distributed within localities. The growth coalitions perspective highlights the danger that alliances may be private sector dominated and pursue a narrow business agenda. In the Judd and Parkinson (1990) review of international experience the task of equitably distributing, as well as creating, wealth had eluded most of the cities studied. Neither is there clear evidence that many of the activities undertaken by local coalitions are effective in actually delivering economic benefits. Cheshire and Gordon (1996) conclude that much of the marketing expenditure of localities is largely symbolic and wasteful, while incentive packages are zero-sum, benefiting one locality at the expense of others in the same region. Finally, some commentators express doubts about the stability and coherence of the growth coalitions that are emerging. Coalitions may be built on a 'fragile consensus that survives by avoiding the kinds of difficult choices that may prove divisive' (Bassett, 1996). Peck and Tickell (1994) point to the shaky commitment of some business representatives and doubt whether a stable form of new urban governance has yet emerged. Indeed the proliferation of local partnerships and coalitions may be adding to the fragmentation and disorganization of local politics and governance and actually undermining capacity.

CAPACITY FOR LOCAL ACTION IN BRISTOL

The remainder of this chapter discusses capacity for local action in Bristol. A number of phases of economic and policy development can be identified, which demonstrate the interaction of wider economic conditions, political factors that influence the scope for local pro-activity and local social relations. The discussion of Bristol's capacity for local action is divided into four periods that closely mirror the phases of economic change and policy development identified by Boddy, Lovering and Bassett (1986), Bassett (1996) and DiGaetano and Klemanski (1993). The four periods are:

- 1945–74: pro-growth consensus, traditional corporatist alliance;
- 1974–9: fractured capacity, contested growth;
- 1979–91: institutional fragmentation and conflict;
- 1991–7: tentative steps towards 'institutional thickness'.

Capacity for local action during 'The Long Boom' – pro-growth consensus, traditional corporatist alliance: 1945–74

Bristol, during the period of the long postwar boom, experienced rapid expansion in the traditional major areas of employment such as the aircraft, tobacco, and printing and packaging industries. Office development expanded rapidly in the mid-1960s, transforming the central area of the city, and the construction of the M4 and M5 and the Severn Bridge made Bristol a focal point for development. The area acquired an image of growth and prosperity.

Political control by moderate Labour majorities was interrupted by brief periods of Conservative rule, but both parties shared a similar vision of Bristol's future as a commercial, industrial and port city. The era was marked by active municipal enterprise, manifest by heavy investment in public infrastructure and backed by a liberal planning regime. Policies were devised for planned development to maintain and diversify the manufacturing base and to provide for the growing demand for warehousing and distribution facilities, providing employment opportunities adjacent to large public housing development in south and east Bristol. The local authority was seen as the natural agent of economic development, and capacity was clearly enhanced by agreement between the local authority and business interests on most policy issues. The business elite, although lacking direct representation on the council, nevertheless had developed a strong network of formal and informal contacts with leading councillors and officers, particularly with respect to planning issues (Clements, 1969). Capacity was further facilitated through the forging of a strong corporatist alliance involving local business leaders, trade unionists and the county borough in efforts to build a new deep-water port at Avonmouth and associated trading and industrial estates (Boddy, Lovering and Bassett, 1986, pp. 172–4).

All of these policies were pursued in the context of economic growth. During this period unemployment was low and cyclical fluctuations comparatively weak. Only towards the end of the 1960s did the long boom falter and a transition phase to international recession begin. This coincided with local government reorganization and a fracturing of institutional competencies and the postwar economic consensus in local economic policy.

Fractured capacity, contested growth: 1974–9

The early 1970s saw the emergence of major changes in the growth patterns of industrialized countries, as the onset of recession signalled the end of the long postwar boom. Manufacturing job loss accelerated in Bristol in the early 1970s and unemployment rose above the national rate. Employment in service industries grew, however, due partly to the relocation of major financial companies from London and the expansion of public sector services. During this period the threat to the aerospace industry, caused principally by the rundown of the Concorde programme, demonstrated the vulnerability of an important sector of Bristol's economy (Lovering and Thrift, 1993). This major restructuring in the local economy and rising unemployment were a source of major concern for the local authority, the Bristol Chamber of Commerce and other bodies concerned with the local economy.

At the start of this period, Bristol experienced another form of restructuring under the Local Government Act of 1972, which stripped away Bristol's county borough status and powers. In 1974 Bristol became one of six districts within the newly established County of Avon. Bristol lost control to the county of the most significant local services (education, social services and highway planning), and the two-tier local government structure created tension between the Labour controlled Bristol City Council, some of the surrounding districts and the Conservative controlled county.

Economic transformation and associated changes in social structure, combined with local government reorganization, brought about a political realignment in the city. The centralized decision-making structures centred on dominant leaders and leadership groupings were dismantled and replaced with a more collective approach to governing. The pro-growth policies that prevailed during the long boom were also questioned. DiGaetano and Klemanski (1993) described this in terms of two competing power centres within the city council, one based on the old pro-growth alliance, and a second which formed around growth management. The result was a dual or fractured regime in which pro-growth and growth management elements coexisted uneasily. However, Bassett (1996) suggests that policy difference in Bristol at this time was more complex than growth versus anti-growth lobbies. All factions of the Labour Party and indeed other parties accepted the arguments for growth, but there was conflict over the form that growth should take. Bassett suggests that these conflicts should also be seen as a local manifestation of what was a long and bitter battle in the 1980s for the soul of the national Labour Party.

Just at the time when local proactivity was required to respond to the problems caused by economic restructuring, Bristol's institutional capacity was fragmented. The competing power bases that emerged within both the city and the county weakened the capacity to act, leading to frustrated attempts over the next three years to construct and coordinate a city-wide development strategy.

Institutional fragmentation and conflict: 1979–91

Industrial restructuring accelerated during the early part of this period. Manufacturing job loss was particularly severe although growth in service employment and buoyancy in the defence and aerospace sector substantially protected the local economy from the impact of the 1979–82 recession. The high level of growth in white-collar services was due to the attraction of mobile investment to the area, most notably from London and the South East. By the mid-1980s Bristol had acquired the image of a prosperous 'Sunbelt City' located at the western end of an M4 growth corridor.

This image and the reality of relative economic success could not be attributed to the institutional milieu which continued to be fragmented and conflict-ridden during this period. There was a growth of left-wing ideas and representation during the first half of this period which led to the adoption of some radical municipal socialist approaches in economic development. However, this New Left group failed to secure overall control which led to disputes on a number of policy issues.

Bassett's (1996, p. 543) view of city council policy in this period was that 'in spite of radical initiatives in some policy areas (economic development, racial equality, etc.) change in many areas was blocked by bitter infighting that often ended in political stalemate'.

Stewart (1990, p. 39) identified a state of indecision over the future direction of policy, diagnosed by many as complacency, which tended to lead to inaction. This inaction was compounded by an absence of civic leadership and was accentuated by the divisions between and within both private and public sectors. Stewart observed that since the city seemed to be able to survive adequately without strategic direction, the culture was one of policy stagnation and administrative inertia. Commenting further on the capacity for local action during this period, Stewart states that:

> In Bristol the tradition has been one of mistrust and competition between organizations and conflict over roles and function. City and County have been in the main at loggerheads since the 1974 reorganization, the private sector fails to speak with a united voice, local government has adopted a conflictual rather than a conciliatory stance towards the new initiatives of the centre. Thus inter-organizational competition is allied to ... complacency ... leading to a marked lack of local capacity to respond to the challenges of change in the 1990s. (1990, p. 40)

In addition, the capacity of the local authority was further limited by central government financial constraints and grant reductions which began in the early 1980s culminating in formal control of local spending through 'rate capping' later in the decade, thereby eliminating discretion over local spending. Central government housing policy change saw the virtual end of municipal house building, and a requirement to cooperate with other agencies in meeting housing needs. At county level, powers and responsibilities were also reducing, with reforms in transport, education and social services. Increasingly, central government policy with respect to local service responsibilities was requiring cooperation with other agencies. Bristol was, for example, forced to start joint working with housing associations in the city and to introduce a programme of land disposals to the private and voluntary sectors. A private sector dominated Training and Enterprise Council was set up to deal with training and labour market issues and an Urban Development Corporation was established in 1989 to bring about the regeneration of a large part of east-central Bristol, although the city and the county resisted its establishment and refused to cooperate with the new agency.

The challenges facing Bristol came into sharp focus by 1990. The recession of the late 1980s affected financial services severely and the continued success of the sector in the city was questioned. Defence-related industries were hit by the changing global political climate and cutbacks in defence expenditure. Competition for inward investment was also being felt from South Wales. The successful local economy of the early 1980s was beginning to look far more vulnerable later in the decade. Indicators of this were much higher unemployment levels and considerable amounts of empty office space in the city centre.

Tentative steps towards 'institutional thickness': 1991 to 1997

The early 1990s saw a significant change in the political and institutional landscape of Bristol. There has been an increasing emphasis on collaboration, the formation of new partnerships between the public and private sectors and the emergence of a more active business elite (Bassett, 1996). One can identify three interconnected strands to this emergent policy regime.

The first is the emergence of a new business elite which coalesced around the Bristol Initiative, launched in 1991. The Bristol Initiative (TBI) was a business leadership team that set out to fill the gap created by the ineffectual Chamber of Commerce. The Initiative secured wide membership from ninety of the largest employers in Bristol, from local government, Bristol Development Corporation and Avon and Somerset Police, and soon established itself as an influential player in a number of partnership activities such as the provision of social housing, the celebration of 'Bristol 97' and the formation of a Bristol Cultural Partnership. In 1993 TBI merged with the Chamber of Commerce to create the Bristol Chamber of Commerce and Initiative, which secured its pivotal role in the increasing number of partnerships that were emerging in the Bristol subregion (Snape and Stewart, 1995).

The second strand of partnership activity relates to attempts to develop a regional profile. There has been a growing awareness among all key actors in the city of the increasing competition between cities for scarce mobile investment. A number of partnerships emerged in Bristol with the explicit purpose of developing a strategy and image for Bristol to compete with neighbouring areas and other cities in Britain and continental Europe (the Western Development Partnership, the West of England Initiative and West of England Development Agency).

The Western Development Partnership (WDP), for example, brought together the business sector, the Training and Enterprise Council, the local authorities and the universities in the area. The organization is oriented to inward investment, with a strong emphasis on the economic competitiveness of the Bristol subregion. At the press conference of the launch of WDP, the chief executive underlined the importance of this collaborative activity by stating that: 'partnership is the only key which will unlock us from the parochialism, rivalries, suspicions, complacency, and procrastinations that have hampered our region in the past, and given other regions, both in the UK and throughout Europe, a free hand to leave us standing' (Bassett, 1996, p. 545).

The third strand of partnership formation relates to the development of a number of city council-led partnerships to promote cultural development (The Cultural Development Partnership), to manage the central shopping district (Broadmead Management Board), to develop Canon's Marsh (Harbourside Partnership) and to gain funding from central government competitive initiatives, the Lottery funds and the European Union (Bristol Regeneration Partnership).

A number of circumstances in the early 1990s brought about this new era of partnership formation. Prime among these was the impact of the 1989–91 recession which sent a series of shockwaves through the local economy, shattering the complacency that had existed in Bristol about the city's economic future. In particular, finance and business services were severely affected, shedding 4 per cent of their employment between 1989 and 1991. The aerospace and related industries also experienced 23 per cent reduction in employment for the same period partly as a result of defence cuts. Unemployment in the Bristol area rose steadily during the early 1990s reaching over 13 per cent by 1993 (Bassett, 1996, p. 544).

Secondly, the continuing fiscal constraints on Bristol through rate-capping (1990–2) combined with the prescription of the 'appropriate' range of economic activities for local authorities in the Local Government and Housing Act 1989 reduced the scope of activities and weakened the potential role of Bristol's economic development. At the same time central government shifted resources and responsibility to the private sector for economic development/regeneration activities, e.g. Urban Development Corporations, Training and Enterprise

Councils and the introduction of City Grant which bypassed local government. Central government has also encouraged a change in the form of local governance through the introduction of Challenge-funded initiatives in which multi-sector partnerships and the establishment of external boards or trusts was essential. This has meant that, increasingly, local authorities have little choice but to seek partnerships with the private sector to combine resources and establish institutional forms appropriate for the pursuit of job creation and growth.

Thirdly, the Conservative Party's fourth consecutive victory at the polls in 1992 led to the pragmatic abandonment of the council's municipal socialist stance. The need to do so was reinforced by two unsuccessful attempts at bidding for City Challenge funding in 1991/92 and 1992/93. In retrospect 1992 represents a watershed in the city in terms of local institutional attitudes and relations. During the first round of City Challenge bidding, limited consultation occurred and few real partnerships were cemented (Lambert and Oatley, 1994). The second bid addressed the issue of partnership more seriously and expanded the range of collaborating interests. One can see the growth of networks and collaborative activity that occurred over the course of the two rounds of bidding in the map of institutions involved in the production of the bids (see Figures 13.1 and 13.2). These networks established for the City Challenge bid were resurrected in response to the establishment of the Challenge Fund element of the Single Regeneration Budget, and the Bristol Regeneration Partnership was formed to respond to and manage the bidding process.

Relations between the city and county began to improve as joint working in relation to the future of the city centre developed, motivated by concerns over traffic growth and the threat from out-of-town retail developments. But just at this point central government announced a review of local government, which concluded with the abolition of the two-tier structure in Avon and the establishment of unitary authorities. This created the possibility of consolidating capacity to deal with a wider range of issues (especially planning and transport) within the city, but threatened the existing strategic capacity to deal with planning and transport issues in the wider city region. One outcome of this process has been the growing realization that joint working between the different authorities in the city and surrounding areas would be necessary.

In summary, capacity for local action in the current period can be characterized as incipient institutional thickness. A range of partnerships have emerged to fill the gaps left by a central government policy

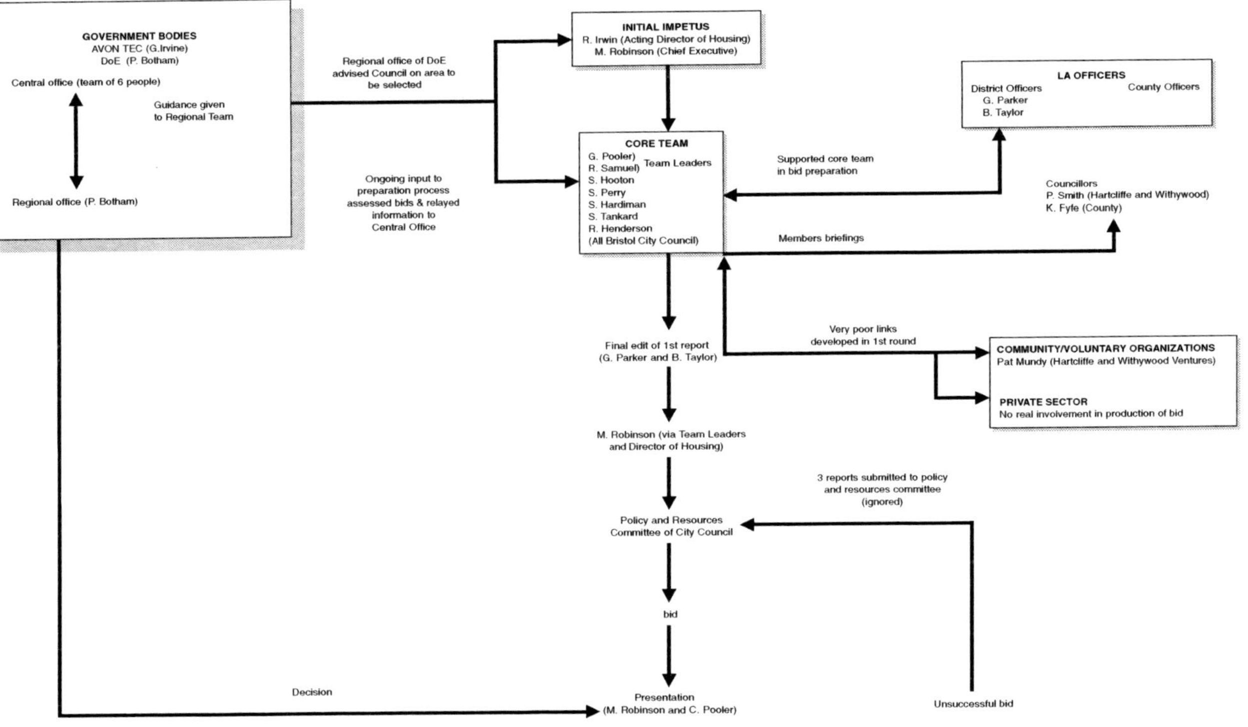

Figure 13.1   Networks established for City of Bristol Challenge bid 1991–2.

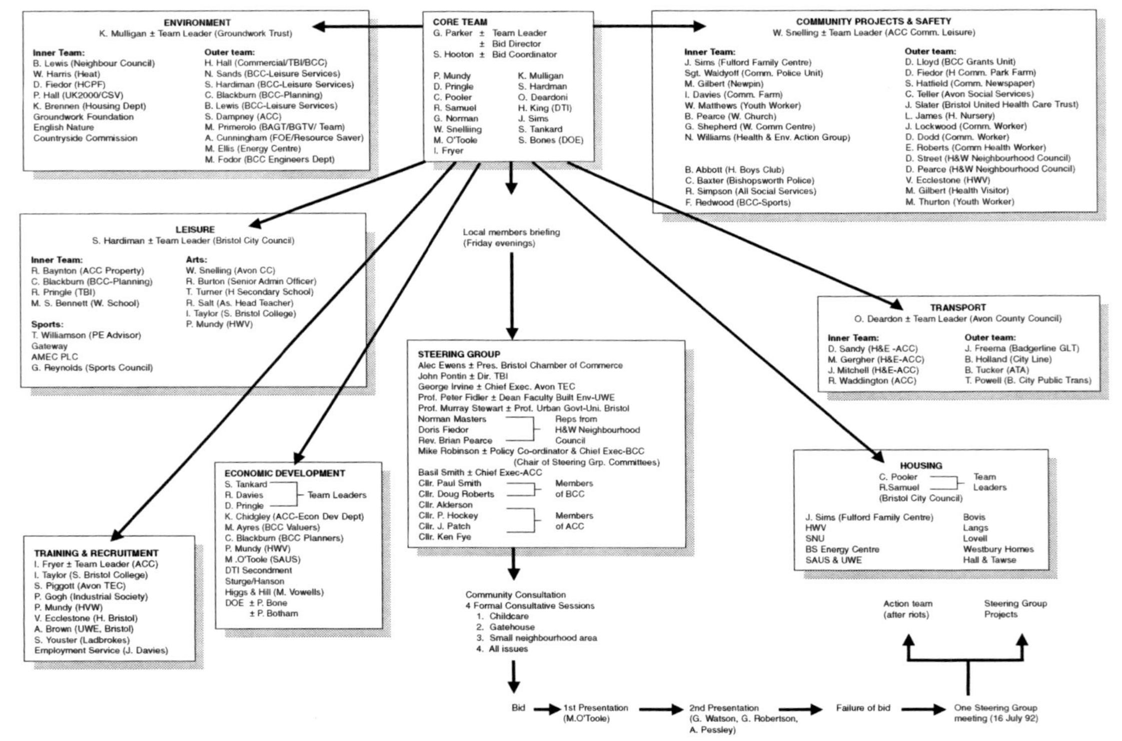

Figure 13.2 Networks established for City of Bristol Challenge bid 1992–3.

of centralization of powers and resources and the absence, in the past, of any civic or business leadership in the locality. Although the new unified authorities offer the prospect of more integrated and strategic approaches towards economic development in time, new structures to coordinate policy across the city region have yet to prove themselves effective.

CONCLUSION

The long postwar boom period of 1945–74 was an era in which there was strong consensus around a pro-growth strategy led by an expansionist city council. The period 1974–9 saw the fracturing of this capacity and the questioning of a Bristol-centred growth strategy with the establishment of a two-tier local government structure involving the creation of Avon County and the stripping away of powers and resources from the ccity Council. The period 1979–91 was characterized by continued fragmentation and conflict, and a significant reduction of local autonomy and centralization of powers and finance. The most recent period, 1991–7, saw the first tentative steps towards the development of 'institutional thickness'.

Despite this history of institutional fragmentation and conflict, Bristol remains, in a national context, a relatively successful city, with below average unemployment and employment concentrated in sectors that (till now) have been growing. This success owes more, however, to central government infrastructure investment (in motorways and rail), spending on defence and a favoured location at the end of the prosperous M4 corridor than to the local institutional milieu. The absence of collaborative working or a strategic policy focus is a marked feature of the period when the city adapted successfully to recession and economic restructuring. Therefore, in the quite recent past 'institutional thickness' does not seem to have been an important ingredient in economic success. The more recent recognition of the need to transform institutional structures and introduce new forms of governance reflects a growing concern about the vulnerability of the local economy, but a key factor is the need to demonstrate partnership in order to effectively access national and European Union funding.

Moreover, this new institutional landscape currently consists of overlapping memberships and ineffective lines of communications between the various partnerships. Although there seems to be a diversity of active partnerships, there is not a coherent, well structured and agreed upon vision for the city with a clear identification of roles and functions for different agencies. One might question the effectiveness of the resulting activity in delivering growth and evenly distributed benefits to the city and subregion. However, some might argue that this apparently chaotic and uncoordinated pattern of institutional arrangements represents precisely the adaptive capacity that is required to respond to the problems currently experienced in Bristol. This perhaps reflects a continuing difficulty in defining and measuring 'local capacity' and evaluating the effectiveness of more or less coordinated arrangements.

It could be argued that Bristol (as a local authority) had a greater capacity to act during the long postwar boom, and that in more recent years this capacity has been diminished by a combination of central government policies and by a local political culture of suspicion and mistrust. Since the break up of the postwar consensus in local politics, the city has been characterized by poor relations between public and private sectors, by negative stereotypes, and by conflict within and between the public and private sectors. Institutional thickness has developed only recently in Bristol as a response to this decline in the local authority's capacity and is part of the changing form of local governance which has been so strongly encouraged by central government. It is perhaps ironic that institutional thickness, a notion often used as a measure of capacity, has developed in Bristol to fill a capacity deficit that has been so apparent in the locality for many years.

References

A. Amin and N. Thrift, *Globalization, Institutions and Regional Development in Europe* (Oxford: Oxford University Press, 1994).

K. Bassett, 'Partnerships, business elites and urban politics: new forms of governance in an English city?', *Urban Studies,* 33 (1996) 539–55

M. Boddy, J. Lovering and K. Bassett, *Sunbelt City: A Study of Economic Change in Britain's Growth Corridor* (Oxford: Oxford University Press, 1986).

P. Cheshire and I. Gordon, 'Territorial competition and the predictability of collective (in)action', *International Journal of Urban and Regional Research,* 20.3 (1996) 383–99.

R. Clements, *Local Notables and the City Council* (London: Macmillan, 1969).

A. DiGaetano, *Ship Shape and Bristol Fashion: Regime Formation in Bristol 1970–1995* (unpublished paper) (1996).

A. DiGaetano and J. Klemanski, 'Urban regimes in comparative perspective; the politics of urban development in Bristol', *Urban Affairs Quarterly,* 29 (1993) 54–83.

S. Fainstein, 'The changing world economy and urban restructuring', in D. Judd and M. Parkinson, *Leadership and Urban Regeneration* (London: Sage, 1990).

A. Harding, 'Growth machines – UK style', *Environment and Planning C,* 9 (1991) 295–316.

D. Judd and M. Parkinson, *Leadership and Urban Regeneration* (London: Sage, 1990).

C. Lambert and N. Oatley, 'Evaluating competitive urban policy: the City Challenge Initiative', in R. Hambleton and H. Thomas (eds), *Urban Policy Evaluation: Challenge and Change* (London: Paul Chapman, 1995).

J. Lovering and N. Thrift, 'Bristol: a city which has reached the end of the old road?', in B. Blanke and R. Smith (eds), *The Future of the Medium-Sized City in Britain and Germany* (London: Anglo-German Foundation, 1993).

M. Mayer, 'Post-Fordist city politics', in A. Amin (ed.), *Post-Fordism: A Reader* (Oxford: Blackwell, 1994).

J. Peck and A. Tickell, 'Searching for a new institutional fix: the after-Fordist crisis and global-local disorder', in A. Amin (ed.), *Post-Fordism: A Reader* (Oxford: Blackwell, 1994).

D. Snape and M. Stewart, *Keeping Up the Momentum: Partnership Working in Bristol and the West* (unpublished paper) (1995).

M. Stewart, *Urban Policy in Thatcher's England*, Working Paper 90 (Bristol: School for Advanced Urban Studies, University of Bristol, 1990).

M. Stewart, 'Competition and competitiveness in urban policy', *Public Money and Management,* July-September (1996) 21–6.

14 Capacity for Action at the Local Level

Hubert Heinelt and Nicola Staeck

INTRODUCTION

Capability and competence in the local policy process have long been a point of controversy in political and scientific debate (see, for example, the opposing views of Mayer (1991) and Häußermann (1991)). Currently, the following issues are being discussed at three different but interrelated levels:

- globalization of the economy with its impact on local competition;
- changes in governance including restructuring of supranational, national and subnational policy level links and the associated shifting balance of power at these different levels;
- the importance of a broadly based local negotiating structure with local authority politicians facing the need to redefine their roles.

It is our intention to begin this chapter with a general summary of the debate on policy capability at the different levels mentioned above before highlighting the relevance of the various views through a survey of European Community structural funds.

THE CURRENT DEBATE ON OPPORTUNITIES IN THE LOCAL POLICY PROCESS

Globalization: 'disappearing cities' versus upgrading local policy

In face of the growing globalization of the economy, local competition is becoming much keener. For Europe, the creation of an economic and monetary union has made this process even more dynamic. Established local economic structures are facing a bleaker future than ever before. In addition to this trend, there is the revolution in communications technology which has rocked the foundations of existing spatial structures and associated traditional concepts of urbanity (Häußermann and Siebel, 1987). Consequently, the debate about disappearing cities (*Verschwinden die Städte?*, Krämer-Badoni 1997) has also been affected.

At the same time, attention is being drawn to opportunities for economic policy at the local level. The issue is that in view of the effect of globalization and the impact of communications opportunities on local decision-making, it is essential that the necessary preconditions are created to address the demands of business. However, these preconditions cannot be created via general structural and economic policy measures introduced by government. They can, however, support endogenous potential through individual case studies of local policy-making.

Changes in governance: back to the Middle Ages or the renaissance of urban policy?

Responsibility for introducing and enforcing binding legislation is becoming less and less a traditional role for the state. This traditional role can be characterized as 'the sovereignty and internal integrated hierarchy of the state in early modern times which replaced the fragmented, polyarchic state at the height of the Middle Ages' (*Staat des hohen Mittelalters*, Mitteis, 1955). In the same way as state sovereignty is being threatened by globalization and cross-border policy networks, hierarchical state domination in internal affairs is also under threat from sophisticated and highly organized social subsystems (see Scharpf, 1992, p. 94; Scharpf, 1994). The changes have produced an institutional reshuffle and shake-up of the political system and institutional structure of governance, resulting in a 'new state architecture' (Grande, 1993). In order to safeguard and restore political governability, governance is to be reshaped beyond the borders of the nation state and within society to incorporate a broad spectrum of policy-makers (Rhodes, 1996).

In order to achieve this, the concept of multilevel governance has been developed specifically in relation to the European Community (Marks, 1993; Hooghe, 1995; Jachtenfuchs and Kohler-Koch, 1996). It does not cover just the importance of the different territorial levels in political processes, but also the role of the various governance mechanisms in and around these levels. It is concerned with how policy instruments of coordinated action can have an impact in a multilevel governance system which is formed by the supranational EC level, member states and the subnational level within the member states, assuming the existing institutional structures. Multilevel governance is also concerned with how the transformation of institutional structures can be brought about. The emphasis on the various governance mechanisms and their (potential) complementary existence in multilevel governance systems is based on the assumption of the existence of a hybrid form of coordination in addition to the market and hierarchical model. This takes the form of policy networks, which link the different, relatively autonomous, public and private sector policy-makers in modern functionally sophisticated societies (cf. Marin and Mayntz, 1991; Kenis and Schneider, 1991).

Policy networks achieve coordinated action by way of negotiation and interaction, and also via debate. They can be characterized as a policy instrument of coordinated action in the same way as democratic majority decisions and hierarchical administrative intervention. They can be seen as distinctive through their deliberate control of the negotiating structure (by the policy-makers involved), instead of coordinating individual interactions via the 'invisible hand' of market controls or exposing modern, functionally sophisticated organizations to the anarchy of uncoordinated interaction.

Within multi-level governance and with the formation of policy networks, development potential at the local or at least the subnational level has increased, according to the consensus in a steadily rising number of publications on the subject (see summary in Kohler-Koch, 1997). At subnational level, this development potential can be seen in both formal and informal decision-making opportunities which have been established within the EC multi-level governance system via the principle of partnership (and subsidiarity) in a range of policy areas (see the next section of this chapter).

There are also the broadly based, local policy networks with their characteristic involvement in negotiations, interaction and debate between public and private sector policy-makers which have been shown to be essential for the success of local policy. As they succeed in overcoming the obstacles in hierarchical relations between public and private sector policy-makers, local and regional innovation networks are being set up (Cooke, 1996). Within these innovation networks, local structural and economic policy measures can be developed and implemented in support of endogenous potential.

Nevertheless, this development potential at local level does have a downside. Innovation networks can be successfully set up, marketed and developed into independent dynamic entities with their 'regional synergy' (Stöhr, 1986, p. 33) building on 'embedded firms' (Grabher, 1993) or 'networked firms' (Morgan, 1992). This occurs where appropriate historical conditions already exist. Where these conditions do not as yet exist, cities and regions are under pressure to catch up. They not only have to catch up in terms of development under local economic competitive conditions, but also need to develop a certain type of 'civicness' (Putnam et al., 1993) in local policy culture to encourage the formation of innovation networks. How difficult this process is for underdeveloped regions can be seen from the fact that regional disparities within the EC have reduced very little over the past twenty years, despite considerable injections of money from the structural funds (European Commission, 1995).

The new formal and informal development potential offered by EC multilevel governance is linked to a loss of influence at nation state level, not just because of increasing local and regional autonomy, but also because of the increasing competence of the EC. This is all the more important given regional and urban rivalry, as cities and regions with innovation networks and a local or developmental competitive advantage are the clear winners. It is irrelevant whether territorial rivalry involves a zero sum or positive sum game, as the ability of redistributive policies to reduce regional and social disparities will disappear with the loss of influence of the nation state. It is unlikely that the EC will take over this function or dismantle the structural funds.

This would have to be subject to the creation of a European entity which would replace the established member states. It does not matter how the European member states came into being, whether through a republican constitution reflecting a community of citizens with equal rights (e.g. France), through ethnic national unification movements (e.g. Germany or Italy), or through ethno-national independence from a multi-ethnic empire (in Eastern or Central Europe). They have one thing in common, i.e. that nationality and citizenship merge and some form of identity is required which supports solidarity, as well as accepting and legitimizing majority decisions on redistributive policy between winners and losers in the marketplace (Lepsius, 1990, 1991; Weiler, Haltern and Mayer, 1995). With the establishment of multilevel governance in European policy-making, nation states that have developed over several centuries since the Middle Ages will lose these policy functions, which will be replaced by new kinds of territorial bodies, including strong city councils, which will take on these functions.

Representatives of city councils: local heroes or policy brokers?

Although local political processes are essential for effective political intervention and for public sector service provision which is tailored to meet demand, nevertheless the legal and financial limitations of local political processes should not be overlooked.

In contrast to other nations, in Germany the independent status of local communities is formally (Article 28, Section 2 of the German constitution) and materially (with respect to the right to levy taxes) laid down in law. However, federal and state legislative levels can limit the development potential of local authorities both formally and in real terms because, against a background of limited local authority resources and overbudgeting (German budget law governs the raising of loans), they can transfer tasks or pass on policy problems. This is particularly evident in the case of the problems that flow from unemployment. In this case, successful budget consolidation measures at federal level which have been applied in the form of amendments to the labour law represent a financial burden on local authorities as the local social security agency. Yet, at the same time, funding is levied from local authorities as a result of federal and state legislation.

In addition, local authority activities are influenced most effectively by way of local confrontation and they are therefore being faced with many policy demands. Although the parties involved are well aware of the limitations of local policies and local authority strategies, in the absence of any direct alternative at state level, an increased role for local policy-making and the local authority is demanded (Bullmann and Gitschmann, 1985).

In examining local policy processes, there is an inherent danger of equating local policy-making with local authority policy-making, due to the superior position of local authorities in law, particularly in Germany. This would reduce local policy-making to the local authority level as defined by state law. It is important to realize that local authority capability is limited, which distorts the entire political system at the local level. One consequence of this, unlike in the UK, is not only that local offices of public bodies (such as the German Labour Office) are overlooked, but so also are the policy-makers who are not directly involved in any particular aspect of local authority policy (companies, associations and chambers of commerce). If this narrow view is abandoned, then the limitations at local authority level and in local authority policy-making disappear, and there is room for policy options based on the development potential of the entire spectrum of local policy-makers. Given the limitations on resources (such as funding or information) and the decision-making powers far beyond those of local authority competence (not least due to private sector investment decisions), the significance of coordination and cooperation, which cannot be demanded by federal or state government but is available only through the local negotiating structure, becomes paramount.

Because of the issue of capability and competence in the local policy process, it is not easy to locate a central policy unit at local level in many policy areas. In these policy areas, the different local service providers tend to rely on one another, and coordinated action is possible via majority voting negotiating structures (Evers, 1988). A substantial role may be assigned to local authorities within this constellation due to the democratic legitimacy of their decisions and the financial resources they can mobilize, despite all the budget problems.

Nevertheless, a mayor will not become a 'local hero' on these grounds alone. He or she can always take on this substantial role by acting as an initiator, organizer or 'policy broker' within majority voting negotiating structures. They can attract interest in decisions on programmes by mediating, or by developing and presenting 'cooperation plans', or by tapping potential willingness to get involved in the various programmes.

LOCAL CAPABILITY AND EC STRUCTURAL FUNDS

On the basis of the more general statements on capability at local authority level, the development potential of subnational policy-makers in Germany is portrayed below, against a background of increasing globalization and Europeanization in policy-making in one particular policy area. As was described in the first section of this chapter, the context for the policy process has changed over the past few decades, and yet concrete programmes are still based largely at the subnational level. Local authorities have to take into account the vertical policy-making procedure of the European Union in their daily work. Local policy is heavily influenced by the distributive policy of the European structural funds (see below). The same applies to the regulatory policies of the EU, such as regulations governing restrictive practices (e.g. local authority invitations to tender for building works and sale of property), environmental protection (e.g. waste disposal, clean water regulation), service provision at local level (e.g. public utilities, banks and local building societies), as well as regulations for the self-employed (architects, lawyers, tax advisers and chemists) (Thränhardt, 1994, p. 69). Although local authorities do not directly feature in European guidelines as these are normally addressed to central government, nevertheless they are indirectly involved via the laws passed by the national legislature (Schmidt-Eichstaedt, 1994, p. 98).

European structural funds are an appropriate policy area for a survey of changing resources at the local authority level. They feature strongly in the interaction between the different levels of the vertical network (European, national, subnational) (Grande, 1995) and there are large numbers of policy-makers involved.

This is one of the major characteristics of policy-making in European multilevel governance (Marks, 1993). It also opens up the political system to regional mobilization and regional autonomy (Hooghe, 1993). In addition to these broad characteristics which make the analysis of structural funds policy a particularly interesting subject for a case study, the content is also relevant. The problem of unemployment was first recognized as a global problem by the EU in the early documentation on the founding of the European Economic Community in 1957 and led to the establishment of the European Social Fund (ESF). Since that time a variety of funding opportunities have been created through the ESF and, despite some stagnation, other elements of European social policy have been introduced. Even regional economic financial support which is provided within the EU via the European Regional Development Fund (ERDF) is having to facing up to new challenges (Sitte and Ziegler, 1994) as a result of increased international competition. The third structural fund is the European Agricultural Guidance and Guarantee Fund (EAGGF) which addresses structural change in agricultural areas. Although problems of structural change are supposed to be countered through help from the European structural funds, the origins and consequences are often international, so initiatives are targeted at local level.

European structural funds policy is aimed at promoting regionalization and supporting decentralized governance structures in addition to its compensatory and redistributive role within Europe. It can therefore be concluded that European policy is designed to have an impact on regional public bodies. The nature of the impact depends on the globalization effects mentioned earlier, on changes in governance and on the importance of broadly based local negotiating structures.

CREATING CAPABILITY IN LOCAL COMPETITION VIA EUROPEAN STRUCTURAL POLICY

The structural funds' subsidies amount to 141.5 billion ECU between 1994 and 1999. A third of the entire EU budget is therefore available to European regions for structural policy measures. The areas of application for structural funding vary. They include productive investment in job creation, infrastructure investment and reintegration assistance programmes for the unemployed and the development of rural areas (Staeck, 1996).

With the growing importance of the location debate due to the effects of globalization, the structural funds have attracted particular attention from policy-makers with responsibility for regional economic funding. In the rivalry between regional and urban areas to offer attractive locations, there is an increasing tendency to rely on European funding, particularly in view of the difficult budgetary situation. However, it should be noted that European regional funding is made available only to a few select regions which have been chosen across the EU according to criteria such as gross domestic product per head, unemployment rates, numbers employed in industry and agriculture, and wage levels (Commission of the European Communities, 1993).

For local authorities, there is a great temptation to make use of the structural funds. Measures are subsidized which would otherwise be carried out without European funding, such as building industrial estates, rural renewal programmes, qualification and employment schemes for the unemployed (Staeck, 1997). Infrastructure measures can underpin long-term plans for projects which can be implemented more quickly with the additional European subsidies from the ERDF and EAGGF (industrial estate construction) or which affect a large group of project sponsors (rural renewal programmes). Through ESF programmes, employment and continuing education projects for special groups among the unemployed can relieve the strain through savings on social security budgets. In addition, local authorities can undertake projects with European funding which would otherwise be considered too innovative or risky. The European structural funds do not appear to limit capability, but the additional funding offers greater development potential. Finally, with certain local authority measures, there is evidence of direct effects on job security and job creation.

The principle of additionality applies in European structural policy. This means that for all European funding, co-funding must be provided from national, subnational, public or private sector sources. The EU money normally accounts for between 25 per cent and 50 per cent of the total cost. The principle of additionality is designed to prevent a bandwagon effect and member states are obliged to maintain their future public expenditure in the subsidized areas at least at the same level as during the programme planning period. However, it is difficult to check whether this regulation has been applied in practice, particularly where structural policy funding is taken from expenditure totals without separate budgeting, as has happened in the UK.

In some cases, the principle of additionality has caused immense problems at local level. The limited public sector budget has meant spending cuts so that there have not been sufficient monies for any co-funding. In Germany, cuts in labour market budgets have meant that local authorities have had to use their own resources for co-funding or raise money from other institutions, such as the German Labour Office. Otherwise, the costs incurred for social security recipients have to be borne by the local authority budget. Local authorities would prefer to use savings in the social security budget as a result of participation in qualification schemes by social security recipients in order to balance their own budgets. In the area of regional policy, a number of local authorities have been unable to take up all the European monies available, as they do not have the resources required for the co-funding. These non-binding European subsidies can be diverted to other projects. As a result, the more active local authorities can absorb subsidies which were intended for less active local authorities. One further consequence of the principle of additionality is that regional and labour market policies at the national level are becoming more structured due to European programme requirements. Since co-funding under the structural policy is based on European directives, this leaves no spare financial capacity for a domestic regional policy. This use of domestic funds in order to co-fund EU regional policy projects has had a sponge effect (Heinelt, 1996, p. 311). This critical situation is currently restricted to the economically weaker member states, such as Greece. Nevertheless, it seems likely that this may extend to other member states with persistent public sector funding problems. The result of this would be (further) Europeanization of subnational structural policy.

Although the European structural funds offer additional resources to local authorities through regional economic funding, support for rural structural areas and integration of social security recipients into the world of work, there is still a bottleneck at the local authority policy level as a result of fiscal cuts at both federal and state level. All in all, the attractiveness of a location depends on broad cooperation between supplier firms, service providers, research and development bodies and the relevant stock of qualified workers in addition to the necessary infrastructure (Junne, 1990, p. 384). In order to achieve this, it is vital to involve all policy-makers in planning and implementation decisions and use the funding offered to improve regional competitiveness. The major responsibility lies with the regions with their existing innovation and strategy skills.

Subnational level as the winners in the Europeanization process?

The ongoing process of integration has far-reaching consequences for the economy, society and polity. For member states it will bring changes to the institutional fabric of their political systems as a result of the shifting balance of power. At the higher supranational decision-making level, only framework conditions will be applied, so that lower policy levels are assigned the task of implementation. Thus, the demands made on those responsible for implementation will rise and there will be more scope for development at regional level. As a result of the changes in governance and the establishment of a multilevel governance mechanism, the European structural funds policy process will be simplified not least because of the application of the principles of subsidiarity and partnership.

On the one hand, the principle of partnership, which was introduced only after the reform of the structural funds in 1988, demands close consultation between the European Commission, the member state involved and the relevant authorities at regional and local level. On the other hand, it prioritizes the involvement of the economic and social partners in programme planning and implementation in accordance with European Community rules and regulations and standard practice in the member states. This is aimed at safeguarding the legal and financial powers of the partners. Coupled with this regulation, there is also the principle of subsidiarity which was allocated special status in the Maastricht Treaty, and by means of which priority is given to competent agencies operating at the lowest level feasible for the policy in question.

Subnational policy-makers will gain more status and influence as they are involved to a greater degree than before in planning and implementation of structural policies, irrespective of their constitutional position. For example, the German federal government will play the roles of mediator and agent and will be responsible for the transfer of funds from European level to subnational level. Its limited role in implementing structural funds programmes is not balanced by its participation in the adoption of European legislation in the Council of Ministers, as there is little scope within that institutional framework to discuss such issues. Some German state ministries are also refusing to accept responsibility for framework planning and guaranteeing basic funding in the light of these principles, as can be seen from the funding position in Lower Saxony. Given the principle of subsidiarity, no state funding will be made available for co-funding local authority economic policy. One consequence of this is that local authorities will have unlimited freedom in regional funding developments within the European guidelines.

Changes in policy-making in the context of the structural funds policy

The structural funds policy of the EU has also contributed to the development of broadly based local negotiating structures which are being shaped by the redefined roles of local authority politicians and new paradigms in regional policy. The structural funds policy specifically supports and even explicitly demands that networking should occur between the relevant policy-makers.

It is not just the principle of partnership as applied to planning and implementation but also the aim of achieving an integrated policy by consolidating the various fund activities which makes broadly based cooperation between policy-makers in social, economic and agricultural policy essential. In addition, Community Initiatives which have been set up as structural funds measures by the European Commission are promoting transnational cooperation and the development of networks between public and private sector policy-makers.

The negotiating arrangements in structural funds policy are primarily used for the better use of resources, such as specialist knowledge, legitimacy and funding. Social structures are likely to develop as a result of sustained links between policy-makers. At the local authority level, education and training sponsors can participate in the planning and implementation programmes, supported by the structural funds. A series of meetings would be held between the programme sponsors, the relevant local authorities and state government representatives. Horizontal and to some extent vertical coordination may also be supplemented by a further vertical component where there are close ties with members of the European Parliament and European Commission, although links to the latter are not common. Within this social system of European structural policy a set of values has been developed which the agencies involved can refer to and which serve as policy guidelines. There are four main points of reference: (a) common goals, e.g. reducing social and regional disparity; (b) principles of action and reference, e.g. partnership, additionality and subsidiarity; (c) common standards, e.g. compensation for economic disparity; and (d) a common language, e.g. Euro jargon, including abbreviations and technical terms for funding conditions (see Staeck, 1997, p. 64). 'A set of values like this provides common ground in problem solving, thereby simplifying interaction between those involved without suppressing conflicts of interest in terms of specific policies' (Pappi, 1993, p. 91).

CONCLUSIONS

Idiosyncracies in local authority policy should not be dismissed out of hand. Although local authorities follow state government rulings and implement supra-local programmes, local authority decisions have a certain clout as they are democratically legitimized. Decisions can be made for the common good. Various interests can be addressed directly, although involvement in the negotiating structure with autonomous local policy-makers is not necessarily guaranteed.

The increasing globalization and Europeanization of policy is reflected in a number of different ways in cities. These include the implementation of European modes of governance, as represented by the principles of partnership and additionality. In this context, there has been a marked development in innovative local policy influenced by European funding guidelines. Capability in local policy is increasing, or, at any rate, not declining, as a result of engagement at the EU level. However, the rise in funding resources and the task of seizing opportunities for project funding in Objective 2 areas, can to some extent be due to the bandwagon effect of structural funds policy.

As has become clear with the problem of co-financing structural funds programmes, cities and regions with superior campaigning power and efficient administration have greater access to European funding. The much quoted notion of the 'Europe of the Regions' continues to play a part in the tension between supranationalization of individual policy areas and effective problem-solving in other policy areas at local and regional level (Nägele, 1995).

References

B. Blanke, S. Benzler and H. Heinelt, 'Explaining different approaches to local labour market policy in the FRG', *Policy and Politics* 20: 1 (1992) 15–28.

U. Bullmann and P. Gitschmann (eds), *Kommune als Gegenmacht. Alternative Politik in den Städten und Gemeinden* [*Local Authorities as a Countervailing Power: Alternative Policy in Cities and Local Communities*] (Hamburg, 1985).

Commission of the European Communities, *Strukturfonds der Gemeinschaft 1994–1999* [*Community Structural Funds 1994–1999*] (Luxembourg, 1993).

P. Cooke, 'Policy networks, innovation networks and regional policy', in H. Heinelt and R. Smith (eds), *Policy Networks and European Structural Funds* (Aldershot, 1996) pp. 26–45.

European Commission, Directorate-General for Regional Policy and Cohesion, *The Structural Funds. Initial Assessment of the 1989–1993 Programming Period*, Info-regio Fact Sheet, 31 October 1995.

A. Evers, *Intermediäre Institutionen und pluralistische Verhandlungssysteme in der lokalen Politik. Eine Problemskizze zur Produktion und Aneignung sozialer Innovationen*, Manuskript (vorgelegt im Arbeitskreis Lokale Politikforschung beim 17. Kongreß der Deutschen Vereinigung für Politische Wissenschaft in Darmstadt) [*Intermediary Institutions and Pluralistic Negotiating Structures in Local Policy: The Problems of Developing Social Innovation*, manuscript (presented at the Local Policy Research Study Group at the 17th Congress of the German Association for Political Science in Darmstadt)] (1988).

S. George, *Politics and Policy in the European Community* (Oxford, 1992).

G. Grabher (ed.), *The Embedded Firm: On the Socioeconomics of Industrial Networks* (London/New York, 1993).

E. Grande, 'Die neue Architektur des Staates [The new architecture of the state]', in R. Czada and M.G. Schmidt (eds), *Verhandlungsdemokratie, Interessenvermittlung, Regierbarkeit* (Festschrift für Gerhard Lehmbruch) [*Democratic Bargaining, Lobbying, Governability*] (Opladen, 1993) pp. 51–71.

E. Grande, 'Regieren in verflochtenen Verhandlungssystemen [Governing through negotiation within networks]', in R. Mayntz and F.W. Scharpf (eds), *Gesellschaftliche Selbstregelung und politische Steuerung* [*Self-regulation in Society and Political Governance*] (Frankfurt am Main/New York, 1995) pp. 327–68.

H. Häußermann, 'Lokale Politik und Zentralstaat. Ist auf kommunaler Ebene eine alternative Politik möglich?' [Local policy and central government: are alternative policies possible at local authority level?]', in H. Heinelt and

H. Wollmann (eds), *Brennpunkt Stadt. Stadtpolitik und lokale Politikforschung in den 80er und 90er Jahren* [*Focus on Cities: Urban Policy and Local Policy Research in the Eighties and Nineties*] (Basel/Boston/Berlin, 1991) pp. 52–91.

H. Häußermann and W. Siebel, *Neue Urbanität* [*New Urbanity*] (Frankfurt am Main, 1987).

H. Heinelt, 'Local labour market policy – limits and potentials', *International Journal of Urban and Regional Research* 4 (1992) 522–8.

H. Heinelt, 'Conclusions', in H. Heinelt and R. Smith (eds), *Policy Networks and European Structural Funds* (Aldershot, 1996) pp. 294–321.

H. Heinelt and R. Smith (eds), *Policy Networks and European Structural Funds* (Aldershot, 1996).

L. Hooghe, *Political-Administrative Adaptation in the EC and Regional Mobilization: The Politics of the Commission Civil Service under Structural Funds*, unpublished manuscript, Nuffield College, 1993.

L. Hooghe, *Subnational Mobilization in the European Union*, European University Institute, Working Paper RSC 95/96 (Florence, 1995).

L. Hooghe (ed.), *Cohesion Policy and European Integration: Building Multi-Level Governance* (Oxford, 1996).

M. Jachtenfuchs and B. Kohler-Koch, 'Regieren im dynamischen Mehrebenensystem [Dynamic multi-level governance]', in M. Jachtenfuchs and B. Kohler-Koch (eds), *Europäische Integration* [*European Integration*] (Opladen, 1996) pp. 15–44.

G. Junne, 'Chancen für eine Reregionalisierung der Politik [Opportunities for a return to regionalization in politics]', in U. von Alemann, R.G. Heinze and B. Hombach (eds), *Die Kraft der Region: Nordrhein-Westfalen in Europa* [*The Power of the Regions – North Rhine-Westphalia in Europe*] (Bonn, 1990) pp. 376–89.

P. Kenis and V. Schneider, 'Policy networks and policy analysis: scrutinizing a new analytical toolbox', in B. Marin and R.Mayntz (eds), *Policy Networks: Empirical Evidence and Theoretical Considerations* (Frankfurt am Main/Boulder, Colo., 1991) pp. 25–59.

B. Kohler-Koch (ed.), *Interaktive Politik in Europa, Regionen im Netzwerk der Integration* [*Interactive Policy in Europe: Regions in the Integration Network*] (Opladen, 1997).

T. Krämer-Badoni, *Verschwinden die Städte?* [*Are Cities Disappearing?*] (Forschungsbericht der Zentralen Wissenschaftlichen Einheit/ZWE 'Arbeit und Region', Universität Bremen [Central Economic Unit Research Report on 'Labour and the Regions', University of Bremen] (Bremen, 1997).

M.R. Lepsius, ' "Ethnis" und "Demos". Zur Anwendung zweier Kategorien von Emerich Francis auf das nationale Selbstverständnis der Bundesrepublik Deutschland und auf die Euopäische Einigung ['Ethnis' and 'Demos': the application of two concepts developed by Emerich Francis to describe the national self image of the FRG and of European unification]', in M.R. Lepsius, *Interessen, Ideen und Institutionen* [*Interests, Ideas and Institutions*] (Opladen, 1990) pp. 247–55.

M.R. Lepsius, 'Nationalstaat oder Nationalitätenstaat als Modell für die Weiterentwicklung der Europäischen Gemeinschaft [Nation state or state of nations as a model for the further development of the EC]', in R. Wildenmann (ed.), *Staatswerdung Europas? Optionen für eine Europäische Union* [*Conception of the State of Europe? Options for the European Union*] (Baden-Baden, 1991) pp. 19–40.

B. Marin and R. Mayntz (eds), *Policy Networks: Empirical Evidence and Theoretical Considerations* (Frankfurt am Main, 1991).

G. Marks, 'Structural policy and multilevel governance in the EC', in A.W. Cafruny and G.G. Rosenthal (eds), *The State of the European Community, 2: The Maastricht Debates and Beyond* (Boulder, Colo./Harlow, 1993) pp. 391–410.

M. Mayer, ' "Postfordismus" und "lokale Stadt" ' ["Post-Fordism" and the "local city"]', in H. Heinelt and H. Wollmann (eds), *Brennpunkt Stadt. Stadtpolitik und lokale Politikforschung in den 80er und 90er Jahren* [Focus on Cities: Urban Policy and Local Policy Research in the Seventies and Eighties], (Basel/Boston/Berlin, 1991) pp. 31–51.

H. Mitteis, *Der Staat des hohen Mittelalters. Grundlinien einer vergleichenden Verfassungsgeschichte des Lehnsmittelalters* [*The City at the Height of the Middle Ages: A Basis for a Comparative Constitutional History of the Feudal Middle Ages*], 5th edn (Weimar, 1955).

K. Morgan, 'Innovating by networking: new models of corporate and regional development', in M. Dunford and G. Kafkalas (eds), *Cities and Regions in the New Europe: The Global-Local Interplay and Spatial Development Strategies* (London, 1992) pp. 150–69.

F. Nägele, ' "Europa der Regionen", Anmerkungen zu einem Leitbild europäischer Staatlichkeit ["Europe of the Regions": Notes on a paradigm of European governance]', in H.-P. Burmeister and C. Hüttig (eds), *Die politische Integration Europas* [*Political Integration of Europe*], Loccumer Protokolle [Loccum Records] 16/94, (Rehburg-Loccum, 1995) pp. 49–60.

U. Pappi, 'Policy-Netze: Erscheinungsform moderner Politiksteuerung oder methodischer Ansatz? [Policy networks: a new political governance or a new technique?]', in A. Héritier (ed.), *Policy-Analyse, Kritik und Neuorientierung*, [*Policy Analysis, Critique and New Perspectives*], PVS-Sonderheft 24 (1993) pp. 84–94.

R.D. Putnam, *Making Democracy Work: Civic Traditions in Modern Italy* (Princeton, NJ, 1993).

R.A.W. Rhodes, 'The new governance: governing without government', *Political Studies* 44 (1996) 652–67.

F.W. Scharpf, 'Die Handlungsfähigkeit des Staates am Ende des Zwanzigsten Jahrhunderts [The capacity of the state at the end of the 20th century]', in B. Kohler-Koch (ed.), *Staat und Demokratie in Europa. 18. Wissenschaftlicher Kongreß der Deutschen Vereinigung für Politische Wissenschaft* [*The State and Democracy in Europe*: 18th Scientific Congress of the German Association for Political Science] (Opladen, 1992) pp. 93–115.

F.W. Scharpf, 'Föderalismus im globalen Kapitalismus [Federalism as part of global capitalism]', in F.W. Scharpf, *Optionen des Föderalismus in Deutschland und Europa* [*Options for Federalism in Germany and Europe*] (Frankfurt/New York, 1994) pp. 156–66.

G. Schmidt-Eichstaedt, 'Die Kommunen zwischen Autonomie und (Über-) Regelung durch Bundes- und Landesrecht sowie EG-Normen [Local authorities between autonomy and (over) regulation under federal and state law and EC standards]', in R. Roth and H. Wollmann (eds), *Kommunalpolitik. Politisches Handeln in den Gemeinden [Local Authority Policy: Political Activity in Local Communities]* (Opladen, 1994) pp. 95–108.

R. Sitte and A. Ziegler, 'Die EU-Strukturfonds nach der Reform [EU structural funds after the reforms]', *WSI-Mitteilungen [Dispatches]* 4 (1994) 214–22.

N. Staeck, 'Die europäische Strukturfondsförderung – Entwicklung und Funktionsweise [European structural funds — their history and impact]', in H. Heinelt (ed.), *Politiknetzwerke und europäische Strukturfondsförderung. Ein Vergleich zwischen EU-Mitgliedstaaten [Policy Networks and European Structural Funds: A Comparison between EC Member States]* (Opladen, 1996) pp. 33–57.

N. Staeck, *Politikprozesse in der Europäischen Union. Eine Policy-Netzwerkanalyse der europäischen Strukturfondspolitik [Political Processes in the European Union: A Policy Network Analysis of European Policy on the Structural Funds]* (Baden-Baden, 1997).

W.B. Stöhr, 'Regional innovation complexes', *Papers of the Regional Science Association*, 59 (1986) 29–44.

D. Thränhardt, 'Die Kommunen und die Europäische Gemeinschaft [Local authorities and the European Community]', in R. Roth and H. Wollmann (eds), *Kommunalpolitik, Politisches Handeln in den Gemeinden [Local Authority Policy: Political Activity in the Local Community]* (Opladen, 1994) pp. 66–80.

J.H.H. Weiler, U. Haltern and F. Mayer, *European Democracy and its Critiques: Five Uneasy Pieces* (European University Institute, Florence, 1995).

15 Changing Cities – Transforming Socio-Ecological Relations in Bristol and Brussels

Colin Fudge

INTRODUCTION

This chapter places Bristol's attempts to move towards a more sustainable future against the context of the emerging European interest in the urban environment and the global urban challenge to be faced over the next 20–30 years. A brief overview records the dimensions of the global urban challenge as discussed by the series of UN conferences that have taken place over the last 25 years of this century. The specific urban focus in Europe is then introduced and the European policy responses to urban and environmental problems elaborated with particular reference to the European Sustainable Cities Project, led by the Expert Group on the Urban Environment following the publication of the Green Paper on the Urban Environment in 1990 (CEC, 1990).

Bristol's and the South West of England region's own approaches to sustainable development are outlined and progress and barriers to implementation examined. The concluding part of the chapter expands on the emerging policy and management orthodoxy to achieve more sustainable futures and raises a number of questions concerning the limits to these new approaches that are raised in the real-world experience of their implementation at the local level in Bristol and in the emerging urban policy discussions in Brussels.

GLOBAL URBAN CHALLENGE

The Conference on Environment and Development (UNCED) held in Rio de Janeiro in 1992 recognized the crucial role of urban communities in seeking global sustainable development and for the improvement of local health conditions. The Conference underlined the key roles of urban settlements and human health for our common future as set out in Agenda 21. At the Earth Summit, the European Union and most national governments signed the conventions on climate change and biodiversity, and committed themselves to Agenda 21, the global action plan for sustainable development in which local governments have a crucial role to play. However, the progress since the Conference, while conditionally positive in terms of Agenda 21, nevertheless leaves cities with major challenges that need to be addressed urgently. The WHO-OECD Madrid Congress (Price and Tsouros, 1996) usefully developed these strands in time to inform the development of the Habitat II conference and agenda. The Rio plus Five Conference (1997) and the Climate Conference in Kyoto (1997), however, remained disappointing.

The world's urban population is now put at 2.6 billion out of a total population of 5.8 billion. Growth rates have fallen but another 86 million people are being added to the world total each year. The gradual drift to urban areas has become an avalanche. In 1950 there were 83 cities with a population of more than 1 million, 34 of the cities in developing countries. Today there are 280, with the number arguably expected to double by 2015. All of the new million population cities are in developing countries, including 11 of the largest 15. Also in 1950 there were two so-called megacities, New York and London, with 8 million population or more. By 1970 there were 11 megacities. By 2015 it is predicted by the UN that there will be 33 megacities, 21 of which will be in Asia and many will be close to a population of 20 million. Many of these megacities, it is argued, will produce 70–90 per cent of their nation's GDP (Brown, 1996; Pearce, 1996; Vidal, 1996).[1]

The European Union is a major part of one of the most urbanized continents in the world. The Union contains approximately 170 cities with more than 200 000 inhabitants and 32 cities with more than a million inhabitants. London and Paris are the only two metropolises with populations approaching 10 million. Some 80 per cent of the European population live in these towns and cities making them the cultural, economic and innovative centres of Europe. They function as the generators of local, regional and national economies but together are the key localities in relation to European global competitiveness. At the same time, many of these localities are confronted with serious problems – high unemployment, social and spatial segregation, social exclusion, concerns over their future economy, crime, the general quality of life, negative impacts on health and pressures on natural and historic assets. In addition, they are handling wider global and societal changes due to the globalization of markets, shifts in demography and family structure, and new technological innovations. Many of them remain crucial meeting places and destinations. They are economically and culturally buoyant, if socially and environmentally in deficit. A number of cities stand out as examples of an urban renaissance in Europe: these include Lyon, Stockholm, Paris, Lisbon, Barcelona, London and Berlin.

Along with cities worldwide, European cities are facing up to these challenges that are reshaping their futures. In the work carried out for the European Commission over the last six years, a number of significant issues can be identified that are closely interrelated and provide the agenda for policy development for cities, member states and the European Union. These include: the increased competition among cities and regions both within the Union and between the Union and the rest of the world; the accumulation of unemployment, poverty and social exclusion in the larger cities; the increasing focus on sustainable urban development; the influence of changes to public expenditure and social insurance on cities; the increasing concern over urban health; the increasing inability to achieve success and mobility within and between cities; the concerns over the quality of local democracy; and the requirements the challenges imply for urban management, urban leadership and governance.

In addition, different concepts and models have been discussed that aid analysis and policy development. These focus on the interrelationship between economic, environmental, social, health and cultural concerns and the significance of integrated and holistic approaches at all levels of government.

EUROPEAN URBAN FOCUS

Since 1991 the European Community, now the European Union, has sought consolidation of its actions for environmental protection and reorientation of environment policy to promote the objectives of sustainable development. These policy shifts have key implications for the urban environment. The principal developments are described and elaborated in *European Sustainable Cities* (CEC, 1996). They include:

- the Treaty on European Union (Maastricht) and the 1996 intergovernmental conference (ICG);
- Towards Sustainability: the Fifth Environmental Action Programme (CEC, 1992a);

- European Spatial Development Perspective and Regional Policy (CEC, 1991, Committee on Spatial Development, 1994);
- Common Transport Policy (CEC, 1992b and 1992c);
- structural funds and their review;
- cohesion policy;
- specific directives, e.g. air quality;
- European Environment Agency Dobris Report (1994);
- Delors White Paper (CEC, 1993b).

The year 1997 saw the publication of *Agenda 2000* (CEC, 1997a) and a report on a possible urban agenda for the European Union (CEC, 1997b). For the purposes of this chapter and for brevity the focus is on the urban environment.

The subsidiarity principle indicates that most urban policies and programmes are most appropriately developed and implemented by member states and the cities themselves. Some member states regard it as particularly crucial that cities continue to have the prime responsibility for policy and action in their local areas and that the identification of appropriate forms of action at different governmental levels should be further debated. However, the Commission, reflecting the wishes of the European Parliament, has now formally recognized the need to give more attention at European Union level to the problems of cities, especially since, with a heavy concentration of the EU's population in urban areas, there is already a strong urban dimension to many of the EU's actions.

Lobbying for Europe-wide action for cities is by no means new. For example, the Council of Europe (COE), of which all EU member states are members, began an urban programme in the early 1980s.

A Better Life in Towns ran from 1980 to 1982. This was followed, between 1982 and 1986, by an urban policy programme which in 1986 became the responsibility of the COE's Standing Conference of Local and Regional Authorities of Europe (CLRAE). In March 1992 CLRAE adopted the European Urban Charter, designed as a practical – although not very detailed – urban management handbook for local authorities (CLRAE, 1992). The Charter also provides the basis for a possible future convention on urban rights and for an annual award scheme for towns subscribing to its principles. Many of these principles have relevance for sustainability and are revisited in the Expert Group report, *European Sustainable Cities* (CEC, 1994c and 1996).

In its 1989–92 programme the European Foundation for the Improvement of Living and Working Conditions broadened its remit to include urban environment issues, having previously concentrated on the economic and social aspects of urban life. In 1993 the Foundation extended this work by initiating a programme on urban innovations contributing to the sustainable city. The programme covers economic and social aspects of sustainability, including questions of social justice, as well as environmental issues. It examines processes and mechanisms – such as environmental auditing and community participation – as well as physical innovations. The Foundation's four-year work programme for 1993–6 includes further projects on urban issues with a strong sustainability component. These cover, for example, the quality of urban life, sustainability indicators for medium-sized cities and a range of projects on economic development and employment.

Explicit recognition of an urban dimension in various EU policies and programmes is relatively recent. The full range of actions is reviewed in *Community Action in Urban Matters* (CEC, 1993a). Examples include the THERMIE and SAVE energy programmes, and URBAN, the Community Initiative concerning urban areas (CEC, 1994b) which the Commission announced in March 1994 as an additional component of regional policy. URBAN proposes a more ambitious and better co-ordinated approach through which cities may benefit from EU actions in the period 1994–9, along with a specific initiative to promote innovative actions and networks for the exchange of experience and cooperation. This initiative is targeted at areas of urban deprivation within large cities, as measured by, for example, high unemployment and environmental decay. The initiative gives priority to innovative projects forming part of long-term urban integration strategies being implemented by the cities concerned.

The Committee on Spatial Development, established in 1991 following a meeting of Ministers on Regional Policy and Planning, regularly discusses urban issues. The Committee has overseen the work contained in the report *Europe 2000+: Cooperation for European Territorial Development* (CEC, 1994a) in which strengthening of the European urban system and sustainable development are central objectives.

The informal meeting of Ministers of Spatial Planning in December 1997 discussed the European Spatial Development Perspective (ESDP) and reached conclusions on the need to make the ESDP more precise, to address questions raised by enlargement, to invite neighbouring countries of the Council of Europe to participate and to support the creation of a European Spatial Planning Observatory Network (ESPON). The European Commission held a series of conferences and seminars throughout 1998 covering a range of urban and European topics culminating in the Urban Forum in Vienna in November 1998 and the ESDP Forum in Brussels in spring 1999.

The Committee of the Regions has established an Urban Affairs Committee which is providing an important political lobby for greater integration of urban policy at EU level.

The Amsterdam Treaty, when it comes into force, will make sustainable development an overarching objective of the European Union and will require that environmental considerations are built into all policies and actions of the EU (Article 6). This change is bound to lead to changes in policy generally but will have a particular influence on urban policy.

The Agenda 2000 document was launched by the Commission in July 1997. It includes a financial perspective which has implications for enlargement of the Union. Enlargement has important implications for spatial planning, regional and urban policy as well as for the range of funding instruments and programmes.

The document *Towards an Urban Agenda in the European Union* (CEC, 1997b) initiated a debate by the European Commission which culminated in an Urban Forum in November 1998 in Vienna. This document introduces a discussion about European urban policy and is developed further later in this chapter.

In the field of environmental policy, integration of the urban dimension has been extensively pursued. An integrated approach was first advocated in the Fourth Environmental Action Programme 1987–92, and this led to the publication of the consultative *Green Paper on the Urban Environment* (CEC, 1990) and to the establishment of the Expert Group on the Urban Environment in 1991.

The rationale for detailed consideration of the urban environment is set out in the Green Paper, which was a response to pressure from three sources – the concern on the part of several European cities that a preoccupation with rural development within the European Commission was overshadowing the interests of urban areas, the commitment of the then Environment Commissioner, Carlo Ripa di Meana, and a resolution tabled in December 1988 by Ken Collins, Member of the European Parliament, urging that problems facing the urban environment be studied in greater detail. This Green Paper is regarded as a milestone in thinking about the urban environment, principally because it advocated a holistic view of urban problems and an integrated approach to their solution.

The Green Paper discussed the key role of cities as the home of increasing proportions of Europe's population and their role as the organizing units of the urban system and the foci of economic, social, cultural and political life. It examined the many and varied problems facing the urban environment and discussed the root causes of urban degradation, seen as linked to the structural changes in patterns of communication, transport and consumption. Questions of economic activity and the health of urban residents were also considered, along with the quality of life, seen as an essential component of the diverse, multi-functional European city. The improvement of the urban environment contributes both to the quality of life and to the development of urban economy. The Green Paper also sparked off a number of debates. The most heated, perhaps, concerned the views on urban form and land use expressed in the Green Paper. While the shape of the built-up and natural areas of cities is clearly important, discussions since have sought to extend the debate to consider ways in which urban society is managed. For the shape of the sustainable city will also reflect the priorities for action identified by urban governments and their communities.

As the Green Paper acknowledged, each European city is to some extent unique. The principles and mechanisms advocated in the Green Paper for urban management for sustainability must be applicable in diverse urban settings, for example in the historic city centres of the north and west as well as in the new settlements of the Mediterranean region. However, the European urban system has characteristics which distinguish it from urban systems elsewhere. In North America, for example, the urban system is more expansive and has a much shorter history, while cities in the developing world are still experiencing very rapid urbanization.[2] A further feature distinguishing European cities from cities elsewhere relates to the effects of progressive political and economic integration of the European Union, although it is important to recognize that cities worldwide are increasingly affected by the globalization of economies and operate in the context of trade area agreements.

EUROPEAN SUSTAINABLE CITIES PROJECT

The European Sustainable Cities Project supported by the European Commission links policies for sustainable cities prepared by the

Expert Group on the Urban Environment with implementation via the European Sustainable Cities and Towns Campaign. These inter-relationships between the policy work of the Expert Group on the Urban Environment and the Campaign, set in the wider context of the European Union's action in the field of urban environment, are focused around Local Agenda 21.

Local authorities and communities throughout Europe are now in the process of evolving their Local Agenda 21 strategies and a good deal of guidance has emerged on approaches and content. The UK is at the forefront of these initiatives and the implementation strategy provided by the UK Local Government Management Board offers a framework for action on a European scale.

The Expert Group on the Urban Environment, established by the European Commission in 1991 following the publication of the Green Paper on the Urban Environment, launched the Sustainable Cities Project in 1993 with the following principal aims:

- to contribute to the development of thinking about sustainability in European urban settings;
- to disseminate best practice about sustainability at local level; and
- in the longer term, to formulate recommendations to influence European Union, member state, regional and local levels of government.

The Sustainable Cities Project is based upon a challenging experiment in European networking which links over forty urban environment experts from 15 member states. The network of experts is supported by EURONET, the European research network based at the University of the West of England at Bristol which provides research expertise to the members of the Expert Group, via its research and consultancy partners in Europe.

A further thirty experts are involved in the Expert Group includ-ing representatives from relevant Directorates-General of the European Commission and a range of international organizations with an interest in urban issues, including the Council of Europe, the Council of European Municipalities and Regions (CEMR), Eurocities, the European Academy for the Urban Environment, the European Foundation for the Improvement of Living and Working Conditions, the International Council for Local Environmental Initiatives (ICLEI), the OECD and the World Health Organization (WHO).

Recent activities within the framework of the European Sustainable Cities Project include the following:

- European Sustainable Cities policy report (CEC, 1996);
- targeted summary reports;
- Good Practice Guide;
- European Good Practice Information System – Local Sustainability;
- travelling dissemination conferences;
- European Sustainable Cities and Towns Conferences; and
- network activities in support of the Campaign.

The policy report

The preparation of the final European Sustainable Cities report for the Lisbon Conference on Urban Sustainability in October 1996 represents one part of a rapidly developing agenda for urban sustainability.

The report on European Sustainable Cities explores the prospects for sustainability in urban settlements of different scales, from urban regions to small towns. However, the main focus is on cities, in line with the EU Green Paper on the Urban Environment. The policy report identifies the challenge of urban sustainability to

> solve both the problems experienced within cities and the problems caused by cities, recognising that cities themselves provide many potential solutions. City managers must seek to meet the social and economic needs of urban residents while respecting local, regional and global natural systems, solving problems locally where possible, rather than shifting them to other spatial locations or passing them on to the future.   (CEC, 1996)

Sustainable development is identified as a much broader concept than environmental protection. It has economic, social, health as well as environmental dimensions, and embraces notions of equity between people in the present and between generations. It implies that further development should only take place as long as it is within the carrying capacity of natural and social systems.

An important argument derived from these principles is that sustainable development must be planned for and that market forces alone cannot achieve the integration of environmental, social and economic concerns. The report seeks to provide a framework within which innovative approaches to the planning of sustainability can be explored. In this respect the report aims to identify a set of ecological, social, economic and organizational principles and tools for urban management which may be applied in a variety of urban settings and which can be used selectively as cities move towards sustainability. It also provides substantive policy recommendations and recommendations for research.

The report is aimed at a wide audience. For while elected representatives in cities, city managers/administrators and urban environment professionals have key roles to play in urban management for sustainability, successful progress, the report argues, depends upon the active involvement of local communities and the creation of partnerships with the private and voluntary sectors within the context of a strong and supportive government framework at all levels.

Local Sustainability – European Good Practice Information System

A core concern of the European Sustainable Cities Project is the widest dissemination of the key messages of the work at both political and technical levels, raising awareness and developing new skills of sustainable urban management.

EURONET and the International Council for Local Environmental Initiatives (ICLEI) have developed an information system entitled Local Sustainability – European Good Practice Information System which addresses the above concerns in disseminating the work of the European Sustainable Cities Project and supporting local action for urban sustainability.

Local Sustainability – the European Good Practice Information System – harnesses new information technologies to offer enhanced opportunities for integration of the work of the Sustainable Cities Project linking policy to implementation, providing a 'hallmark' standard for good practice across Europe and the widest possible dissemination of this work. A system for researching and describing cases of good environmental practice by local authorities is being developed and evaluated through this two-year development and pilot project.

The system incorporates written information (case studies) including illustrations, which are being made available through printed leaflets and provision on a world wide web site for on-line access.

The tangible benefits of the information system include:

- full integration of Sustainable Cities policy with good practice examples delivered on the Internet;

- positive linkage of new policy approaches and good practice with the work of the Campaign and Local Agenda 21;
- a fully specified database of good practice targeted at both technical and policy users;
- a 'showcase' for the work of both the Expert Group and the Campaign based on a practical and user-orientated demonstration of the positive influence of the European Union on the development of sustainable urban policy;
- a mechanism for horizontal integration of the work of the European Commission in respect of the themes of urban sustainability.

THE EUROPEAN SUSTAINABLE CITIES AND TOWNS CAMPAIGN

The European Sustainable Cities and Towns Campaign was initiated by 80 European local authorities through signing the Charter of European Cities and Towns Towards Sustainability. It was launched by the EU Environment Commissioner at the first European Conference on Sustainable Cities and Towns in Aalborg, Denmark, on 27 May 1994. Any local authority (city, town or network of local authorities from any part of Europe) may join the Campaign by adopting and signing the Charter.

The objective of the Campaign is to encourage and support cities, towns and counties in working towards sustainability and to promote development towards sustainability at the local level through Local Agenda 21 processes. This is to be achieved by strengthening partnership among all actors in the local community as well as inter-authority cooperation, and relating this process to the European Union's action in the field of urban environment, and the work of the Urban Environment Expert Group. It may be considered as the European Local Agenda 21 campaign.

Campaign structure and tasks

The Campaign is formed by municipal signatories of the Aalborg Charter as Campaign participants. Its supporters are major European networks and associations of local authorities which coordinate their efforts through a coordinating committee. The networks and associations work with their member local authorities in various ways to carry out projects supporting the Campaign.

The coordinating committee supports the work of the Campaign office and provides recommendations to it. The European Commission (DG XI) and the city of Aalborg, both sponsors of the Campaign, also have seats on the coordinating committee in addition to the chair of the Urban Environment Expert Group.

The Campaign office's primary function is to facilitate the adoption of Local Agenda 21 processes and promote sustainability objectives among the participating cities and to support the networks involved in the Campaign by providing general information and guidance, and ensuring regular communication among the networks and between the networks and outside partners. This is achieved by, among other things, the following:

- supporting the development of concrete projects of cooperation both within some of the participating networks and between cities;
- collecting and disseminating information on good examples at the local level, and making them available to Campaign participants through the good practice guide of the Expert Group on the Urban Environment and Campaign newsletters;
- facilitating mutual support between European cities and towns in the design, development and implementation of policies towards sustainable development through workshops;
- follow-up on EU initiatives relevant to sustainable urban development in order to inform local authorities of Commission initiatives;
- supporting local policy-makers in implementing appropriate recommendations and legislation from the European Union through dissemination of information on European Union actions, policies and legislation in the Campaign newsletter, which is provided on a regular basis in English, French and German;
- reviewing and further developing the Aalborg Charter.

There are now over 350 local authorities actively involved in the campaign with growing representation from Central and Eastern Europe.

Network activities in support of the Campaign

The European Sustainable Cities and Towns Campaign is supported by major European networks and associations of local authorities which coordinate their efforts through a coordinating committee. The supporting networks and associations have officially signed the Charter of European Cities and Towns Towards Sustainability (Aalborg Charter) and thereby committed themselves to the principles and goals laid down in the Charter. These organizations include: the Environment Committee of the Council of European Municipalities and Regions (CEMR), the Environment Committee of Eurocities, the International Council for Local Environmental Initiatives (ICLEI), the United Towns Organization (UTO), and the World Health Organization's (WHO) Healthy Cities Network.

Council of European Municipalities and Regions

Activities in support of the Campaign include supporting a network of 15 national coordinators to assist the Local Agenda 21 process, presentations at Habitat II and at the second Sustainable Cities Conference, organizing a special workshop on Local Agenda 21 plans at the General Assembly, the development of an annual sustainable city award scheme, and the training of national Local Agenda 21 coordinators.

Eurocities

Activities in support of the Campaign include an environmental awareness project to stimulate communication of the Local Agenda 21 concept, an air quality project to gather local practical experiences on the Framework Directive on Ambient Air Quality Assessment and Management, a sustainable development project with presentations at Habitat II and the second Sustainable Cities Conference, a soil clean-up and an urban planning project to produce good practice examples for dissemination across Europe.

ICLEI

Activities in support of the Campaign include the development of more training material, the stimulation of Local Agenda 21 plan preparation, and a presentation at the second Sustainable Cities Conference. A one-year training initiative has been developed covering the officers and politicians of nine local authorities to develop Local Agenda 21 plans. In addition, the European Local Agenda 21 Planning Guide published in English by ICLEI will be translated into the other languages of the European Union.

UTO

Activities in support of the Campaign include the preparation of Local Agenda 21 plans for UTO members, the production (in French) and translation (into English) of training material, the gathering of good practice examples, and a presentation at the second Sustainable Cities Conference. In addition, UTO will disseminate an environmental audit guide (in English, German, Spanish and Italian), develop a city award in cooperation with CEMR and undertake an inventory of local needs.

WHO Healthy Cities Network

Activities in support of the Campaign include the gathering of good practice examples in the field of health and sustainable development, and the presentation of a working paper at the second Sustainable Cities Conference. In addition, a Handbook on Health and Local Agenda 21 plans will be published after testing in eight cities.

FUTURE DIRECTIONS

The Sustainable Cities Project has mobilized and supported different levels of government, different geographic areas of Europe and different sectors including local authorities, non-government organizations and the private sector in both policy thinking and, increasingly, implementation of Local Agenda 21 plans and moves towards more sustainable futures within towns and cities. The policy thinking has an institutional as well as an environmental focus. It is concerned with the capacity of local governments in particular to deliver sustainability and provides a framework for local action as well as recommendations for different levels of government, different sectors and the research agenda.

The project has moved to its second phase and until 2000 will focus on implementation issues generally, the geographic regions of Southern, Central and Eastern Europe and the further expansion of the Campaign. Four regional conferences were to be held in 1998, with a third European-wide conference organized for the year 2000 in Central Europe. Currently, there are emerging projects with the Expert Group on 'Urban Management and Governance for

Sustainability', a 'second interactive web site' to improve dissemination of practice and active involvement in 'the discussions on the Urban Communication' (CEC, 1997b).

SUSTAINABLE BRISTOL?

Bristol City Council published its first State of the Local Environment report in August 1995. Since its publication the local environmental agenda has progressed, and there have been discussions and feedback from environmental groups, officials and members of the public on the content, value and usefulness of the report. As part of the State of the Local Environment report, the council has developed 62 sustainability indicators based on 11 sustainability themes including: resource use, pollution, biodiversity, basic needs, work, health, access, freedom, information and education, leisure and culture and beauty. The indicators have been developed from the National Sustainability Indicators Research Project, funded by the Local Government Management Board alongside a range of supporting materials for local government in the UK (LGMB, 1992a, 1992b, 1993a, 1993b, 1994).

A supplementary Sustainability Update consultation document published in 1996 is divided into three parts providing:

- maps of the city showing 62 ward indicators;
- a table showing citywide indicators 1992–6;
- a leaflet summarizing trends and key points.

Indicator trends show that for some indicators Bristol is moving in a direction towards sustainable development, while for others Bristol is either reflecting very little change or moving away from sustainable development.

In a Local Agenda 21 survey of UK local authorities conducted by the University of Westminster for LGMB, Bristol responded to questions for the July 1997 meeting in New York of the Commission for Sustainable Development as follows:

- the authority is committed to participating in a Local Agenda 21 process;
- the commitment involves strong support for change in the authority's operations;

- a Local Agenda 21 strategy document is to be published at the end of 1996 or early in 1997;
- new staff have been appointed for the Agenda 21 process, and sustainability and healthy city work;
- integration of Local Agenda 21 takes place throughout the authority through both existing and new officers' working and liaison groups;
- local authority members are involved through the Local Agenda 21 steering group, other committees and specific training initiatives;
- awareness has been raised across the authority through seminars and other activities for officers and members;
- environmental management systems involving the principles of eco-management and audit (EMA) have been introduced without registration although EMA schemes are currently under consideration;
- the approach is holistic, involving all policy areas and across the whole of the authority;
- sustainable development is a major driver of policy in corporate activities, land use planning, energy management, transport strategy, welfare and equal opportunities strategies, anti-poverty strategies, local food links and youth and community services, but not necessarily in relation to economic development and inward investment strategy and implementation;
- explicitly environmental services are a major driver of policy towards sustainable futures;
- additionally, green housekeeping, waste management, some aspects of economic regeneration, procurement, housing, health and major funding bids are significant contributors to sustainable development;
- Bristol involves the wider community mainly through environmental education, awareness raising events, support for voluntary groups, publication of local environmental information, library displays, press releases and an environment centre;
- the community participation requirements of Local Agenda 21 are being met through adapting existing structures such as planning consultation and tenant consultation procedures, and adopting new arrangements including focus groups, a Local Agenda 21 forum, planning for real, visioning and future search exercises;
- the authority has formal partnership arrangements with business, academia and non-governmental organizations;
- the authority has established links with other countries;

- state of the environment reporting has commenced and indicators have been established;
- the Bristol Local Agenda 21 campaign involves women, ethnic minorities, older people and people with disabilities.

In terms of implementation the city council responded to the same survey by suggesting the following barriers to implementation:

- lack of statutory status for Local Agenda 21;
- Lack of real commitment at national level for sustainable development (prior to the election of the new government in May 1997)
- lack of local tax-raising powers;
- lack of an integrated transport policy;
- jobs and environment seen as being in competition;
- language of sustainability.

In relation to the future, Bristol's answers to the survey considered that the three key issues for further work were on transport, climate change and its implications and how to meet housing demand as a result of changing household size and growth in single person and elderly households and its impact on the urban and rural environment.

Expanding the information reported so far to give some concrete examples of the range and level of activity on sustainability it is important to include:

- the Create Centre – Bristol's Environment Centre;
- Western Partnership for Sustainable Development (WPSD);
- the ecological house demonstration project;
- environmental performance advice to small businesses;
- healthy city campaign, conferences and multi-city programme;
- expansion of cycle routes and facilities;
- Choices for Bristol consultation;
- improvements in air quality monitoring and results;
- innovative examples of new forms of public transport, e.g. non-polluting buses;
- the cultural development policy of the city;
- extensive waste recycling.

Following a series of conferences hosted by the Government Office for the South West in the winter of 1996–7, which explored how the region could be made more sustainable, the following conclusions were suggested:

> Bristol and the South West owes much of its attraction and success to the quality of its environment. Ensuring the region develops in ways which protect and enhance that quality, building on its strengths, will be vital, it was suggested, to future quality of life and prosperity.   (GOSW, 1997)

Much is already under way in the region to explore how it can develop more sustainably. For example:

- There is an active network of local authorities and others concerned with Local Agenda 21, building local participation and tackling environmental issues;
- successful energy and environmental groups offer a forum for companies to improve their performance; and
- work on land use planning, regeneration and transport is increasingly concerned at every level with promoting more sustainable patterns.   (GOSW, 1997)

The principal regional challenges were seen to involve the need to manage demand to more sustainable levels in relation to housing, the extraction of minerals, pressures from traffic, energy and its input to the region and waste management. However, there was also concern that any measures be economically beneficial as well as good for the environment and socially. Tensions were perceived between current demands of inward investment and other economic development policies for large greenfield sites and sustainable policies designed to reuse land and minimize travel pressures. There was an 'anxiety' over the appropriate policy stance to be taken with respect to economic competition in relation to other parts of the UK, Europe and globally, and the policies necessary for the maintenance of the quality of life and supporting local assets that also contribute to the attractiveness of the city and the region to inward investment.

At a regional level the Government Office for the South West is to set up a Round Table on Sustainable Development, mirroring the national set-up with a technical secretariat and a regional database of relevant practice.

At a city level, Bristol has been active and seems politically committed to making its contribution at local level to regional, national,

European and global concerns. This is being implemented through environmental programmes, the Local Agenda 21 process, and innovatory and pioneering partnerships between business, academia, voluntary and community sectors with the City Council (Snape and Stewart, 1996). What is not so clear is how well this policy initiative is owned across the authority, whether economic imperatives are in any way affected positively or negatively by the policy drive for sustainability, and whether Bristolians understand their contribution to the local and global issues facing the world in the next century.

URBAN MANAGEMENT FOR SUSTAINABILITY

Earlier in this chapter some of the discussions of a global urban challenge for the next 20–30 years that have emerged from the UN series of conferences, international non-governmental organizations, some national governments and many local government networks as well as from science and social science research were outlined. There is a certain orthodoxy over the general scenario and the fundamental actions that need to be addressed, although global issues and concerns are not readily or easily grasped at the local level despite the early rhetoric of thinking globally, acting locally.

The European urban focus was then discussed, raising some of the tensions within it and again noting the emerging policy thinking in relation to both urban sustainability and notions of sustainable futures in terms of Europe's regions. Indeed, in discussions over the Fifth Framework Programme for Research in the European Commission, the 'City of Tomorrow' is identified as a key theme, as are developing concerns with the interrelationship of socio-economic and environment/ health issues associated with the transformation of cities.

The European Sustainable Cities Project was described and its influence both within European policy thinking in the Commission and the Parliament can be noted as well as the ongoing influence and support for different sectors, but particularly local government. In concluding the description of the project, which is continuing in its second phase until 2000, the main issues underpinning the detailed discussion and recommendations of the policy report were identified.

Against this backcloth questions were then asked about Bristol as a European city in its region and whether it is moving towards a more sustainable future. The actions of the city council in conjunction with other partners and the community were described, and some of the barriers and obstacles that place limits on what can be achieved were identified.

In this concluding discussion two different levels of intervention are considered, the local and the European. At the local level the chapter discusses the emerging policy and management orthodoxy to achieve more sustainable futures for urban areas, and discusses these in terms of their limits and the wider issues that are raised in the reality of their implementation. At the European level, the emerging urban policy is discussed and the implications and questions that this raises.

City level

Despite considerable work by cities and by national governments, cities continue to face economic and social problems and environmental degradation and ill health. New ways of managing the urban environment, it is agreed, need to be found so that cities can both solve local problems and contribute to regional and global sustainability.

Sustainable development in the Expert Group Report (CEC, 1996) is identified as a much broader concept than environmental protection. It has economic and social as well as cultural health and environmental dimensions, and embraces notions of equity between people in the present and between generations. It implies that further development should take place only within the carrying capacity of natural and social systems. In relation to work on the ecological footprint of cities (Rees, 1993, 1997), it could be suggested that a sustainable city is one that is attempting to reduce its ecological footprint (Douglas, 1995).

A developing argument deriving from discussion of these principles is that sustainable development must be planned for and that market forces alone cannot achieve the necessary integration of environmental, social, health and economic concerns. A form of urban management and urban governance is suggested which provides a framework within which innovative approaches to the planning of sustainability can be explored. In this respect, a set of ecological, social, economic, organizational and democratic principles and tools for urban management have been identified, which may be applied in a variety of urban settings and which could be used selectively as cities move from different starting points and different circumstances towards contributing to local and global sustainability. The case study examples from practice across Europe and from Bristol clearly demonstrate an institutional as well as a policy focus. The capacity of different levels of government, and particularly local government, to deliver sustainability is seen as crucial.

This may require fundamental reviews of the internal structure and working of local authorities and their relationship with their communities, as well as an examination of the relationship between central and local governments. A further dimension is that thinking about cities is undergoing a reappraisal with a return to a view of the city as a complex system requiring a set of tools which can be applied in a range of settings. Although the system is complex, it is appropriate to seek practical solutions, especially solutions which solve more than one problem at a time, or several solutions that can be used in combination. Illustrative examples of this are numerous – a Sheffield UK example in housing captures the essence of this approach (Price and Tsouros, 1996).

The challenge of urban sustainable development involves both the problems experienced within cities, the problems caused by cities and the potential solutions that cities themselves may provide. Managers of cities, if they are to meet more sustainable futures, must seek to resolve the social, economic, cultural and health needs of urban residents while respecting local, regional and global natural systems, broadly solving problems locally where possible rather than shifting them to other spatial locations or passing them on to future generations. This prescriptive advice must, however, be interpreted within the complexity of regional and global economic and environmental relationships. This interpretation may raise broader issues about the 'production of space' and the 'production of nature' (Harvey, 1996) and may also raise issues about the role of local political leadership, the partnership approach to resolving urban issues and the responsibilities of chief executives of cities (SOLACE, LGMB, LGA, 1998).

The preceding overview of the changes argued to be necessary to achieve a more sustainable future for cities is both proactive, coherent and potentially radical. However, for it to be implemented, a number of deeper questions and issues are raised that must also be addressed.

We have witnessed considerable 'local' changes and achievements that support sustainable futures (recycling, environment centres, Agenda 21 coordinators, Agenda 21 plans, use of sustainability indicators, expansion of cycling provision, etc.) but at the same time we have also witnessed considerable growth in inward investment and economic development initiatives that appear to have little in common with policy or practice changes for more sustainable futures.

Similarly urban regeneration schemes, often successful in their own economic and physical development terms, have not engaged with nor helped to improve the environmental and social aspects of the city's problems. We seem to be at a stage where the integration of social, economic and environmental aspects of all policies, programmes and projects appears to be somewhat beyond the capacity of local government. Does this mean that an approach like comprehensiveness in town planning in the 1960s is too complex and too idealized for the reality of everyday governance, or is something more fundamental needed which will transform the socio-ecological and political-economic processes and relations both within a city and also at national, European and global levels? Tackling these difficult issues is an urgent area for interdisciplinary research, education, training and new forms of consultancy, but it also requires considerable leadership and cultural change at the local level.

EUROPEAN LEVEL

Towards an Urban Agenda in the European Union (CEC, 1997b) sees the main challenges facing European cities revolving around the dynamics of urban change in Europe, due to net immigration, national economic performance, structural change in the employment market coupled with the rapid growth and size of the service sector, the increasing importance of environment and quality of life conditions, the skills base and responsiveness of labour in locational decisions, the expansion of the EU through the reunification of Germany and the accession of countries in Central and Eastern Europe. Globalization and the shift to services has nevertheless not diminished the importance of space for economic development. There is, however, an emerging imbalance in the European urban system with central gateway cities such as Antwerp, Bremen, Rotterdam, Hanover, Lyon and Vienna, and medium cities located in the core of Europe, profiting more from European integration than cities on the periphery.

As these economic changes shape urban futures, inhabitants are increasingly concerned about the quality of their natural and physical environment and the quality of life their city provides. There is a growing dissatisfaction with the quality of air, water, natural environment, safety, quality of the built environment and the contribution of urban planning. Inhabitants' 'voice' in relation to these issues, although growing, is often fragmented, frustrated or missing. There is clearly an imbalance in local democratic influence within and between cities across the Union. In terms of institutional response, cities across Europe are operating in very different legal, institutional and financial systems. Some local authorities, for example, operate within a greater tradition of local autonomy and wield larger spending power than other local authorities.

The Communication concludes that the European city is at a cross-roads asking 'Why are people no longer happy to live all their lives in the city?' We need to ask of this question: which people, what parts of the city, and what are the components of a lifestyle that apparently cannot be satisfied for some in the city?

Although the Communication provides an understanding of urban change and suggestions for policy responses that integrate social, economic and environmental concerns, the main issue that remains is the real politics of integration both horizontally and vertically within the Commission which becomes crucial if the Urban Agenda Communication is to lead to a more coherent urban policy.

Included within the Urban Agenda Communication is the work of the European Sustainable Cities Project. This is considerably more developed compared with the stage of development of urban policy. The main findings of the European Sustainable Cities report (CEC, 1996) point to the following policy directions for cities:

- rethinking urban management, governance and leadership;
- organizational, governmental and policy integration;
- continued development of ecosystems thinking and the notion of the ecological footprint of cities;
- expansion of partnership, cooperative and participatory approaches;
- maintaining notions of equity now and inter-generational equity.

These broad policy themes suggest new thinking for cities and city authorities but equally for national governments and Europe (Van den Borg, 1996; Free Hanseatic City of Bremen, 1997).

Further, the Fifth Framework Programme for Research in the European Union funded by the European Commission (DG XII) which began its four-year programme in 1998 contains a strong focus on the 'City of Tomorrow'. Fudge and Rowe (1998) in a report on a research seminar on the development of socio-economic environmental research suggest some of the priorities for urban researchers:

- how to upgrade (towards sustainability goals) current urban stock – which will also comprise the fabric of the 'City of Tomorrow';
- developing models for the future of access and mobility which are affordable and sustainable;
- how to reduce inequality, counteract unemployment and social exclusion;
- investigating methods of implementing healthy public policy including community safety;
- attuning urban economies to sustainability goals, at the appropriate scale and without exporting problems, so the research agenda must include city and hinterland;
- underpinning research into the changing nature of urban and social values;
- examining approaches to urban management and governance that are required for sustainable futures for cities.

Cities are increasingly at the centre of European policy thinking, even though the legal and constitutional competence is less clear. The Urban Agenda Communication (CEC, 1997b) provides the stimulus for active debate in Europe leading to the Urban Forum in late 1998. As a contribution to the debate the Expert Group on the Urban Environment is finalizing its own response and will include the suggestions contained in Figure 15.1 for changes to European policies, legislation, funding programmes and research to enhance the possibility of urban sustainability in the future. However, fundamental questions remain to be addressed:

- What would a European urban policy look like and how would it be implemented?
- How will the accession of countries in Central and Eastern Europe affect this policy?
- How will a European urban policy – indeed how will the European Union – fare in the much discussed 'Pacific century' at the beginning of the next millennium?

In an era of apparent global environmental change and rapid urbanization, it becomes essential to reconsider our thinking about how cities are changing and how we can change cities. It is clear from the global discussions over the last 25 years that cities all over the world are in different development phases and in different states of vulnerability to global forces. It is also apparent that, despite these differences, cities are increasingly coming together to solve problems and share practice. But

- As a prerequisite evaluate impact of existing EU policies, programmes and instruments on towns and cities.
- The workshop commented on the lack of attention given in the Communication to Central and Eastern Europe. In looking forward to the Urban Forum and any emerging urban policy changes, the expansion of the European Union should be included in this policy thinking as an integral part.
- The contribution of towns and cities in Europe at their local levels to global concerns such as climate should be made more explicit when considering changes to urban policies. Thus integrating both local and global concerns and making explicit to European citizens their global responsibilities were required.
- The notion of 'urban' in the Communication should be reframed to include the urban–rural interdependency and relationship. This emphasises notions of ecological footprint and city region both of which should be pursued via a research programme in DG XII. In addition, the workshop considered that further understanding was needed of the urban–rural relationship at the end of the 20th century.
- There was some concern that the 'natural environment' and biodiversity issues were apparently omitted from the Communication even though they are important issues for urban areas. As well as policy inclusion of this issue suggestions were made in relation to inclusion in both revised urban pilot projects and research.
- There was considerable discussion of the nature of urban economy and the relative influence at the local level. A dual urban economy was postulated made up of a global component that is difficult to control locally and a local economy that can be influenced. Pilot projects and research were put forward as suggestions for examining how the 'two economies' can be interrelated positively in urban areas.
- Some cities have been exploring the development of local food production as part of their sustainable urban policy. These cities are suggesting that European agriculture policy and funding needs to be changed to support such initiatives.
- All economic development and regeneration programmes funded by the European Commission should be recast to ensure achievement of sustainable objectives and include sustainability criteria. In addition, some urban projects should be recast to combine urban and rural areas in joint proposals.
- The workshop discussed local authority procurement fairly extensively and the need for liberalisation of rules to achieve sustainable objectives. It was suggested that pilot projects should be set up with some zones in Europe being free of procurement rules. These zones should be evaluated to see if procurement achieving sustainability objectives can be advanced.
- In addition it was suggested that European wide local authority procurement consortia be organised to improve the influence of purchasing towards sustainable objectives.
- Reallocate funding and policy to provide a strong focus on transport problems of towns and cities. DG VII to take the lead in association with DG XI. This is the most common issue facing all towns and cities.
- Continue with the development of the spatial development perspective, urban audit approaches and sustainability indicators. Combine work of the European Environment Agency and Commission to avoid duplication.
- Support further work on 'urban management and governance' as seen as critical at all levels of government and involving cultural change, institutional capacity and change, training, education and practice dissemination.
- Continue and expand education and awareness programmes. Develop these within a new across Commission strategy focusing on urban sustainability. Utilise and build on existing approaches, e.g. the Campaign.
- Expand and implement, as a matter of urgency, the sharing of practice through a database, interactive web sites, partner forums and seminars/workshops such as the Campaign day.

Figure 15.1   Changes to European policies – suggestions from the EU Urban Environment Expert Group in response to the Urban Communication (CEC, 1997b).

as Rees (1997) says: 'What happens to the cities of 1 million, 10 million or 20 million population if the distant sources of food, water, energy etc. are no longer secure?' If cities are to reduce their dependence on external resources, to reduce their ecological footprint, they may need to reconsider their regional and local natural capital, for example Bristol's work on local food chains. This means thinking of cities as whole systems and thinking of cities in relation to their hinterlands. This implies not only changes to urban policy and urban management, but crucially for Europe changes to policies in relation to agriculture and food production. However, whether we define cities with or without their supportive hinterland or whether we argue for compact urban forms, linear transport corridor cities or looser sustainable lattices, the best designed cities and most creatively managed and governed cities cannot be sustainable until their citizens also adopt more sustainable lifestyles.

ACKNOWLEDGEMENTS

This chapter draws directly on the work of the EU Urban Environment Expert Group and its two policy reports (CEC 1994c, 1996); the work of the Campaign for European Sustainable Cities and Towns; work on Healthy Cities for WHO; policy development contributions for the European Commission on urban policy and urban research; and the developing work of the Western Partnership for Sustainable Development in Bristol. It acknowledges the many who contributed to this work but particularly Dr Liz Mills (DG XI), Stefaan de Rynck (DG XVI), Andrew Sors (DG XII), David Ludlow and Susann Pauli (EURONET UWE), Vincent Nadin (UWE), Anthony Payne (Campaign Co-ordinator, Brussels), John Pontin, Mo Mulligan (Western Partnership for Sustainable Development).

Notes

1.	Satterthwaite (1996), a British researcher, argues that the statistical basis for megacity arguments are suspect. As a result he raises concerns about the proportion of national budgets and international aid going to megacities and the overlooking of continents such as Africa with the fewest megacities but severe problems of poverty, poor sanitation and health.
2.	Rapid urbanization is, of course, occurring in certain parts of Southern Europe in relation to the growth of large cities, e.g. Madrid, and in relation to tourism.

References

P. Brown, 'Swelling cities face collapse', *Guardian*, 30 May 1996.

CLRAE, *The European Urban Charter*, Standing Conference of Local and Regional Authorities of Europe (Strasbourg: Council of Europe, 1992).

Commission of the European Communities (CEC), *Green Paper on the Urban Environment*, COM(90) 218 (Brussels: CEC, 1990).

Commission of the European Communities, *Europe 2000: Outlook for the Development of the Community's Territory*, COM(91) 452 (Brussels: CEC, 1991).

Commission of the European Communities, *Towards Sustainability: A European Community Programme of Policy and Action in Relation to the Environment and Sustainable Development*, COM(92) 23 (Brussels: CEC, 1992a).

Commission of the European Communities, *The Future Development of the Common Transport Policy: A Global Framework for Sustainable Mobility*, COM(92) 494 Final (Brussels: CEC, 1992b).

Commission of the European Communities, *Green Paper on the Impact of Transport on the Environment*, COM(92) 46 Final (Brussels: CEC, 1992c).

Commission of the European Communities, *Community Action in Urban Matters* (Brussels: CEC, 1993a).

Commission of the European Communities, *Growth, Competitiveness, Employment – The Challenges and Ways Forward into the 21st Century*, White Paper, COM(93) 700 Final (Brussels: CEC, 1993b).

Commission of the European Communities, *Europe 2000+: Cooperation for European Territorial Development* (Brussels: CEC, 1994a).

Commission of the European Communities, *Community Initiative Concerning Urban Areas (URBAN)*, COM(94) 61 Final (Brussels: CEC, 1994b).

Commission of the European Communities, Urban Environment Expert Group, *European Sustainable Cities*, Part One (Brussels: CEC, 1994c).

Commission of the European Communities, Urban Environment Expert Group, *European Sustainable Cities*, Final Report (Brussels: CEC, 1996).

Commission of the European Communities, *Agenda 2000* (Brussels: CEC, 1997a).

Commission of the European Communities, *Towards an Urban Agenda in the European Union* (Brussels: CEC, 1997b).

Committee on Spatial Development, *Principles for a European Spatial Development Policy*, paper to the Informal Council of Spatial Planning Ministers, Leipzig, 21–22 September 1994.

I. Douglas, Reported at the Commonwealth Heads of Government meeting, Auckland, New Zealand (1995).

European Environment Agency, *Europe's Environment: The Dobris Assessment* (Copenhagen: EEA, 1994).

European Institute of Urban Affairs, *Urbanisation and the Functions of Cities in the European Community*, Regional Development Studies No. 4, CEC Directorate-General for Regional Policies. Prepared by the European Institute of Urban Affairs, Liverpool John Moores University (Brussels: CEC, 1992).

European Sustainable Cities and Towns Campaign, *Charter of European Cities and Towns Towards Sustainability* (1994).

Free Hanseatic City of Bremen, *The Bremen Declaration, Business and Municipality. New Partnerships for the 21st Century* (1997).

C. Fudge and J. Rowe, *Urban Environment and Sustainability: Developing the Agenda for Socio-Economic Environmental Research*, research report for DG XII (1998).

Government Office of the South West (GOSW), *Draft Report on Sustainability Conferences held in 1996 and 1997* (Bristol: GOSW, 1997).

D. Harvey, *Justice, Nature and the Geography of Difference* (Oxford: Blackwell, 1996).

International Council for Local Environmental Initiatives, *The Local Agenda 21 Initiative – ICLEI Guidelines for Local and National Local Agenda 21 Campaigns* (Toronto: ICLEI, 1993).

Local Government Management Board (LGMB), *A Statement on Behalf of UK Local Government*, UNCED, February (1992a).

Local Government Management Board, *Agenda 21: A Guide for Local Authorities in the UK*, Earth Summit Rio '92 Supplement No. 2 (Luton: LGMB, 1992b).

Local Government Management Board, *A Framework for Local Sustainability* (Luton: LGMB, 1993a).

Local Government Management Board, *Greening Economic Development* (Luton: LGMB, 1993b).

Local Government Management Board, *Local Agenda 21 – Principles and Process – A Step by Step Guide* (Luton: LGMB, 1994).

F. Pearce, 'The rise and fall of the megacity', *Guardian*, 30 May 1996.

C. Price and A. Tsouros (eds), *Our Cities, Our Future: Policies and Action Plans for Health and Sustainable Development* (Copenhagen: WHO, 1996).

W.E. Rees, 'Ecological footprints and appropriated carrying capacity; what urban economics leaves out', *Environment and Urbanisation*, 4 (1993) 121–30.

W.E. Rees, 'Is "Sustainable city" an oxymoron?', *Local Environment*, 2 (1997) 303–10.

D. Satterthwaite, private communication at Habitat II, Istanbul (1996).

D. Snape and M. Stewart, *Keeping up the Momentum – Partnership Working in Bristol and the West* (Bristol: Bristol Chamber of Commerce and Initiative, 1996).

SOLACE, LGMB, LGA, *Sustainability Stocktake for Chief Executives in Local Authorities* (London: LGMB, 1998).

Van den Borg, *Organising Capacity of Metropolitan Cities*, EURICUR (Rotterdam, 1996).

J. Vidal, 'Global warning: cities harm people', *Guardian*, 11 June 1996.

M. Wackernagel and W. Rees, *Our Ecological Footprint: Reducing Human Impact on Earth* (British Columbia: New Society Publishers 1995).

16 Implementing Sustainable Development at the Local and Regional Level

Sabine Kunst

INTRODUCTION

Since the term 'ecological sustainability' was revised at the Environment Summit in Rio de Janeiro, it has brought fresh impetus into the environmental debate and has had a broad impact on the specialist literature. However, it has also inevitably triggered a flood of definitions of what sustainability means in different technical contexts. In the water management disciplines, there is talk of introducing a closed loop system for water, raw materials and energy, of not consuming more than can be regenerated, so that the next generation can enjoy the same conditions as we do now. This typology relates to the development of a responsible environment policy. Environment problems of all kinds, such as water, ground and air pollution, as well as the use of natural resources will have to be re-evaluated in line with these criteria.

This chapter aims to provide a brief summary of what the various approaches for implementing sustainable development at the local and regional level might look like. This will take the form of a case study in two areas of application (domestic and industrial water management) in Lower Saxony. These examples have been chosen because water is such a precious resource. According to the predictions of the expert standing committee for environmental issues, the study groups attached to Agenda 21 (United Nations, 1994), the international EXPO programme on people, nature and technology, the Environment Ministry in Berlin and the German Research Association water research group, water will be our greatest problem in the twenty-first century. Northern European nations with plentiful water supplies will be preoccupied with water management-related questions about securing resources, such as decontamination, ground water quality, expanding waterways and oceanic properties. For Southern Europe, the dominant issue will be adequate availability and provision of essential water supplies in view of the water shortage.

In ancient cultures water used to be viewed as an element with magical powers. The smooth surface of a calm stretch of water served as the first mirror for the human race. The secrets hidden behind this reflective area played an important role in dream analysis and for consulting the oracle. Now, water is seen as a general consumer durable which can apparently be used without harm, dirtied and reused (at least in the regions on earth with enough water). We seldom remember that we would be lost without clean water. In addition to waste water treatment, the supply of water is the responsibility of domestic water management agencies. This will be described in brief in relation to current problem areas in this sector and trends associated with implementing sustainable use of technology.

DOMESTIC AND INDUSTRIAL WATER MANAGEMENT IN GERMANY

Domestic water management

Waste water treatment is clearly facing a crisis. In recent years, there have been numerous reports of cost explosions in sewage treatment and sewer building projects. To cover their costs, local authorities are compelled to pass on connection costs to owners in the form of charges determined at the local level. In many communities, waste water treatment costs now account for over 10 DM per cubic metre. With all the controversy about cause and effect in this area, it should be noted that Bonn was partly to blame for the exorbitant costs. Realistic time-scales were not employed to enable local authorities to adapt to the new legal position with their long-term structural redevelopment strategies at the end of the 1970s when waste water regulation was first introduced. Instead, the water pollution control levy act was passed five years before it was introduced, and the situation has worsened considerably over the past decade. As soon as sewage treatment plants were converted for nitrification, there were calls for denitrification systems to be introduced. There were also extremely contradictory statements from the Environment Ministry about recycling sewage slurry in agriculture.

Industrial water treatment

Water treatment experts aim to safeguard and protect water supplies as far as possible. In 1992 common European agreements on reductions to halve the eutrophy nutrient deposits in the North Sea were concluded. In Germany, a higher water quality (Class II) was to be achieved for flowing water with water management programmes, including specifically sewage treatment plant development. As the ecological stability and properties of Class II flowing water represent extremely high quality, in many areas these conditions were not attainable. In spite of numerous efforts, it has been impossible to achieve this target. Decontamination of many of the major selective sources was not sufficient by itself. Other factors, such as the water structure and large numbers of diffuse nutrient inputs from agriculture, soil erosion and so on, have also significantly affected the class of water quality (see Figure 16.1). Consequently, the class target has not been achieved despite efforts and initiatives by individual expert disciplines, e.g. with sewage plant development excluding agricultural input. Non-particularist multilevel interdisciplinary concepts are required.

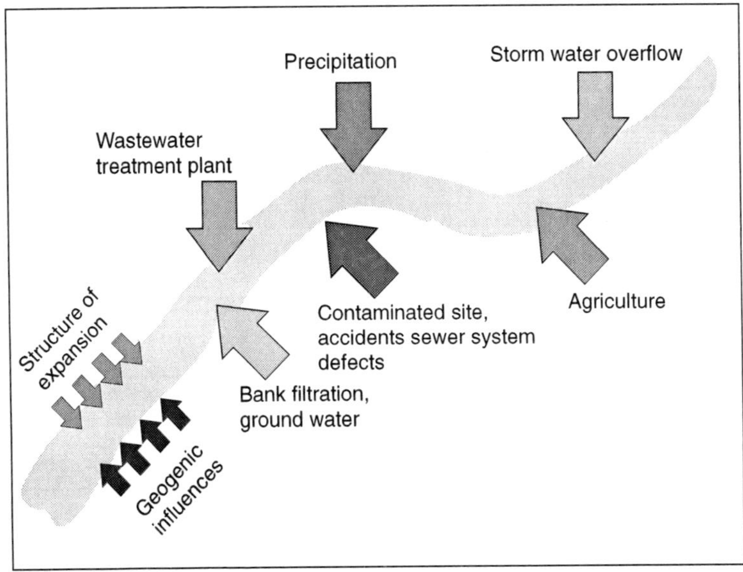

Figure 16.1 Influences on water quality.

In recent years traditional methods of evaluating water management measures have been widely criticized by professionals in the field. The following points have been identified as the main problem areas:

- particularist approach;
- lack of sufficient interaction with natural surroundings;
- economic accountability in terms of area of expertise only;
- shortcomings in evaluation methods (Strigl, 1996).

As a result, integrated approaches to development, management and use of water are essential if we are to protect the quality and quantity of freshwater resources.

In future, evaluations will not just address the cause and effect of programmes, but their sustainability too. If traditional values and development capacity criteria are combined, the following questions arise concerning water management measures:

- How should measures be designed to achieve an ecologically sustainable impact? Is it more worthwhile to build sewage plants or purchase land to ensure that river banks are not farmed when comparing and contrasting the effects of a range of measures, such as restoring water levels, sewage plant development, responsible farming methods, hedgerow cultivation schemes? On what basis should ranking decisions be made?
- What local and regional effects do the various measures have?

In the next section, a current example illustrates this point.

IS DECENTRALIZED WASTE WATER TREATMENT MORE ENVIRONMENTALLY WORTHWHILE AND 'MORE SUSTAINABLE' THAN A CENTRALIZED SYSTEM?

This issue is the subject of a lively and heated debate in Lower Saxony, not just in terms of sustainable development, but also because in Lower Saxony the reform of section 149 (water pollution control levy) of the Lower Saxony Water Regulation attaches equal weight to decentralized and centralized waste water treatment. Local authorities were required to present a waste water treatment plan by the end of 1998 and they were free to base the plan on the notion of decentralization.

Unfortunately, in local authority debate little importance is attached to the argument in favour of sustainable development, and the traditional profitability calculations normally take overriding priority. Nevertheless, there are isolated exceptions where ideas are being developed to solve practical problems based on criteria such as sustainability or development capacity. The following example is intended to illustrate the extent to which this can be applied to decentralized waste water management:

In Lower Saxony 87 per cent of the population are on mains drainage. Waste water is treated in 1062 local authority sewage plants, 372 of which serve more than 1000 of the population equivalent. The remaining waste water is treated in 275 000 private small-scale sewage plants, of which 3000 are natural purification plants. In regions with rural structures, the average number of householders with mains drainage will remain below average due to the topographic situation, i.e. around 20–30 per cent of the local population will continue to rely on waste water disposal by small-scale sewage plants. Whereas the effectiveness of treatment in large-scale sewage plants has risen following investment in continuing waste water treatment projects up to 1990, there is no doubt that the smaller plants are in urgent need of overhaul. Beyond the small sewage plants and smaller treatment plants, pond-based and natural purification plants stimulate natural processes, produce good process concentration levels and are extremely reliable in contrast to small-scale technical systems.

Trace nutrient deposits entering into the water in Lower Saxony from large and small sewage plants may be calculated from the average process concentration levels. Those causing long-term harmful effects consist of 4.1 per cent nitrogenous and around 8.3 per cent phosphorous output from small-scale sewage plants (total input: $N = 47.4$ tonnes/day and $P = 5.6$ t/d). The output from agriculture is greater, so that in the region overall there is no significant damage to the ground water from small-scale sewage plants.

By contrast, the evaluation of the local situation produces the following picture. The waste water of one resident contains 12 g/resident/day of nitrogen, of which 4.8 g/resident/day will remain in the ground water as a potential pollutant following biological treatment, whereas around 0.4 g/resident/day of phosphorus is left from 2.8 g/resident/day of phosphorus. Therefore, for a property of 1000 square metres and a household of four, this produces an annual ground water pollution level from treated waste water of 70 kg N/hectare p.a., or 5.8 kg P/hectare p.a., or, in other words, considerable selective ground water pollution on virtually the same scale as land which is farmed intensively.

For the sake of our environment it is therefore vital that we try and improve process values and employ nutrients as fertilizers in the garden if we want to implement decentralized waste water treatment as sustainable development as well. In addition to the individual nutrient chain it has also been shown to have a positive effect on the water balance.

DECENTRALIZED WASTE WATER TREATMENT IN THE LOCAL AUTHORITY DEBATE

So far it has been stressed that there is room for improvement in waste water treatment in scattered settlements. It is therefore hardly surprising that at the local level an in-depth controversial debate is currently raging about a satisfactory solution for the environment at a reasonable cost. A series of local action groups have been set up to implement ideas based on decentralization. One of the main lines of argument concerns safeguarding existing supplies with a closed loop system which is essential for any sustainable development.

These local action groups assume that decentralized recycling will serve the essential life cycle processes in nature better than central processing. In order to maintain natural water levels, it is absolutely vital to restore water where it is taken out of the earth. The following arguments also form a fundamental part of this approach:

- decentralized waste water treatment is cheaper;
- natural water levels remain intact;
- residents can influence their own costs;
- the use of artificial fertilizers is reduced.

The relevant local action groups frequently argue in favour of decentralized waste water treatment on ideological grounds, without providing firm evidence to prove their case.

DECENTRALIZATION AS A POLITICAL PRINCIPLE: 'PERSONAL EXPERIENCE DEVELOPS A SENSE OF RESPONSIBILITY FOR SUSTAINABLE PLANNING AND DEVELOPMENT'

Environmental lobbies and political parties are demanding a more environmentally minded and sustainable industrial policy, although there is still no clear consensus on the criteria for such a policy. One solution is to demand the replacement of so called central policy. There are calls for a commitment to smaller, less complex structures. The demand for decentralization can therefore also be interpreted as an opportunity for political emancipation and scope for the development of ecological solutions. Decentralized structures are meant to bring about independent regional development.

SUMMARY AND CONCLUSION

In regional terms, we may safely assume that small-scale sewage plants do not constitute a major pollutant and that seepage volumes of waste water do not contribute substantially to artificially inflating water supply and consumption figures. Our local survey reveals that waste water seepage produces selective ground water pollution and it would be possible to effectively improve the ground water quality. Nevertheless, the building and operation of small-scale sewage plants in isolation would still make no significant contribution to sustainable domestic water management development.

Moreover, sustainable ecological planning and development is designed to have two areas of impact: influence on the spatial environment and on individual and social treatment of the environment. The latter is primarily a question of communications. However, these are more suited to decentralized structures, i.e. clear-cut areas with scope for individual participation, rather than centralized structures.

APPROACHES TO THE EVALUATION OF WATER MANAGEMENT PROGRAMMES

In order to define criteria for implementing sustainable development in future environmental policy, it is essential to evaluate past measures. The most important water management measures need to be monitored and inputs from the various pollutant trails, such as agriculture, selective and diffuse input, should be documented. Furthermore, it is important to find out what costs are incurred by the various measures and whether the impact of decontamination is environmentally effective or sustainable.

In Lower Saxony, there are a number of research projects under way with a similar general background, including one European Union and several regional projects which are designed to monitor nutrient deposits in water and calculate the costs of a series of measures and develop economic environmental cost-effective links. On the basis of the findings of the nutrient monitoring, quota fixing scenarios can be drawn up to produce effective and sustainable nutrient purification. The following questions are particularly relevant in this respect:

- What environment quality targets are feasible?
- Is the achievement of these ecologically based targets financially viable?
- How much of sewage treatment plant development is economically worthwhile in terms of the environment?

The following water monitoring factors were taken into consideration:

- precipitation;
- evaporation;
- drainage effluent;
- intermittent effluent;
- ground water effluent;
- surface effluent.

For the nutrient monitoring, ten different input trails were identified:

- sewage treatment plant intake;
- rainwater drains;
- direct input (fertilizer loss, small-scale sewage plants);
- drain water;
- intermittent effluent;
- ground water;
- erosion;
- woodland area concentrations;
- atmospheric deposits;
- restoring and reducing water levels.

From nutrient monitoring conducted on flowing water in heath land, 30 per cent of the nitrogen originated from sewage plant processes and 70 per cent from diffuse sources. The picture for phosphorous input was different. There, 47 per cent of the input was from sewage treatment plants with 15 per cent from surface effluent and 12 per cent from erosion. According to the impact analysis, with responsible farming methods and extensive land use, the following results were obtained (February 1995):

- For nitrogen reduction, measures affecting selective sources are more effective; for phosphorus on the other hand, measures influencing selective points of entry are favoured.
- The desired quality targets cannot be achieved with sewage plant development.
- Measures affecting sewage plants and additional implementation of responsible farming methods with alternate fruit tree plantation produces an adequate reduction.
- The most effective strategy for achieving sustainable nitrogen reduction is to practise more extensive agriculture.
- The most effective strategy for reducing phosphorous deposits is sewage plant development.
- In addition to responsible farming methods, riverbank and hedgerow schemes, leaving ploughed fields in areas suffering from erosion to lie fallow as green spaces is apparently particularly effective for the environment.

To establish the order of priorities for the various scenarios, individual quota-fixing scenarios are evaluated in terms of cost-effectiveness. It was surprising to learn that even in the worst case scenario, with sewage plant development, responsible farming methods, hedgerow schemes and extensive farming, prices were not exorbitant and it remained a viable alternative at 4.00 DM/cubic metre. It was particularly noticeable that the block of measures aimed at significantly impacting on diffuse input, i.e. responsible farming methods, involved only a slight rise in specific costs.

Furthermore, people are beginning to realize that surveys and scenarios need to be based on natural space and use if sustainable development is to be achieved in the regions. Only then is it possible to estimate what measures might have a particular impact in certain locations. Approaches like this are therefore an important part of the methodical process of development (see Figure 16.2), and bring us a

      Sabine Kunst

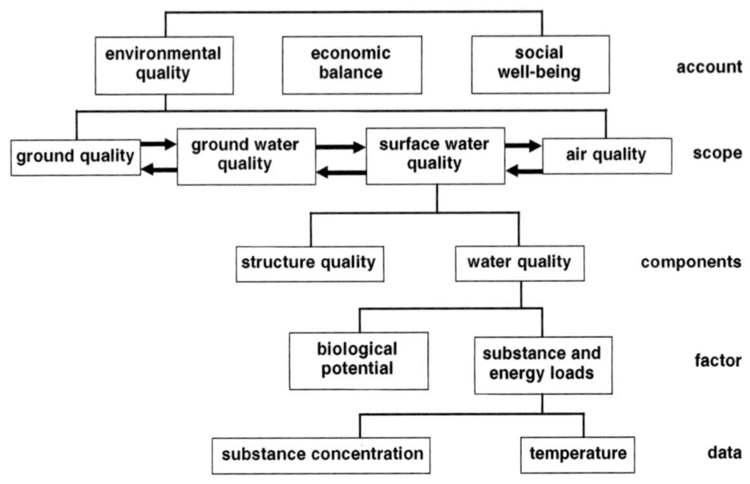

Figure 16.2   A comprehensive approach to water quality management.

step closer to notions of sustainability for water management measures at regional level too. The first few steps have already been taken, but there is still a long way to go.

References

G. Strigl, 'Hydrologie und Entwicklung der Wasservorkommen in einer ver-wundbaren Welt [Hydrology and the development of water resources in a vulnerable world]', *DGM*, 40: 3 (Bonn, 1996).
United Nations, 'Agenda 21: Umweltpolitik, Konferenz der Vereinten Nationen für Umwelt und Entwicklung 1992 im Rio de Janeiro [Agenda 21: UN Conference on Environment and Development, Rio de Janeiro 1992]', in *Information der Bundesumwelt – 'Ministerismus'* [Information from the Environment Ministry] (1994).

17 Challenges to Urban Policy: Modernization and the Mobilization of Local Resources in the Twenty-first Century

Bernhard Blanke and Randall Smith[1]

INTRODUCTION

The need for action at the local level can be addressed from four different but interrelated perspectives:

- the *globalization* of economic competition, which is often associated with the problem of a huge public budget deficit (the economic dimension);
- the transfer of welfare state responsibilities to local level and the shift of the costs of provision onto the private sector. These changes, especially in the big cities, aggravate the problems of *social exclusion* and *poverty* and pose the question of whether and to what extent local authorities are in a position to develop the capacity to focus their services and match them to modern social problems and challenges (the social dimension);
- the challenge which the idea of sustainable development presents for *local environment policy-making* and ecologically informed urban restructuring. This has to be addressed through the development of specific, long-term action plans and innovative packages of particular measures (the ecological dimension);
- the reform of *urban governance*, whereby a 'negotiating administration' and the enhancement of opportunities for participatory democracy are associated with overarching strategies for modernization (the political-institutional dimension).

GLOBALIZATION AND COMPETITION BETWEEN CITIES

The climate of competition is creating significant pressure to modernize policy at the local level. With the breakdown of national economic boundaries, 'there is a paradoxical increase in the economy's sensitivity to the diversity of cities' (Schridde, 1997b, p. 173). City councils have an incentive to be innovative in their policy-making in order to develop their particular strengths and competitiveness through marketing strategies, improvement of their infrastructure and stimulation of a climate of innovation.

Globalization is accompanied by a concentration of government and decision-making in the cities as jobs in production and sales move to peripheral localities. Labour markets are being restructured in ways which vary locally depending on their degree of integration in global, national or regional economic networks. This process tends to lead towards social polarization in terms of jobs, incomes and standards of living. However, cities are not all equally involved in the globalization process. While the more prosperous cities are witnessing more dynamic career patterns, more individualization and pluralization and more risks in individual people's lives (with intermittent poverty among some individuals), the old industrial cities tend to be characterized rather by the social structures of industrial society and traditional forms of poverty. In other words, the 'Fordist' life pattern is clearly shaped by the traditional labour market and sustained by the social policy of the welfare state. The contrasting dynamics and patterns are a reflection of differing economic, social and institutional contexts. As far as policy at the local level is concerned, this means that, because of the changes in the social structure of those cities more engaged in the globalization process, the conventional social security systems are losing their effectiveness. A growing number of people are becoming dependent on the bottom line of income support and on any additional support that can be provided at local level (Schridde, 1997a).

Globalization is, however, directly linked to a second and increasingly important issue, namely regional integration. Europe has been 'regionalizing' itself since the 1980s for two reasons. First, the consequences of crises in economic and employment policies usually extend well beyond individual local authority areas and have in many places led to the creation and implementation of regional development ideas. Second, 'the globalisation of entrepreneurial decisions is making it necessary to adopt a regional position' (Priebs, 1998, p. 123), since it is usually only at the regional level that individual municipalities can mobilize those strategic financial or infrastructure resources needed to tackle intense international competition.

Unfavourable characteristics of a particular location can be countered by a regional strategy and a pooling of resources. Action is therefore needed to develop an effective functional region, with appropriate institutional arrangements, competitive profiling and a distinctive character. Urban policy should, therefore, be seen in the context of its functional integration in the region. This means more than setting up local and regional associations, which typically undertake a range of regional administrative tasks, geographically mirroring formal structures. They tend to constitute just another level of administration, frequently leading to duplicated responsibilities and a growing administrative burden. What is needed above and beyond this is the formation of city or district networks, that is areas of cooperation and coordination, to function as creative promoters of the locality, to develop in accordance with clearly defined objectives and to address particular issues such as economic support, technology and transport.

These networks should develop within and between individual cities but can also extend beyond national boundaries. In particular, linkages have developed between localities facing similar problems or with similar characteristics in different member states of the European Union (Church and Reid, 1996). The Coalfields Communities Campaign is one example of a focused transnational interest group of local community representatives. Another is the more broadly conceived Eurocities which addresses a wide variety of issues facing large, but not capital, cities in the European Union.

The European Commission itself requires transnational partnerships on the part of local and regional authorities in any bid for funds from Community Initiatives such as HORIZON (promotion of employment opportunities for disadvantaged people) or ADAPT (retraining of workers in the light of technological change) (see Staeck, 1996, pp. 56–7). As well as globalization pressures, there are, therefore, other kinds of administrative supranational developments which can encourage cities to depart from a traditional inward-looking localism and to redefine themselves as part of a transnational European enterprise.

URBAN POLICY AND SOCIAL DIVISION

In the light of social and economic upheaval and ever tighter cost-cutting strategies, the question of what form a society should take and what rights of participation it accords to individuals or social groups is clearly a very important local matter. The thrust of social policy at the local level is crucial for the distribution of opportunities and the general shaping of people's lives.

Since the 1980s, a twofold socio-economic division has become apparent in both Germany and the UK. First, there are the regional inequalities between north and south and in Germany since reunification, between east and west. Second, there is the rise of social divisions and exclusion, especially in the larger cities. As a result of economic restructuring and the crisis of a social security system based on the labour market, social policy at the local level in the 1990s has increasingly had to take on the burdens resulting from the modernization of the welfare state. The phenomenon of 'double exclusion', i.e. exclusion from earnings-related benefits and broader exclusion of an increasingly large group of people not in the formal labour market, has increased the likelihood of poverty and placed a heavier burden on the social security system. The growth of poverty, underprivilege and social exclusion seems unstoppable in the cities. The repercussions of economic and social restructuring and thus the specific impact of poverty and social exclusion in the cities flow from a number of political and institutional factors, both local and national, such as the current structure of the welfare state's social security system (see Hamnett, 1996).

Against the background of social and economic modernization, social policy at the local level is faced with the tasks of addressing the consequent risks of exclusion and of identifying new possibilities for integration tailored to local circumstances. If national social policy is no longer able to provide lifelong integration in the labour market for all citizens, then a responsibility falls upon local social policy to ensure social integration outside the labour market of a group of people who are fully capable of work but are not actually employed (Blanke et al., 1987). Despite attempts, at least in Germany, in the 1980s to achieve this social integration, there has been increasing decentralization and fragmentation of the welfare state in the 1990s. The new risks of exclusion in 'postmodern' society and the move towards a residual 'income support state' – marked by the shifting of responsibility for a range of social problems and predicaments from the central to the local level – have increasingly forced local authorities to become crisis managers with limited local powers of decision-making and little room for financial manoeuvre. They have been largely left to their own devices. Although local authorities are not in a position to ameliorate the causes of poverty and exclusion, they are the least able to escape the problems.

Social policy at the local level must therefore be both more than poverty administration and more than a shock absorber of a general local policy influenced by globalization. The local authorities have the clear task of both encouraging and formalizing inclusion and reintegration processes. How this will be implemented 'depends primarily on the local context, the perception of the problem, and political perspectives and objectives ... at the local level. In this respect, social policy at the local level differs both within and between cities' (Schridde, 1997a, p. 878). Programmes of action of varying complexity, some more complex than others, have been launched in many cities to combat poverty and social exclusion.

The potential of local policy is based on its involvement, in cooperation with the citizen and with people in positions of social responsibility, in the dynamics of social conflict and on its ability to find ways forward in a manner which takes account of cooperative social responsibility and self-regulation. At the same time there is a tendency in many industrial countries for state policy to exploit, on the one hand, the social integration function of local policy and, on the other hand, to wield its power in order to pursue a 'welfare to work' strategy, whereby programmes are developed to cushion the effects of social exclusion and to open up opportunities for resocialization. Whether cities will become further divided or will come to play a vital part as places of integration depends on local commitment to the struggle against social exclusion and for economic regeneration.

URBAN POLICY AND ENVIRONMENTALLY INFORMED STRUCTURAL CHANGE

Environment policy has joined social policy as a central concern at the local level. The range of city responsibilities for environmental policy has changed radically in the last twenty years. The defensive position into which national environmental policy in the 'old' industrial countries has slipped in the wake of the competitiveness debate and high levels of unemployment stands in marked contrast to the diversity of reorganization at local level, where both ideas and measures are being discussed and implemented in order to protect resources and reduce the impact on the environment. Local authorities have therefore become the focal point of hopes and expectations.

At the UN conference on environment and development in Rio in 1992, the view was strongly expressed that global environmental problems could be resolved only with the active and interdisciplinary cooperation of local authorities and other key players. Chapter 28 of the final document, 'Agenda 21', accordingly emphasized the special role of local authorities as an essential component at an independent level of action, and not only for addressing the problems of the urban environment. The phrase 'sustainable development' was already being promoted before the earth summit as the focus for local discussion, as something which – 'complementing national agendas and with a weight of its own' (Hahn, 1997, p. 285) – needs to be turned into specific measures on local agendas and embedded in local policies. Local authorities have come together not only at the national level but also internationally with the aim of developing a joint environment policy.

It is due both to its positive connotation and to the openness of its definition that, depending on who the actors are, fundamentally different interpretations and approaches have become associated with the concept of local sustainable development. An examination of proposed specific sustainable development programmes reveals some very controversial views about their implementation, such as the instruments to be used, the strategies for effecting them, the stated objectives, the timescales and the cost-sharing arrangements. The term 'sustainable development' has become so overused that it is in danger of becoming meaningless. While there is consensus both about the basic idea and about the will to make local activity responsive to Agenda 21, it is nonetheless clear that there is a serious discrepancy between the introduction of concrete measures for achieving the stated objectives and the perfectly sincere declarations of intention. Putting into practice a local Agenda 21 in big cities is a huge problem.

This should not hide the fact that, in many cities, the Earth Summit in Rio has triggered debates which are aimed at a reassessment of local strategies for the sustainable use of resources and which have succeeded in establishing new ideas institutionally and normatively in local policies and in bringing together the ecological, social and economic dimensions. What matters above all is to get as many social groups as possible into a constructive dialogue.

Practical measures for the restructuring of cities on ecological lines (for example, in the areas of traffic, energy, sewage and water, waste disposal, urban development and open space provision) can be successful only if – at the *level of the administration* – the measures are developed across departments and understood as an integrated common strategy. The more comprehensively the ideas are discussed and developed and the more seriously the participants are involved in the planning and shaping of programmes, the greater will be the likelihood of success – *at the level of action* – of changes in the urban environment directed towards a sustainable future along Agenda 21 lines. There is a key role here for 'effective information systems, communications structures, and instruments of governance geared to local initiatives, economic strengths and powers of self-help in the districts of cities' (Hahn, 1997, p. 294). They must offer clear opportunities for new forms of cooperation between the various actors in debating, planning and implementing commonly agreed measures and they must at the same time stimulate the 'desire for experiment and the sense of possibility' (Hahn, 1997, p. 294) for the development of an overall concept for the ecology of the city.

ADMINISTRATION UNDER PRESSURE TO REFORM: MODERNIZATION THROUGH CITIZEN PARTICIPATION

The styles, instruments and notions of administrative action and the question of change have been the subject of intensive and wide-ranging debate. The internationalization of this debate has proved a catalyst and has provided a new impetus. A common starting point for reflections about reform is that traditional forms of democratic and decision-making processes are increasingly being seen as functionally and culturally inadequate in the face of rising demands for public participation and local authorities' growing need to work through mediation, coordination and consent. The various schools of reform ('traditional' approaches, 'New Public Management' or 'alternative' concepts) address different shortcomings in the modernization of local policy-making. In doing so, however, they systematically ignore the fact that a real reform of the way policy is made at the local level can succeed only by integrating different approaches.

While, from the point of view of administrative modernization, a redefinition of the relationship between district councils and their administrations plays an important role and the restructuring of the organization on business management principles (efficiency and effectiveness) remains central, the question of mobilizing citizen participation emphasizes elements of democratic policy. The latter is not directly compatible with the impact on internal modernization (the competitive spirit, modernization of organizational and staffing structures, reduction of responsibilities) of wider administrative reform in Germany, which is aiming in essence at 'a de-bureaucratization and an entrepreneurialization of local administration' (Heinelt, 1997, p. 18) and which regards citizens as customers. This points to the need to coordinate interactive negotiations and the strategic use of *resource cooperation* by developing new forms of citizen participation, which in turn require that the modernization of local policy-making be interpreted much more broadly.

Local environmental policy is not the only area in which there are signs that, despite the fact that the participatory dimension (and thus the input into local policy-making) still plays only a marginal role in thinking about local authority reform, local authorities are more willing in the 1990s to experiment with new forms of citizen participation in planning and decison-making and to make better use of the hitherto underused potential for creativity (see Burton and Duncan, 1996, Schridde, 1997b and Spitzer, 1998 for overviews). Key players at the municipal level are increasingly looking for new ways of handling conflicts and for initiating cooperative procedures for solving problems. There is a readiness to respond to unproductive conflicts, crises in decision-making, ineffective performance, lack of information and knowledge, and the growing complexity of problems in sensitive and potentially hazardous areas such as incineration plants and waste disposal sites, as well as in connection with large-scale traffic projects. It is clear from various studies of environmental policy (on local waste disposal, see Lamping, 1998 and Porter, 1998) that local authorities which not only have a regard for quality and propriety but also focus on solutions to problems were the more successful, when they managed to make decision processes transparent, to decentralize responsibility and to act vigorously to improve communications. 'Management by dialogue' (Spitzer, 1998, p. 132), whereby the administration is a partner in the dialogue, can be an important vehicle for consensus and innovation, if intelligently used by local authority personnel. In the joint search for appropriate solutions to problems, those affected become participants and 'planning victims become planning partners' (Spitzer, 1998, p. 136). Dialogue groups in settings can be the source of communication and negotiation where interests, evaluations, objectives and solutions are usefully discussed and coordinated with relevant actors in an extended policy and learning process. The practical and social effects of learning and synergy are an important product, not to be underrated, of this informal mode of paving the way to decisions by debate over time in discussion groups.

Even in the face of competition between localities, the development of styles of negotiation in which citizens participate, such as city or regional forums, can provide a means of 'breaking down blocks to decision-making, planning and implementation in the local administration and other local agencies. This can be achieved through reaching agreement – publicly, by means of debate and with the direct participation of the people involved – about policy aims and the best ways to realise them' (Heinelt, 1997, p. 21).

This reflects some of the 'old' discussion about governance, for the mobilization of *citizen participation and partnership* is linked to three issues of political governance (Mayntz, 1987):

- *implementation*, i.e. carrying out policies in conformity with objectives;
- *motivation*, i.e. integrating target groups and generating acceptance;
- *knowledge*, i.e. gathering information and becoming aware of the complexity of the consequences of taking action by exploiting the existing potential in society and by establishing direct feedback.

The aim of modernizing policy and administration in the twenty-first century should therefore be to develop in innovative ways the formal problem-solving competence of citizens, to integrate citizen activity as a source of information, knowledge and engagement, and to include the views of citizens in the process of public decision-making and service provision. The creation of favourable conditions for communications, the facilitation of communications networks and sustained public debate are necessary to the process of modernizing internal structures in local authorities and are also a necessary complement to the long established means of underpinning core values.

One of the ways in which the opinions of citizens can be introduced into local decision-making is by creating a strong sense of identity with a particular locality. This leads to an engagement with local issues, such that the formal leadership in any urban setting would be failing in its functions if it did not take seriously the views of local residents.

The practical issue is that local communities may well be very diverse in their views – the residents of an affluent area near to a city centre will have different priorities from those living on a peripheral housing estate ten kilometres from the city centre. The local leadership will need to have a clear strategic sense of its priorities. Is more attention (and resources) to be paid to those disadvantaged in social and economic terms through no fault of their own or are investment in cultural heritage and an active tourism policy key elements of an inward investment strategy to support the overall economic health of the city?

The role of urban leaders is therefore to produce a broad outline picture of the desired future of their city and to devise techniques whereby local residents can have some influence over the events and decisions that affect them personally. In this volume, Nigel Thrift outlines how imaginative administrations might think about the future of cities and the earlier part of this final chapter identifies some of the key socio-economic changes that need to be included in any well based planning for the future.

In his contribution, Paul Burton points up a middle way between total political disengagement and full involvement by citizens in the local political arena. Community visioning may be one way in which the device to have a say but not take full political responsibility can be offered to the population of cities, and it can include children who are not yet eligible to vote, thereby making an important investment for the future in the relationship between the city administration and the citizen.

Note

1.   We would like to thank Isabella Aboderin, Wolfram Lamping and Henning Schridde for their suggestions and support.

References

B. Blanke, H. Schridde, and M. Metje, *Bürgerschaftliche Aufgabenkritik und Aktivierender Staat. Erste Ergebnisse des Projekte 'Bürgerbefragung'* [*The Scope of Government and the Voice of the Citizen in the Enabling State: Preliminary Results of a Citizens' Survey*] (Universität Hannover, Abteilung Sozialpolitik und Public Policy [University of Hanover, Centre for Social and Public Policy], 1998).

B. Blanke, H. Heinelt, C.-W. Macke and F.W. Rüb, 'Staatliche Sozialpolitik und die Regulierung der Nicherwerbstätigkeit [National social policy and the regulation of unemployment]', in H. Abromeit and B. Blanke (eds), *Arbeitsmarkt, Arbeitsbeziehungen und Politik in den 80er Jahren [Labour Markets, Labour Relationships and Policy in the 1980s]*, *Leviathan*, [Special Issue], 8 (Opladen, 1987) pp. 296–314.

P. Burton and S. Duncan, 'Democracy and accountability in public bodies: new agendas in British governance', *Policy and Politics*, 24: 1 (1996) 5–16.

A. Church and P. Reid, 'Urban power, international networks and competition: the example of cross-border cooperation', *Urban Studies*, 33: 8 (1996) 1297–318.

E. Hahn, 'Ökologischer Stadtumbau in der Praxis. Zwischenbilanz eines Modellprojektes in Leipzig [The ecological restructuring of cities in practice: results from a model project in Leipzig]', in F. Biermann, S. Büttner and C. Helm (eds), *Zukunftsfähige Entwicklung. Herausforderungen an Wissenschaft und Politik [Sustainable Development: Challenges for Science and Politics]* (Berlin, 1997) pp. 285–98.

C. Hamnett, 'Social polarisation, economic restructuring and welfare state regimes', *Urban Studies*, 8 (1996) 1407–30.

H. Heinelt, 'Neue Debatten zur Modernisierung der Kommunalpolitik. Ein Überblick [New debates on the modernization of local politics: an overview]', in H. Heinelt and M. Mayer (eds), *Modernisierung der Kommunalpolitik. Neue Wege der Ressourcenmobilisierung [The Modernization of Local Politics: New Ways of Mobilising Resources]* (Opladen, 1997) pp. 12–28.

W. Lamping, *Kommunale Abfallpolitik. Ökologischer Strukturwandel und politisches Lernen [Local Waste Disposal Policy: Ecological Restructuring and Policy Learning]* (Wiesbaden, 1998).

R. Mayntz, 'Politische Steuerung und gesellschaftliche Steuerungsprobleme – Anmerkungen zu einem theoretischen Paradigma [Political governance and societal problems of governance: comments on a theoretical paradigm]', in *Jahrbuch zur Staats- und Verwaltungswissenschaft [Yearbook of Government and Administrative Science]* (1987) pp. 89–110.

M. Porter, 'Waste management', in P. Lowe and S. Wand (eds), *British Environmental Policy and Europe* (London, 1998).

A. Priebs, 'Neubau der Region [Remodelling of the region]', in B. Blanke, S. von Bandemer, F. Nullmeier and G. Wewer (eds), *Handbuch zur Verwaltungsreform [Handbook of Administrative Reform]* (Opladen, 1998) pp. 122–31.

H. Schridde, 'Lokale Sozialpolitik zwischen Integration und Ausgrenzung [Social policy at the local level: between integration and exclusion]', *Zeitschrift für Sozialreform [Journal of Social Reform]*, 43 (1997a) 872–90.

H. Schridde, 'Verfahrensinnovationen kommunaler Demokratie. Bausteine für eine Modernisierung der Kommunalpolitik [Innovation in local democratic processes: building blocks for the modernization of local politics]', in H. Heinelt and M. Mayer (eds), *Modernisierung der Kommunalpolitik. Neue*

Wege der Ressourcenmobilisierung [*The Modernization of Local Politics: New Ways of Mobilising Resources*] (Opladen, 1997b) pp. 171–91.

M. Spitzer, 'Bürgeraktivierung und Verwaltungsmodernisierung [Involving the citizen and modernizing the administration]', in B. Blanke, S. von Bandemer, F. Nullmeier and G. Wewer (eds), *Handbuch zur Verwaltungsreform* [*Handbook of Administrative Reform*] (Opladen, 1998) pp. 131–9.

N. Staeck 'The European structural funds – their history and impact', in H. Heinelt and R. Smith (eds), *Policy Networks and European Structural Funds* (Aldershot, 1996).

Index